An Annotated Edition of

Lectures on Moral Philosophy

An Annotated Edition of

Lectures on Moral Philosophy

by John Witherspoon

Edited by Jack Scott

Newark
University of Delaware Press
London and Toronto: Associated University Presses

© 1982 by Associated University Presses, Inc.

Associated University Presses, Inc.
4 Cornwall Drive
East Brunswick, New Jersey 08816

Associated University Presses Ltd.
69 Fleet Street
London EC4Y 1EU, England

Associated University Presses
Toronto, Ontario, Canada M5E 1A7

Library of Congress Cataloging in Publication Data

Witherspoon, John, 1723-1794.
    An annotated edition of Witherspoon's Lectures on
moral philosophy.

    Bibliography: p.
    Includes index.
    1. Ethics.   I. Scott, Jack, 1933-   II. Title.
BJ1005.W5   1981   170   80-24404
ISBN 0-87413-164-2

Printed in the United States of America

Contents

Introduction

"He is as high a Son of Liberty, as any Man in America."[1] Thus John Adams described John Witherspoon in his diary entry of August 27, 1774. Adams and the rest of the Massachusetts delegation to the First Continental Congress spent several days in Princeton enroute to Philadelphia. After discussing with Witherspoon the agitated state of affairs between America and Great Britain, Adams was pleased to discover the Scottish immigrant's fervent attachment to the American cause. Adams reiterated this warm opinion of Witherspoon in his diary a few days later (September 3, 1774) after breakfasting with him in Philadelphia. "Dr. Witherspoon," he said, "enters with great Spirit into the American cause. He seems as hearty a Friend as any of the Natives—an animated son of Liberty."[2]

Adams' enthusiastic estimate of Witherspoon was an accurate appraisal of a man who so intensified his involvement in the colonial cause that by July 4, 1776, he was one of the fifty-six signers of the Declaration of Independence. And for six years during the Revolutionary War he served with distinction as a member of the Continental Congress. Thoroughly committed to the new American nation, Witherspoon is best known as a patriot, although this is a reputation somewhat amiss. Though his identification with the revolutionary cause was complete, he was more powerful, more influential as a cleric and educator than as a political activist. Indeed, Witherspoon dedicated a far greater portion of his life to the church and higher education than he did to government service. Admittedly, he was best known to his own generation for his political contribution, but contemporary fame and permanent influence do not always coincide. This is particularly true in the realm of thought, and it is here that Witherspoon's influence was most far-reaching.

Witherspoon's thought is best revealed in his *Lectures on Moral*

1

Philosophy. Composed shortly after his arrival in America in 1768, these lectures were delivered yearly to the senior class at Princeton. Touching on many subjects—ethics, epistemology, theology, political theory—the lectures testify to the broad scope of Witherspoon's mind. Further, they indicate his ideological grounding at the very time that his striking tripartite career emerged. In the 1770s Witherspoon functioned ably as a clergyman, college president, and political activist.

But these lectures accomplish more than outlining the thought of a forceful personality. They have general importance as well, for they proved congenial to American society with an impact soon felt far beyond the lecture halls of Princeton. Some students of Witherspoon used their copies of lectures to teach at other colleges. For instance, William Graham, class of 1773, found them valuable when he assumed direction in 1780 of the Liberty Hall Academy at Lexington, Virginia.[3] More important, perhaps, Witherspoon's lectures were used by many who were not his students at the College of New Jersey.[4] Taught in college classroom, collected in private libraries, and shaping student's lives after graduation, *Lectures on Moral Philosophy* was an influential intellectual document during the Revolutionary era.

The importance of this document, however, does not rest in its originality. Witherspoon was no original thinker, as the extensive annotations to this edition attest. But the absence of creative thought does not, of course, invalidate his work; its very derivativeness can and does make it representative of a particular intellectual milieu. Witherspoon captures the interest of the intellectual historian precisely because he was such a representative thinker. And he appeared on the American scene at a propitious moment, just when the colonies were trying to break away from the British Empire to set up a new nation. Since questions still remain unanswered about the intellectual context in which this separation occurred, a fresh look at an effective leader of the period is appropriate. Witherspoon's *Lectures on Moral Philosophy* provide a microcosm of the collective mind of the Revolutionary period.

It would be misleading, however, to represent Witherspoon as merely a passive receptor of other men's ideas. Rather, he was a forceful personality who dynamically interacted with his environment. His thought was synthesized in the vortex of activity; his ideas usually bore the mark of personal experience. Thus an evaluation of Witherspoon's thought necessitates some knowledge of his life, and a summary of salient biographical details follows.[5]

A BIOGRAPHICAL SKETCH

John Witherspoon was first a cleric. He was, in fact, born to the manse. His father, James, was minister in the Scottish parish of Yester from 1720 until his death in 1760. His mother, Anne, was the daughter of the Reverend David Walker, minister of Temple Parish in the county of Edinburgh. Calvinist divines dominate both lines of his ancestry. His great grandfather, also named John Witherspoon, had signed the famous Solemn League and Covenant in 1643. Into this clerical atmosphere John Witherspoon was born at Gifford, Scotland, on February 5, 1723.

Witherspoon's family gave him the advantage of a good education. His first schooling occurred in Haddington Grammar School, four miles from his home village of Gifford. Here he received the customary grounding in Latin language and literature plus the unusual benefit of studying French. After finishing grammar school, he enrolled in the University of Edinburgh at thirteen, a normal age for university matriculation in Scotland during this period.

A university of genuine distinction in the eighteenth century, Edinburgh had abolished the archaic regent system in which one teacher continued with a class through varied subjects until graduation. In its place the university had instituted chairs of humanity (chiefly the study of Latin), Greek, logic, and natural philosophy, which provided the curriculum that was studied in successive years. There were also professors of mathematics, moral philosophy, and universal history, but attendance at their lectures was optional.

The major weakness in this new system was that many students chose only those courses that appealed to them. Consequently, although the number of students at the University of Edinburgh increased, the actual number of graduates declined. This trend was encouraged by a society in which the favor of a wealthy patron was often more important to advancement than a university degree. Witherspoon was among the minority, however, whose studies led to graduation. On February 23, 1739, he defended his Latin thesis in the university common hall and three days later was awarded the Master of Arts degree.

Witherspoon then continued his studies at Edinburgh for four more years under the Faculty of Divinity. Divinity was still the most prestigious profession in Scotland in the eighteenth century. On the Edinburgh divinity faculty at this time were three pro-

3

fessors: John Gowdie, professor of divinity; Patric Cuming, professor of ecclesiastical history; and William Dawson, professor of Hebrew. Alexander Carlyle (1722–1805), classmate of Witherspoon and later a prominent churchman, recorded his impression of Gowdie in his autobiography. He candidly observed that Gowdie's class "had no attractions," for the professor "was dull, and Dutch, and prolix."[6] Gowdie lectured from a standard Calvinist text, Benedict Pictet's *Compend of Theology*. Cuming, teacher of church history, evidently taught with greater ability than Gowdie and was later honored by being elected three times as moderator of the General Assembly of the Church of Scotland. Little is known about Dawson's class in Hebrew, but later Witherspoon felt competent to teach it at Princeton.

At the conclusion of his studies in 1743, Witherspoon's theological views were formed; they remained essentially the same throughout his life. The religious instruction, first given in his father's home, had been systematized by the divinity faculty at Edinburgh. The nature of that religious thought is aptly described by one of Witherspoon's biographers, Ashbel Green: "Dr. Witherspoon's Theology was Calvinistic, according to the system of Calvin himself; subject only to the modification it has received in the Standards of the Presbyterian Church."[7] In no other country had Calvinism taken deeper root or more profoundly affected national life than in Scotland. Witherspoon was of this tough and gnarled Scottish stock. Until his death he resisted any doctrine that he considered inimical to orthodox Presbyterianism.

In fact, what first catapulted Witherspoon before the Scottish public was his orthodox stance in an ecclesiastical conflict. When he began his ministerial career at Beith (he had been formally ordained on April 11, 1745), the Church of Scotland was embroiled in a quarrel between the Moderate and Popular parties.

Two issues were basic to the tension between the Moderates and Evangelicals (or Popular party). The first of these was lay patronage: should the local landowner or the congregation possess the right to select the pastor? To the Moderates, lay patronage was the law of the land, established by Parliament in the Patronage Act of 1712 and partially affirmed by the Church's General Assembly in 1732. In addition, the Moderates were convinced that this method of selection maintained and even upgraded the quality of the clergy. To the Popular party, however, lay patronage denied the basic right of the congregation. The Evangelicals were usually willing to permit the patron to make nominations for the pulpit, but they asserted that in the end only the congregation could select its pastor.

4

The other issue dividing these two wings of the Scottish church was more fundamental and more theologically significant. Moderates tended to be men of good education and genteel manners. On good terms with the nobility and gentry, the Moderate clergy enjoyed various forms of secular entertainment such as dancing and theatre. Latitudinarian in their theology, they frowned upon orthodox Calvinism and evangelical piety. To the Popular party the activities and attitudes of the Moderates smacked of worldliness and heresy. Evangelicals felt that the Moderates had sacrificed the fundamental dogmas of the church on the altar of culture and humanism.

Perhaps nothing better illustrates the feeling of the Popular clergy toward the Moderates than an excerpt from Green's biography of Witherspoon. Since Green was personally unacquainted with the quarrel, his chief source of information must have been Witherspoon. In this passage, Green describes John Home, a Moderate leader whom he considers representative of the party. Although admitting Home to be a generous man and eminent scholar, Green adds:

> But Home was completely a man of the world. It is not known indeed, that he ever spoke against religion; but some of its most decided enemies were among his dearest and most intimate friends. Of this number was Adam Smith and David Hume; the latter of whom showed his special affection and admiration, was attended to by him with the greatest assidity and a journal kept of his conversation and actions, while he was sinking to the ground. Thus striking is the contrast formed by such a character, with that of the minister of the gospel of Christ, "who watches for souls as one that must give account."[8]

Thus, early in his ministerial career Witherspoon sided with the Evangelicals in their battle with the Moderates.

Witherspoon soon emerged as a leader of the Popular party, particularly after his publication of *Ecclesiastical Characteristics, or the Arcana of Church Polity* in 1753.[9] In this biting satire, he excoriated the "paganized Christian divines" of his day. Although the pamphlet was published anonymously, Witherspoon's authorship soon became known. The popularity of *Ecclesiastical Characteristics* is attested by the fact that it went through five editions in ten years. Of particular interest in *Ecclesiastical Characteristics* is Witherspoon's sharp attack on Francis Hutcheson (1694–1746), succinctly stated in his conclusion entitled an "Athenian Creed." All Moderates, he suggested with heavy sarcasm, subscribe to the last dogma that reads: "In fine, I believe in the divinity of Lord Shaftesbury, the saintship of Marcus Antoninus, the perspicuity and sublimity of Aristotle, and the perpetual duration of Mr, Hutcheson's works, notwithstanding their present tendency to oblivion. Amen.''[10]

Witherspoon's antipathy toward Hutcheson is understandable. During Hutcheson's tenure as professor of moral philosophy at the University of Glasgow (1730–46), he effectively championed the Moderate cause. His influence was central in bringing the liberal minister William Leechman to Glasgow as professor of theology, a move that Hutcheson predicted in his correspondence would put "a new face upon theology in Scotland."[11] Hutcheson particularly appealed to a younger generation: his liberality in theology, his erudition, and his gentility made him the epitome of the Moderate ideal. Alexander Carlyle, an Edinburgh student who traveled to Glasgow and heard Hutcheson lecture, noted that when he explained the moral virtues, "he displayed a fervent and persuasive eloquence which was irresistible."[12]

Paradoxically, Hutcheson's thought, a target of Witherspoon's attack in Scotland, becomes the central source for Witherspoon's composition of *Lectures on Moral Philosophy* in America. Yet Witherspoon fails to acknowledge his obvious debt to Hutcheson. It is clear that his unacknowledged mentor's identification with the Moderate party still rankled, though he had been dead for more than forty years.[13]

Witherspoon's involvement in this quarrel between the Evangelicals and the Moderates intensified from the time of the publication of *Ecclesiastical Characteristics* in 1753 until his departure for America fifteen years later. Illustrating this was his leadership in an Evangelical attack upon the Moderate party, occasioned by a theatrical event on December 14, 1756. On this date *Douglas* was presented on the stage of the Canongate Theatre in Edinburgh. John Home wrote the drama, and other Moderate clergymen such as Alexander Carlyle attended the performance. Evangelicals were scandalized by this connection between clergymen and the stage; a pamphlet war ensued between the two parties. Heresy trials were initiated, and Home himself resigned his pastorate under pressure. Witherspoon joined the fray with a broadside entitled *Serious Inquiry into the Nature and Effects of the Stage* (Glasgow, 1757).[14] In this pamphlet, Witherspoon reasoned that man's obligation was "to supremely and uniformly aim at the glory of God." He argued that the stage did not serve this purpose and thus should not be supported by professing Christians. As is evident from a comment in the lectures and from a letter written in 1793, Witherspoon's opposition to the stage did not lessen with the years.[15]

Witherspoon continued his offensive against the Moderates, but it was a losing fight. In 1763 William Robertson (1721–93), former classmate of Witherspoon at Edinburgh and now principal of the university, was elected moderator of the General Assembly of the Church of Scotland. For sixteen years the Moderate leader held this position, thereby solidifying the firm control that his party exercised over the Church of Scotland.

In spite of the fact that Witherspoon's views did not prevail in ecclesiastical politics, his reputation grew both in Scotland and abroad. His writings were widely read: they were reviewed regularly in London and often translated for Reformed audiences on the Continent. In 1757 Witherspoon accepted a call to the pastorate in Paisley, a flourishing industrial town on the outskirts of Glasgow. Other honors came his way: in 1759 the Synod of Glasgow and Ayr elected him moderator and in 1764 the University of Saint Andrews awarded him the honorary doctorate in divinity. He also received invitations from prestigious Reformed pulpits in Dublin and Rotterdam shortly before leaving Scotland.

This widening clerical reputation brought Witherspoon to the attention of the trustees of a small Presbyterian college in America, the College of New Jersey. His orthodox Calvinism was attractive to them; his obvious gifts of leadership could be put to real advantage. Furthermore, because of a particular situation in the colonies, the trustees were inclined to look across the sea for their president. Tensions between the Old Side and New Side parties still plagued American Presbyterianism, despite their ostensible reconciliation in 1758. As a Scottish divine, Witherspoon identified with neither faction; additionally, his theological orthodoxy and ministerial prestige made him appealing to both parties.

Therefore, in 1766 the trustees tendered Witherspoon an invitation to head the College of New Jersey. But persuading Witherspoon to come to America was not easy. He was an established minister in Scotland with a secure future. To risk this loss of position for the uncertainies of adjusting to a new role in a new country would have to be a painfully difficult decision. Not only was Witherspoon reluctant to make the move, but his wife was even more hesitant to leave Scotland. He refused this first invitation, but a series of importunate letters from friends of the College of New Jersey finally led him to change his mind and accept the challenge.[16]

About May 20, 1768, the forty-five-year-old Witherspoon and his family set sail for America, arriving in Philadelphia harbor on August 7. Seven members of the Witherspoon family stepped off the boat onto American soil: John Witherspoon; his wife of twenty years, Elizabeth; and their five children—Anne, 19; James, 16;

John, 11; Frances, 9; and David, 8. After a brief stay in Philadelphia, the new president was escorted to Princeton by friends of the College of New Jersey. Here he found the college edifice, Nassau Hall, brilliantly illuminated with candles to welcome him. Formally inaugurated on August 17, 1768, Witherspoon continued as president of the College of New Jersey until his death in 1794. Healing most of Princeton's doctrinal and financial wounds, he was the college's most effective administrator during the eighteenth century.

What explains this success? Certainly it was not experience, for Witherspoon had no background as an educator when he assumed the presidency in 1768. Rather, the achievement of this remarkable man was due to the varied talents he brought to the post of college presidency: churchman, fund raiser, and teacher. For instance, Witherspoon quickly used his clerical reputation to lift the sagging financial condition of the College of New Jersey, a task requiring all his energies. The trustees had so poorly managed the college funds that bankruptcy was a genuine threat in 1768. In fact, the trustees could not even pay the entire ship fare for the Witherspoon family when they arrived in Philadelphia.[17]

Fortunately, Witherspoon's journeys throughout the colonies soon began to reap dividends for the college. He preached in pulpits from Boston to Charleston, South Carolina.[18] Everywhere he traveled, Witherspoon stressed the needs of the College of New Jersey as well as its good influence on society. In November 1769 he spoke before a crowd in the capital yard at Williamsburg, Virginia. They responded with a contribution of £66 that was supplemented by a personal donation of £50 from Governor Norborne Berkeley Botetourt. In the spring of 1770 a trip to New Haven, Providence, and Boston netted gifts to the college of £1,000. In this manner, Witherspoon changed the Princeton ledger from red to black within two years.[19]

Witherspoon's skill as a fund raiser is indicated not only by his personal efforts but also by his ability to encourage others to solicit donations for the college. For example, in 1769 the Presbyterian synod appointed twenty-five members to "use their utmost endeavors to obtain subscription" for Princeton in Pennsylvania, Maryland, New Jersey, Virginia, and South Carolina.[20] The Reverend James Caldwell raised £700 in Charleston alone. From 1768 to 1770, the College of New Jersey received over £6,000 in contributions.[21]

Yet Witherspoon's major objective as a college administrator was not financial stability. Rather, this new stability created the context in which the more important goal—educational reform—could be attained. Witherspoon had definite eduational views that he began to implement at the College of New Jersey. The realization of his program was made easier in 1769 by the action of the trustees. In formal resolution they affirmed that President Witherspoon was "invested with the sole direction, as to the methods of education to be pursued in this Seminary."[22]

Witherspoon's imprint in every aspect of the curriculum of the college is easy to detect. For he directly influenced instruction by entering the classroom himself. (Most eighteenth-century college presidents combined teaching and administration.) Ashbel Green writes that he was the first to use the lecture method at Princeton.[23] By this he meant that Witherspoon carefully prepared his material and delivered it orally to his students, whereas previous instructors had assigned material for their students to read and then quizzed them in class. Witherspoon's formal lectures included four subjects: composition, taste, and criticism; moral philosophy; chronology and history; and divinity. He also taught French and Hebrew occasionally, and whenever possible, personally conducted the competition in speaking and writing Latin.[24]

Witherspoon also eagerly advanced the study of subjects of which he was not personally knowledgeable. For instance, although his understanding of mathematics and natural sciences was general and elementary, he appreciated the values of these studies and thus created a professorship of mathematics and natural philosophy at Princeton in 1771. In the same year, Witherspoon installed at the college the celebrated orrery of David Rittenhouse. This delicate bit of astronomical machinery was a marvel in its day, representing accurately the motions and phases of the planets and satellites in the solar system. In purchasing his orrery Witherspoon accomplished quite a coup, for the Philadelphia Academy also desired it and thought its acquisition by the Academy was assured.[25] The College of New Jersey was justly proud of this purchase, and an additional order of scientific equipment in 1772 led Witherspoon to boast that Princeton's "apparatus for Mathematics and Natural Philosophy will be equal, if not superior, to any on the continent."[26]

A pamphlet dated 1772 and written by Witherspoon gives a brief outline of the Princeton curriculum during Witherspoon's early administration. In an appeal for funds he briefly described the course of instruction:

In the first year they read Latin and Greek, with the Roman and Grecian antiquities, and Rhetoric. In the second, continuing the

9

study of the languages, they learn a compleat system of Geography, with the use of the globes, the first principles of Philosophy, and the elements of mathematical knowledge. The third, though the languages are not wholly omitted, is chiefly employed in Mathematics and Natural Philosophy. And the senior year is employed in reading the higher classics, proceeding in the Mathematics and Natural Philosophy, and going through a course of Moral Philosophy. In addition to these, the President gives lectures to the juniors and seniors, which consequently every Student hears twice over in his course, first, upon Chronology and History, and afterwards upon Composition and Criticism.[27]

This description indicates a well-ordered curriculum under Witherspoon's guidance.

All in all, Witherspoon gave the College of New Jersey new life during the first few years of his presidency. Under his leadership the college's finances, faculty, and student body steadily increased. Princeton attracted students from all sections of colonial America, thus becoming the least provincial of the contemporary institutions of higher learning. For instance, in 1769 only nineteen of the eighty-four students at Princeton were from New Jersey. This gathering of students from various regions widened Witherspoon's influence.

While Witherspoon capitalized fully on the prestige that the post of college president afforded, his impact in those early years of American residence was not confined to higher education. A thorough understanding of the forms and principles of historic Presbyterianism naturally prepared him for leadership in the fledgling Presbyterian Church of America. And this American denomination used Witherspoon almost from his first day in America. On August 10, 1768, three days after his arrival, he preached at the Second Presbyterian Church in Philadelphia, and on the following Sunday delivered his first sermon in the Presbyterian Church at Princeton, a pulpit he occupied until his death in 1794. From Witherspoon's journal of 1768, it is evident that he traveled widely and preached from many pulpits.[28]

At this time, the highest Presbyterian body in the nation was the Synod of New York and Philadelphia. Formed in 1758 when the schism between the Old Side and New Side Presbyterians was healed, this synod was composed of ten presbyteries and ruled over two-thirds of the Presbyterian membership in America. In April 1769, Witherspoon joined the New Brunswick Presbytery which subsequently selected him as a delegate to the meeting of the national synod, held the following month. At Witherspoon's first synodical meeting (May 17–25), he was appointed to serve on eight different committees. The minutes of the Synod of New York and Philadelphia, from Witherspoon's first attendance in 1769 to the synod's dissolution in 1789, clearly underscore his importance. Time and time again, his name is connected with substantial documents and committees.[29]

Particularly significant among Witherspoon's varied religious activities was his involvement in the effort to prevent the establishment of an Anglican episcopate in America. Concern of long standing over this matter had led to the formation of the Society of Dissenters in 1766. The convention of this society, composed of representative Presbyterians and Congregationalists, met annually to formulate plans against an American episcopate. In May 1769, the Presbyterian Synod selected Witherspoon to head their delegation to the convention scheduled for September. Minutes of the Society of Dissenters show that he was an active participant in the 1769 convention and in subsequent conventions until the society dissolved temporarily in 1776. In addition Witherspoon corresponded with Scottish ministers, encouraged other American ministers to join the battle against the Anglican episcopate, served as chairman of the 1773 convention, and supported the society with all the prestige he could command.[30]

This concerted effort of Congregational and Presbyterian clergymen against an American episcopate was no small tributary in the stream of colonial liberty. No less an authority than John Adams considered the role of the dissenters especially pertinent to kindling an awareness of governmental power. Writing to Jedediah Morse in 1815, Adams declared: "The apprehension of Episcopacy contributed, fifty years ago, as much as any other cause, to arouse the attention, not only of the inquiring mind, but of the common people, and urge them to close thinking on the constitutional authority of Parliament over the colonies.[31] Careful studies on this subject by Arthur Lyon Cross and Carl Bridenbaugh document Adams's assertion.[32] For Witherspoon, personally, these Dissenter conventions were strong motivating influences. The semi-seditious discussions of these Reformed ministers aroused zeal for religious battle similar to his earlier conflict with the Moderates of Scotland. This time, however, what began as a relatively narrow theological campaign rapidly developed into a broad-gauged, thoroughly secular protest movement.

Yet even without such militants as the Reformed ministers, the entire climate of American Presbyterianism was favorable to any resistance against the English—theological or otherwise. With the exception of its sister faith, Congregationalism, no other religious body cast its lot so completely with the American cause as did Presbyterianism. The huge wave of Scotch-Irish immigration during the eighteenth century gave the Presbyterians the second largest church membership in America at the outbreak of the Revolutionary War. Many of these recent arrivals from Ulster came to American shores with deep-seated animosity toward the English. Exorbitant land rents and brutal English economic policies had driven many of these men from their homes in northern Ireland. High-handed Anglican policies had deeply insulted their religious convictions, adding salt to their already existing economic wounds. The churches helped organize and institutionalize a latent hostility into an effective instrument of opposition to British imperium. In fact, many English and American loyalists believed the Presbyterians to be the major force behind the Revolution. For instance, Ambrose Serle, British clerk of reports who accompanied the English army in America from 1776 to 1778, wrote Lord Dartmouth that "though it has not been much considered at Home, Presbyterianism is really at the Bottom of this whole Conspiracy, has supplied it with Vigor, and will never rest, till something is decided upon it."[33] British soldiers often vented their wrath on Presbyterian churches, asserting that Presbyterianism and rebellion went hand in hand. The Presbyterian inclination to resistance created a situation ripe for the forceful politico-religious leadership of Witherspoon.

Indeed, John Witherspoon and American Presbyterianism on the eve of the Revolution represent a fortunate convergence of personality and circumstance. Witherspoon was president of the only Presbyterian college in America. Scotch-Irish America looked to Princeton as its religious and educational capital. Furthermore, Witherspoon effectively exercised clerical leadership from the congregational level to the highest Presbyterian body, the Synod of New York and Philadelphia. In 1768 American Presbyterians had been favorably disposed toward Witherspoon, hoping that this prestigious Scottish clergyman would become an ecclesiastical leader. In the subsequent years, Witherspoon more than fulfilled that expectation: no voice would have equal influence in Presbyterian circles during the Revolutionary era.

Yet Presbyterianism was only one of the sources of Witherspoon's intense involvement in America's struggle against Great Britain. Obviously many factors produced the metamorphosis of Witherspoon from loyal British subject of 1768 to American rebel of 1776. It was the total colonial environment that accounted for his identification with the patriot cause. Witherspoon himself described how quickly the Americanization process occurs: "A man will become an American by residing in this country three months, with a prospect of continuing, more easily and certainly than by reading or hearing of it for three years, amidst the sophistry of daily disputation.''[34]

Significantly, at the time Witherspoon came to the New World in 1768, the country's mood was one of discontent and defiance toward the British. Three years earlier the colonists had fiercely resisted the Stamp Act, thus forcing the Parliament to repeal it in the following year, 1766. Yet the respite from taxation was short-lived, for Charles Townshend, Chancellor of the Exchequer, pushed a new revenue act through Parliament in 1767. Import duties on glass, paint, paper, and tea were to be collected from the Americans. The colonists immediately resisted the measure by the revival of non-importation and non-consumption agreements. The Massachusetts legislature sent a circular letter to the other colonies, denouncing the Townshend Acts as unconstitutional. When the legislature refused to rescind its action, Governor Francis Bernard of Massachusetts promptly dissolved the legislature on July 1, 1768. During the same summer, British customs officials attempted to collect duties from John Hancock's sloop *Liberty*, but a Boston mob forcibly prevented them from doing so. After this incident, two regiments of redcoats were sent to Boston to teach the rebellious populace a lesson.

This was the volatile situation that Witherspoon discovered when he arrived in America. As a result, he must have heard many heated discussions on colonial rights and liberties during his frequent travels on behalf of the College of New Jersey. In these early years as its president Witherspoon was simply a listener to the informal debates. His unremitting labors in behalf of the college and his pulpit at Princeton left little time for a deeper involvement in the slowly emerging conflict between Great Britain and the colonies.

Nevertheless, the frustrations of the colonists and the arguments he heard influenced Witherspoon's thinking. By late spring 1771, a definite trend is discernible in a letter he wrote to the *Scots Magazine* entitled "Ignorance of the British with Respect to America."[35] Witherspoon's ire had been aroused by a writer in this magazine who had confused the New England Congregationalists with the Presbyterian Synod of New York and Philadelphia, and his letter encouraged European writers to acquire correct knowledge of the British North American colonies before attempting judgments.

Evidently the British writer had denounced a sermon preached by John Lathrop, Congregationalist minister of Boston. Lathrop's stinging remarks, "Innocent Blood Crying for Vengeance," had been delivered on the Sunday following the Boston Massacre when British soldiers under mob pressure killed five Bostonians.[36] Notice Witherspoon's guarded, yet sympathetic, identification with the colonial cause:

> Now Sir, as to this author's observation on Dr. Lathrop's sermon, I shall say little—because, perhaps it cannot be wholly justified; yet, if all circumstances are duly attended to, there is as little reason to insult or glory over the people of Boston, as there was to excite the public resentment against Captain P—.[37]

He could appreciate the colonists' resentment of British troops on American soil.

Another manifestation of Witherspoon's early attachment to the cause of colonial liberty is his tolerance of the patriotic fervor frequently expressed by Princeton students. In July 1770, they publicly burned an intercepted letter from New York merchants. These merchants had broken the colonial non-importation agreement after the English Parliament had repealed all the duties of the Townshend Acts except the one on tea. They then wrote to encourage the Philadelphia merchants to follow suit, but the Princeton students viewed the action of the New York merchants as cowardly and expressed their disdain accordingly. Later that year the graduating seniors further showed their approbation of the non-importation agreement by wearing American-made cloth at the September commencement exercises. Significantly, James Witherspoon, the eldest son of President Witherspoon, in the Latin oration of the occasion, argued for the right of resistance against a king who ignored the laws of the state or treated his subjects cruelly.[38]

Witherspoon's failure to suppress such patriotic ardor is of consequence. Although he may have occasionally regretted the impetuosity of the students, there is no evidence of disciplinary action. Not all observers viewed the spirited Princeton students with such equanimity. For example, one person present at the 1772 commencement exercises expressed his alarm in a letter to the *Pennsylvania Chronicle* dated October 19, 1772. Under the title "A Friend to Impartiality," he wrote: "With many others, I was surprised to hear most of the young Gentlemen discussing in their performances the most perplexing political topics. The most difficult and knotly [sic] questions, relating to the British constitution, were solved in a jerk."[39]

Witherspoon not only tolerated the students' spirit of liberty, but his own teaching was no small factor in the genesis of that spirit. His lectures on moral philosophy articulated the right of resistance by the governed.[40] In response to those who might argue that such a right would lead inevitably to anarchy, Witherspoon countered: ". . . to refuse this inherent right in every man, is to establish injustice and tyranny, and leave every good subject without help, as a tame prey to the ambition and rapacity of others."[41] The Whig tradition of rebellion to tyrannical authority was an underlying theme in many of the president's discourses before the Princeton students.

Even more significant than his formal lectures was Witherspoon's encouragement of speeches and discussions on contemporary topics. The college erected a stage for formal speaking, and at least three evenings a week Princeton students were "pronouncing orations from this platform."[42] Here lively topics such as freedom and colonial rights were argued. Here patriotic fervor was intensified. This repeated arousal of patriotic spirit helps account for such an act as Princeton students wearing only American cloth to the commencement exercises in 1770. James Hasting Nichols, in his study of Witherspoon's views on church and state, describes the College of New Jersey as a "chief center of agitation for the colonial cause."[43]

One student deeply affected by Princeton's patriotic climate was James Madison, who came to Princeton in 1769, graduated in 1771, and remained for several months afterward to study a diversity of subjects under Witherspoon's tutelage. While a student, Madison was the effective poetic satirist for the newly formed American Whig Society. In this club he mingled with classmates such as Philip Freneau and Hugh Henry Brackenridge, both of whom were noted for their patriotic writings during the American Revolution. From letters written at this time it is evident that Madison was concerned with and participated in the patriotic activities of Princeton undergraduates. The spirit of revolutionary fervor breathed by Madison and his fellow students led naturally to their later involvement in the Revolutionary War. Irving Brant, biographer of Madison, points out that Witherspoon first introduced Madison to writers of political philosophy such as Montesquieu, Grotius, and Pufendorf. Witherspoon also instilled in Madison "a peculiar blend of knowledge and self-sufficiency" in political thought that remained his permanent heritage. Although he later transcended his mentor, Madison had no teacher so influential in shaping his thought as Witherspoon.[44]

What occurred in the life of Madison was repeated in the lives of many Princeton students. Of the 469 graduates during Witherspoon's administration (1768-94), an impressive number held prominent political offices. Six were members of the Continental Congress, twenty-one were United States senators, thirty-nine were representatives, three were justices of the Supreme Court, and one became president.[45] This prestigious roll call indicates some of the power emanating from Witherspoon's Princeton. As a later president of Princeton, Woodrow Wilson, commented in 1896:

> It would be absurd to pretend that we can distinguish Princeton's touch and methods in the Revolution, or her distinctive handiwork in the Constitution of the Union. We can show nothing more of historical fact than that her own President took a great place of leadership in that time of change, and became one of the first figures of the age; that the college which he led, and to which he gave his spirit, contributed more than her share of public men to the making of the nation, outranked her elder rivals in the roll call of the Constitutional Convention, and seemed for a little, a seminary of statesmen rather than a quiet seat of academic learning.[46]

The spirit of liberty pervading the college was yet confined to mere opinions. When news of the Boston Tea Party reached Princeton in January 1774, the students burst into the college storehouse to confiscate the winter's supply of tea and then searched other students' rooms for any private cache. All the tea was then gleefully destroyed in a huge bonfire, enlivened by an effigy of Governor Hutchinson of Massachusetts with a "tea cannister tyed about his neck."[47] This event, though it destroyed college property, must not have greatly disturbed Witherspoon, for in the summer of that same year he proudly told John Adams that his students were "all Sons of Liberty."[48]

By now Witherspoon himself had begun the intensive political activity that was to characterize most of the remainder of his life. The "Coercive Acts" of Parliament in March and April of 1774 and the summary closing of the port of Boston in June caused American tempers to boil. Provincial and county committees of correspondence, first suggested in 1773, now multiplied in the colonies. Significantly, the name of John Witherspoon joined eight others on the committee formed in Somerset County, New Jersey on July 4, 1774. In turn, the various county committees of correspondence in New Jersey met together on July 21 to 23. Witherspoon, who headed the Somerset delegation to this convention, successfully argued for the adoption of a non-importation and non-consumption agreement against British tea. A series of resolutions were passed calling for the repeal of the "dangerous and destructive" acts passed by Parliament. However, in a procedure standard for this time, all members of the New Jersey convention professed their loyalty to King George and detested "all thoughts of an independence on the Crown of Great Britain."[49]

The action of this statewide assembly coincided with Witherspoon's own thinking during this period of mounting tension. During the summer of 1774 he wrote an essay entitled *Thoughts on American Liberty*, in which he expressed his loyalty to the king and "backwardness" to break connection with Great Britain. But Witherspoon made it clear that resistance to the present course of British policy was absolutely essential. He advised the First Continental Congress, scheduled to convene in September, to declare the claims of the British Parliament illegal and unconstitutional. In a statement prophetic of Patrick Henry's later remark ("Give me liberty or give me death"), Witherspoon wrote "We are firmly determined never to submit to it, and do deliberately prefer war with all its horrors and even extermination itself, to slavery riveted on us and our posterity."[50]

At this juncture one can understand why John Adams described Witherspoon in glowing terms as "an animated Son of Liberty." These two men obviously agreed on the course of action that they believed the First Continental Congress should follow. Although not a delegate to this intercolonial assembly until two years later, Witherspoon clearly concurred with the measures and resolves adopted by it in 1774.

On December 15, 1774, the freeholders of Somerset County met at the invitation of that county's committee of correspondence. This meeting unanimously approved "the proceedings of the later Continental Congress in general." Witherspoon, along with eight others, was once again elected to serve on the committee of correspondence. Additionally, committees of inspection were selected to enforce the non-importation, non-consumption, and non-exportation agreements formulated by the Continental Congress.[51] Thus the patriot party tactically controlled Somerset County by late 1774, and Witherspoon was by this time a foremost member of that group.

As Witherspoon continued his political activity in the winter of 1774–75, Massachusetts patriots were building up a stockpile of arms in opposition to the British garrison stationed in Boston. Finally, the fateful shot was fired on April 19, 1775, when British troops marched into the Massachusetts countryside to Lexington and Concord. Political disagreement had escalated into armed conflict before the Second Continental Congress convened on May 10.

The mood of this congress was much more militant than the session of the preceding year. Delegates were not yet ready to declare independence, but neither did they shrink from battle with the British. On May 15 they passed a resolve to put the colonies in a state of military readiness, and two weeks later they adopted an address to the Canadians asking them to join the rebellion. Congress also took a series of steps to organize a Continental Army to support the Bostonians in their resistance. This culminated on June 15 with the election of George Washington as commander-in-chief. In many forthright statements the members of Congress decried the "tyranny" of Whitehall's ministers.

Meanwhile, Witherspoon was exerting crucial leadership for the American cause within the Presbyterian Church. He attended the annual meeting of the Synod of Philadelphia and New York on May 17–23, 1775, in New York City. The synod selected him to head the committee to compose a general pastoral letter, which the synod then officially adopted and circulated.[52] This letter addressed itself to the explosive national situation, since armed hostilities had begun at Lexington a month earlier. On the whole, its tone was conciliatory, and it assumed that the English king had been the victim of poor advice. The letter called for peace and made no mention of the radical solution of independence, but it did refer to the present hostilities as "unmerited oppression" and warned that if "the British ministry shall continue to enforce their claims by violence, a lasting and bloody contest must be expected."

Particularly significant was the pastoral letter's unstinted approval of the Continental Congress:

As the Continental Congress, now sitting in Philadelphia, consists of delegates chosen in the most free and unbiased manner, by the body of the people, let them not only be treated with respect, and encouraged in their difficult service—not only let your prayers be offered up to God for his direction in their proceedings—but adhere firmly to their resolutions.[53]

Thus the fate of American Presbyterianism and the Continental Congress were inseparably linked. When the latter body declared independence the following year, the Presbyterians were authorized by their highest ecclesiastical body to follow suit. At least one loyalist clergyman believed this action by the Presbyterian synod to be significant. The Anglican Charles Ingliss, in a letter written from New York on October 31, 1776, observed the following:

I have it from good authority that the Presbyterian ministers at a synod where most of the middle colonies were collected passed a resolve to support the Continental Congress in all their measures. This and only this can account for the uniformity of their conduct; for I do not know one of them, nor have I been able, after strict inquiry, to hear of any, who did not, by preaching and every effort in their power, promote all the measures of the congress, however extravagant.[54]

Furthermore, Witherspoon's conspicuous political stand must have emboldened many Presbyterian laymen to identify with the American cause.

In Philadelphia the Continental Congress made a final effort to resolve the impasse between England and America. The "Olive Branch Petition" was drawn up on July 5, 1775, asking George III to rescind the Coercive Acts and effect a reconciliation between the home country and the colonies. But King George was in no mood to heed a petition from an extra-legal assembly, particularly one which had just authorized a military expedition to bring Canada into union with the thirteen colonies in their opposition to England. So instead, George III issued a proclamation of rebellion on August 23. "Utmost endeavors" were urged in order "to suppress such a rebellion and bring the traitors to justice."

Now the colonial revolt was cast in a more dangerous light. The Crown had labeled the resistance "treason," and conciliation was impossible. The Americans had backed into a revolution in which a complete break with England was the only honorable alternative. This was Witherspoon's conviction at the time, as he later recalled in a tract written in 1778. In it he referred to the fact that the king had treated Congress's petition with "absolute contempt" and that "all intercourse" was broken off. He concluded that

we were declared rebels; and they themselves must confess, that no alternative was left us, but either to go with ropes about our necks, and submit ourselves, not to the king, but to the kingdom of England, to be trampled under foot, or risk all the consequences of open and vigorous resistance.[55]

Yet the commitment to a total break with the mother country was not easy for the colonists. America was going through the agonizing travail of casting aside her deep-rooted British loyalty. In late 1775 a majority of the public spokesmen of the American people still claimed to desire only a restoration of colonial liberty under the British Crown. For instance, the Assembly of Witherspoon's own state, New Jersey, assured Governor William Franklin of their "utmost abhorence" of independence on November 25.[56]

But the half-way house of declaring allegiance to the king while resisting his forces by arms could not be occupied indefinitely. Highly influential in accelerating the colonists' total break with England was the pamphlet *Common Sense*, published anonymously on January 9, 1776. In this broadside, Thomas Paine effectively articulated the major reasons for American independence. He argued that liberty was impossible under George III or, for that matter, under any monarch. Furthermore, he asserted that foreign aid was impossible unless the break with Great Britain was complete. With boldness the right word had been spoken at the right time.

Fierce debate ensued and Witherspoon sided with those who supported *Common Sense*. Witherspoon indicated this support by his response to *Plain Truth*, one of the more effective pamphlets taking issue with *Common Sense*.[57] Writing under the name "Aristedes," Witherspoon attacked *Plain Truth* in the May 13 issue of *Pennsylvania Packet*. Rhetorically he inquired into the options before America in the spring of 1776: "Shall we make resistance with greatest force, as rebel subjects of a government which we acknowledge, or as independent states against an usurped power which we detest and abhor?" To Witherspoon, the latter course was the wiser.[58]

Other actions during the first few months of 1776 corroborate the increased tempo of Witherspoon's involvement in the patriot cause. As chairman of the Somerset County committee of correspondence, he was concerned about New Jersey's defense against British troops. On February 14 he wrote a letter to Philadelphia requesting "one Tun of Powder" for use by the local militia.[59] Another letter from Witherspoon, dated March 19, indicated his willingness to cooperate with Lord Stirling, commander of the First New Jersey Regulars, in the military defense of the state.[60]

The first clear-cut indication that Witherspoon had opted for independence comes from an event recorded in the journal of Elias Boudinot. An anonymous notice appeared in *Pennsylvania Packet* requesting that all New Jersey counties choose delegates for a meeting in New Brunswick on April 18. Witherspoon was the moving force behind this meeting, actually called to encourage New Jersey to separate from Great Britain and to form an independent constitution. However, the stated purpose of the meeting, as advertised in the public notice, was to discuss the "present state of affairs." At the meeting Witherspoon ably argued the case for independence, believing it unwise to continue opposition to Great Britain merely as rebellious subjects. Elias Boudinot spoke strenuously against such a step, labeling it imprudent. Most of those present concurred with Boudinot, and according to his account, only three or four of the thirty-six present sided with Witherspoon.[61] Although Witherspoon's desire had been frustrated, his own stand for independence was now quite public. And as each day passed, this cause gained momentum. On May 20, 1776, John Adams exuberantly wrote James Warren from Congress that "every post and every day rolls in upon us Independence like a torrent."[62]

Certainly Witherspoon was doing his part for the cause of independence. On May 17 he spoke from his Princeton pulpit on the "Dominion of Providence over the Passions of Men," probably Witherspoon's most significant statement to his Presbyterian constituency during the Revolutionary War.[63] The occasion was a fast day ordained by the Continental Congress. Witherspoon began his sermon by stating his normal reluctance to introduce politics into the pulpit. Although not demagogic in his approach, he did denounce the cruelty of the British and the "inhumanity" of their soldiers. Pleased at the success that had thus far attended the American efforts, he asked, "Has not the boasted discipline of regulation and veteran soldiers been turned into confusion and dismay, before the new and maiden courage of free men, in defence of their property and right?"[64]

The main purpose of the address was to seek God's blessing for the American cause. Thus Witherspoon encouraged holiness and concern for the salvation of one's soul in such trying times. He was confident that the colonies would triumph in their battle with Great Britain, although he warned of disappointments along the way. That he viewed the struggle as a holy cause is evidenced by these stirring words: "There is not a single instance in history, in which civil liberty was lost, and religious liberty preserved entire."[65]

This fast day sermon was widely read, being published in Philadelphia and later reprinted in London and Glasgow. In the Scottish edition the sermon was acccompanied by severe annotations in which Witherspoon was labeled as a traitor. But to a majority of Americans, these were the stirring words of a patriotic preacher. William Warren Sweet, dean of American church historians, assessed it as "one of the most influential pulpit utterances during the whole course of the war."[66] Overall, the sermon tended to sanctify the revolutionary effort for America's Presbyterians. Their leading clergyman had placed his enormous prestige squarely behind the colonial rebellion.

In Witherspoon's generally moderate state of New Jersey the mood was becoming more radical. Such a trend was altogether pleasing to Witherspoon. On May 28 he was elected as one of the five delegates from Somerset County to the New Jersey Provincial Congress. When this congress convened at Burlington on June 10, those favoring independence were manifestly in the majority.

One of the first acts of this body was to move against New Jersey's royalist governor, William Franklin, an illegitimate son of Benjamin Franklin. He had recently summoned the state assembly to meet on June 20, thus hoping through this moderate body to dampen New Jersey's ardor for independence. The Provincial Congress proclaimed Franklin's action to be "in direct contempt and violation of the resolve of the Continental Congress of the fifteenth of May last," ordered his salary stopped, and declared him to be "an enemy to the liberties of this country." He was subsequently arrested and brought before the Congress at Burlington. When Franklin refused to answer charges before this extra-legal body, Witherspoon bitterly denounced him even to the point of taunting him for his illegitimate birth. On June 25 Franklin was deported to East Windsor, Connecticut, where he was confined in the home of Captain Ebenezer Grant.[67]

Another important item on the agenda of the Provincial Congress was the drafting of a new state constitution for New Jersey. Witherspoon had little chance to participate in this particular task, however, for on June 22 he was selected as a delegate to the Continental Congress. Also included on this "independence slate" were Richard Stockton, Abraham Clark, John Hart, and Francis Hopkinson.

The New Jersey delegation arrived in Philadelphia on Friday, June 28. Before the Continental Congress at this time was the monumental issue of independence, since it had been formally introduced on June 7 by Richard Henry Lee's motion, "that these United Colonies are, and of right ought to be, Free and Independent States." On Monday, July 1, the Congress resolved itself into a committee of the whole to consider the question. Stockton, Hopkinson and Witherspoon requested a recapitulation of the preceding debate, and John Adams publicly obliged them. After this, according to Adams's own recollection, "the Jersey Gentlemen said they were fully satisfied and ready for the Question, which was then put and determined in the Affirmative."[68]

On the following day, July 2, Congress formally adopted the course of independence with twelve states in the "yes" column (only New York abstained). Many works record that Witherspoon spoke out strongly on this occasion. When one member of the Continental Congress—presumably Jonathan Dickinson—argued that the country was not ripe for independence, Witherspoon testily replied, "In my judgment the country is not only ripe for the measure, but in danger of becoming rotten for the want of it."[69] The authenticity of this statement, however, is open to question. It does not appear in contemporary accounts and is first related in Ashbel Green's manuscript biography of Witherspoon, written over three decades after his death.[70] Whether or not the words were actually spoken by Witherspoon, they do reflect accurately his sentiment at that time.

After proclaiming independence, the Congress had to decide upon the actual formulation of their declaration. Thomas Jefferson, who had been commissioned to write the declaration, presented his draft for consideration. Although the Congress finally accepted substantially all of Jefferson's draft, they made several revisions in wording. Witherspoon, for example, strenuously objected to the sentence that denounced George III's use of "Scotch and foreign mercenaries" against the Americans. In deference to Witherspoon, the Congress deleted this unfavorable reference to the Scotch. Finally the group approved the document, and Witherspoon joined fifty-five other Americans in proudly affixing their signature to the Declaration of Independence.

During the remainder of the Revolutionary War, Witherspoon supported the American cause with sermons, pamphlets, and addresses. On July 30, 1776, British troops acknowledged their awareness of Witherspoon's leadership when they burned an effigy of him along with the effigies of the American generals Washington, Lee, and Putnam. These English soldiers had staged a mock scene in which Witherspoon was haranguing the generals to greater efforts. They incisively assessed Witherspoon's talent, for he was an articulate spokesman of the religio-political creed of his day. In this role he was both a catalyst and a vindicator of the American Revolution.

To the reader, Witherspoon's life after 1776 is not as central to understanding the *Lectures on Moral Philosophy*, as those years prior to that date. Witherspoon's study and life experiences prior to the composition of the lectures helped to mold the essays. Furthermore, his activity immediately subsequent to their composition validated them, as was evident in the two-year period of intense political involvement that preceded his signing of the Declaration of Independence. Indeed, it is clear that Witherspoon lived by the credo he had elucidated in *Lectures*. Although Witherspoon's life from 1776 to 1794 is not as relevant to the *Lectures* as his first eight years in America, nevertheless, it certainly deserves to be examined.

From 1776 through 1782, Witherspoon was pre-eminently occupied with his tasks as a member of the Continental Congress, which showed its confidence in Witherspoon by placing him on over one hundred committees. Three of these were particularly important: the board of war, the committee of secret correspondence, and the committee of finance. As a member of this finance committee, Witherspoon wisely opposed the flood of paper money, prophesying that such a move would be financially disastrous. Polemical skill, forged earlier in the crucible of ecclesiastical debate, was now used effectively in the halls of Congress. Even in the moments of despair, Witherspoon believed resolutely in the eventual triumph of the American cause. It was only after military victory was assured that Witherspoon left his congressional seat in November 1782 to resume his duties as president of Princeton.

And Princeton desperately needed his services. Nassau Hall was largely in ruins, having been extensively damaged by British and American troops during the battle of Princeton in 1777. The college purse was depleted. Enrollment had plummeted during the war, since many students had volunteered for the Continental Army. Although matters improved after Witherspoon's return in 1782, he was never able to restore the institution to the prominence it had enjoyed before the war. A fund-raising trip to the British Isles in 1784 was a fiasco. Evidently the indefatigable energy that had fueled Witherspoon in the decade of the 1770s had been lessened by age. More and more of the administrative duties of the college were turned over to Samuel Stanhope Smith, Witherspoon's son-in-law and eventual successor. Witherspoon began to spend more of his time at his country home, "Tusculum," in these declining years.

But there remained yet another important contribution that Witherspoon made to his beloved church. For some time there had been sentiment within American Presbyterianism to reorganize the denomination along national lines. The first major step toward such a restructuring was taken at the synodical meeting at Philadelphia in May 1785. Following the suggestion that the Synod of New York and Philadelphia be divided into four separate synods under a general assembly, the Synod appointed Witherspoon to head a committee to study these proposed changes. For the next three years Witherspoon played a major role in the work that was necessary to effect the reorganization of the Presbyterian Church in America. It was he who composed the short preface to the Plan of Government and Discipline, which was officially adopted by the Synod in 1788. Appropriately, the Synod selected

Witherspoon to open the first session of the General Assembly in May 1789 with a sermon. The delegates then elected Witherspoon as their first Moderator—thus culminating his long career of churchmanship with the highest office in the Presbyterian Church.[71]

Just as Witherspoon responded to the church in his later years, so he could never refuse a call to governmental service in his adopted nation. Although his political activity during this period never equalled his prominence as a member of the Continental Congress, his interest in political affairs remained keen until his death. In 1787 he was a delegate to the New Jersey convention that ratified the national Constitution. In 1783 and in 1789 Somerset County elected him to one-year terms in the New Jersey legislature.

In 1789 Witherspoon was saddened by the death of his wife of forty-one years, Elizabeth. But two years later considerable comment was engendered by his marriage to the widow Anne Dill, a young woman of twenty-four. Witherspoon was so enthusiastic about the nuptials that he granted the Princeton students a three-day holiday. Two daughters were born to this union, one dying in infancy. In 1792 Witherspoon became totally blind; in spite of this, he continued to fill his Princeton pulpit. Finally on November 15, 1794, the career and life of this remarkable man came to an end. In his twenty-six years of residence in America, Witherspoon had left an indelible imprint on the ecclesiastical, educational, and political life of the nation.

AN ANALYSIS OF THE LECTURES

Fortunately, a sense of the power of Witherspoon is preserved in his *Lectures on Moral Philosophy*. Although the dynamic quality of his personality is inadequately conveyed in these lectures, the wellsprings of his thought are clearly revealed. The lectures themselves were prepared for the senior class at Princeton; Witherspoon's class on moral philosophy was considered the culminating course of the college curriculum. In it Witherspoon brought together wide-ranging thought dealing with man's responsibilities in his individual and social state.

Witherspoon was not the first to teach moral philosophy at the College of New Jersey. It was first introduced into the course of instruction in 1764 during the presidency of Samuel Finley.[72] In fact, by mid-eighteenth century moral philosophy was becoming a staple item in the curricula of American colleges. It continued to be a standard course for American college students after the Revolutionary War and well into the nineteenth century. One evidence of this is that *Elements of Moral Science*, a textbook written by Francis Wayland, president of Brown University, sold 200,000 copies between its publication in 1835 and 1890.[73]

But few teachers of moral philosophy in America could match Witherspoon's background in the subject. He had been reared in Scotland, a nation rich in the tradition of moral philosophy. The eighteenth century was the golden age of the Scottish universities, and no discipline equalled the intellectual prestige of moral philosophy in these institutions. Among those filling the chair of moral philosophy at the University of Glasgow during this period were such luminaries as Francis Hutcheson (1730–46), Adam Smith, (1752–64), and Thomas Reid (1764–96). Although the other Scottish universities could not match Glasgow in this respect, nevertheless there were Adam Ferguson (1764–95) at Edinburgh and James Beattie (1760–97) at Aberdeen. Also contributing to this dialogue in Scotland were two eminent philosophers who were not university professors—David Hume and Henry Home (Lord Kames).

This stimulating philosophical atmosphere deeply affected Witherspoon, although its religious heterodoxy frequently horrified him. But he read the books and understood the philosphical issues of his day. His first systematic exposure to moral philosophy was at Edinburgh in a class taught by John Pringle (1707–82). Pringle—who later made outstanding contributions to military medicine—was evidently a better physician than teacher, for Alexander Carlyle thought Pringle's class of little or no value. "Had it not been for Puffendorf's small book, which he made his text," said Carlyle, "we should not have been instructed in the rudiments of the science."[74] Witherspoon probably gained most of his knowledge of moral philosophy from his own reading and conversation with others. For instance, Carlyle writes of frequent gatherings of friends, including Witherspoon, in an Edinburgh tavern in 1743 where the chief topics of conversation were "the deistical controversy and moral philosophy."[75] This type of dialogue probably continued in Witherspoon's life during his pastorates at Beith and Paisley (1745–68). Certainly he continued to read books on moral philosophy, for both his library (see Appendix 2) and *Lectures* evidence a thorough acquaintance with contemporary writings on the subject. Hence Witherspoon was no neophyte when at Princeton he was faced with the task of preparing a set of lectures on moral philosophy.

This knowledge of contemporary philosophy is evident in Witherspoon's *Lectures*, because the one characteristic that stands above all else in this work is eclecticism. Evidently he built his own intellectual structure from varied material. For instance, in political theory he draws upon several traditions: Lockean republicanism, Scottish Whiggism, Grotius-Pufendorf thought on international law, and even on the ideas of thinkers such as Montesquieu and Burlamaqui. Epistemologically, Witherspoon blends Lockean empiricism and a rudimentary form of Scottish Common Sense. This characteristic of combining diverse thought highlights both the strengths and weaknesses of the *Lectures*.

Obviously, Witherspoon's eclecticism and extensive borrowing create problems. For one, the use of a variety of sources, unless they are carefully sifted, inevitably leads to some inconsistency. For example, Witherspoon attacks Hume for his utilitarian ethic, particularly as it relates to justice and chastity, and yet Witherspoon's own discussion of marriage and incest betrays a utilitarian leaning in ethical philosophy.[76] Elsewhere in the *Lectures*, Witherspoon emphasizes moderation in his exposition of one's duty to oneself.[77] This virtue is hardly compatible with Witherspoon's Calvinist theology; he was probably blinded to this incongruity because of his extensive reading from the ancients on this subject. Other subtle contradictions appear repeatedly in the *Lectures* and is the type of contradiction that is usually avoided by one who has constructed his thought originally and carefully.

In particular, Witherspoon's great dependence upon Francis Hutcheson especially weakens the *Lectures*. Although Witherspoon did not slavishly copy Hutcheson's *System of Moral Philosophy* (London, 2 vols., 1755), he did use the work to structure his own lectures. Considering that Hutcheson's book contains at least five times as much material as Witherspoon's *Lectures*, condensation is a Herculean task. It is true that Witherspoon often abridges Hutcheson's material adeptly and clearly.[78] On the other hand, Witherspoon sometimes does not accompany borrowed material with adequate exposition or does not link diverse topics with sufficient transition. This is especially apparent in Lecture XVI, in which he discusses several unrelated topics, mostly borrowed from Hutcheson.

Furthermore, it is disappointing that Witherspoon nowhere acknowledges his debt to Hutcheson, despite the fact that his borrowing borders on plagiarism. Perhaps the fact that Witherspoon never intended his *Lectures* to be published helps explain this omission. At the same time it is clear that Hutcheson's identification with the Moderate party in Scotland had prejudiced Witherspoon against him. Hence Witherspoon does not convey to his audience this dependence upon Hutcheson. Rather he seems to enjoy the opportunity of taking issue with Hutcheson in the *Lectures*. For instance, while generally following Hutcheson in Lecture VII, Witherspoon interjects near the beginning of Lecture VIII his disagreement with the Hutchesonian tenet that general benevolence toward all could grow from particular affection toward family and friends. Again, in Lecture VII, he declaims against "loose moralists" who believe punishment is only justified if it serves the public interest—an obvious reference to Hutcheson. Even when he agrees with Hutcheson, Witherspoon seems reluctant to admit it. For example, in his discussion of the innate moral sense, Witherspoon writes that

> Though there is no occasion to join Mr. Hutcheson or any other, in their opposition to such as make reason the principle of virtuous conduct, yet I think it must be admitted, that a sense of moral good and evil, is as really a principle of our nature as either the gross or reflex senses.[79]

Indeed, the scars of an ecclesiastical battle occasionally surface in *Lectures on Moral Philosophy*.

Perhaps Witherspoon's appropriation of material from many sources contributes to his tendency to synthesize facilely conflicting views. It is to Witherspoon's credit that he frequently lists the various contemporary opinions as he discusses a controversial subject. But then, rather than state forthrightly his position, he often indicates that there is merit in each of the varying views and concludes that the truth of the matter is a combination of the differing opinions. In Lecture IX he deals with Thomas Hobbes's contention that the state of nature is the state of war versus Hutcheson's affirmation that the state of nature is the state of society. Witherspoon is convinced that it is "no hard matter to reconcile them," but his few sentences on the issue are unconvincing.[80] On another occasion, he settles the issue of the ground of divine dominion simply by suggesting that the various opinions be combined.[81] Repeatedly Witherspoon offers this type of surface solution to intellectual disputes. Such an approach exposes the reader of the lectures to diverse opinions on a subject, but it hardly wrestles adequately with the genuine intellectual problems often involved.

One other weakness of the *Lectures* is connected with Witherspoon's treatment of contemporary intellectual disputes. This fault is his tendency to deal unfairly with some of his opponents.

Occasionally he will create caricatures rather than honestly grapple with the strength of an opposing intellectual position. The views of two men that Witherspoon especially handles in this manner are the twin demons of eighteenth-century orthodox religion—Thomas Hobbes and David Hume. On pages 123 and 136 he attributes to Hobbes doctrines that are actually those of Robert Filmer, noted royalist and author of *Patriarcha* (1685). And Witherspoon is grossly inaccurate in accusing Hobbes, the father of the modern social contract theory, of treating the social compact "with great contempt." Similarly, he erroneously places Hume in the philosophical camp of Berkeleian idealism, when, in reality, Hume had rejected the epistemological views of George Berkeley as he had those of John Locke.[82] Witherspoon's penchant to attack and occasionally to misrepresent Hutcheson has already been noted. Had he dealt with fewer thinkers in the *Lectures*, he could have probed their thoughts more thoroughly and represented their positions more accurately.

Yet these criticisms of the lectures should not go unqualified. In the first place, Witherspoon prepared them as a syllabus for his class on moral philosophy at Princeton. Ashbel Green indicates that Witherspoon's "enlargements at the time of recitation were indeed often considerable, and exceedingly interesting.[83] Consequently, the sketchy quality of the lectures is understandable. Obviously, they were not in the expanded form most suitable for publication. For this reason Witherspoon resisted efforts to publish these lectures during his lifetime and the first edition of *Lectures on Moral Philosophy* did not appear until six years after his death.[84]

Furthermore, it is unfair to judge Witherspoon by the rigid standards of twentieth-century scholarship. He fails to credit properly his sources and, even when quoting, often does so incorrectly: for example, on page 64 he quotes from Cotton Mather and merely refers to him as "an author from New England." He commits the egregious error of quoting from Tacitus and attributing it to Cicero.[85] Many other illustrations of inaccuracy and imprecision could be cited. But eighteenth-century writing was not characterized by the exacting research and careful documentation of present scholarship.

Modern scholars, in fact, would eschew an enterprise such as moral philosophy because of the breadth of knowledge involved. Yet this very extent and diversity of subject matter is the strength of the *Lectures*. Witherspoon drew from respectable sources in writing the *Lectures* and generally developed his material in an orderly, logical manner. No speculative genius, Witherspoon was nevertheless knowledgeable—a dilettante in the best sense of the term. The *Lectures* is a microcosm through which the larger world of eighteenth-century thought is revealed.

In organizing his lectures, Witherspoon chose to divide moral philosophy in the customary manner: ethics first and then politics. Bifurcation of the subject, common to the eighteenth century, can be traced back to Aristotle. H. Rackham, translator of Aristotle's *Politics*, comments in his preface, "For Aristotle Political Science is the second half of a subject of which Ethics is the first half; indeed in the opening chapters of *The Nicomachean Ethics* the term *Politike* is applied to the whole subject."[86] Similarly, the course of study at Harvard in 1642 included philosophical disputations about "Ethicks and Politicks."[87]

Witherspoon's discussion of ethics is in Lectures I to IX. Here he touches on many subjects, some of which would not normally belong in a systematic philosophical treatment of ethics. Rather he includes material relating to such themes as epistemology, aesthetics, and theology. Furthermore, Witherspoon's treatment of these topics is not always clear and orderly. For instance, he introduces the subject of the foundation of virtue in Lecture II, discusses it superficially, and then expounds on it more fully in Lecture IV.[88] Yet despite these weaknesses, the ethical section of the *Lectures* does mirror the philosophical controversies of the time. It reflects a clear image of an important body of thought during the last half of the eighteenth century.

One of the liveliest issues of eighteenth-century thought concerned epistemology. John Locke (1632–1704) had first raised the central question: How do we know what we know? His answer is in the *Essay Concerning Human Understanding* (1690), the purpose of which is "to inquire into the origin, certainty, and extent of human knowledge." Locke concludes that all ideas come from experience and thus denies the existence of innate ideas. The human mind assimilates experience in two ways: sensation (sense experience received from external objects) and reflection (sense experience combined and abstracted by internal processes). Locke, however, is aware that sense experience is not direct knowledge of the world as it is. And the opening of this epistemological Pandora's box occupied British philosophy throughout the eighteenth century.

Following Locke, the next significant contribution to epistemological theory was made by George Berkeley (1685–1753). Fearful of the mechanistic implication of Locke's thought, Berkeley erected his philosophy on the dictum *esse est percipi* (to be is to be perceived). Properties do not exist prior to, or independent of, the mind. Matter, which is inert and has no metaphysical reality, cannot be the cause of one's ideas. Rather they are the ultimate product of an infinite, omnipotent God. Berkeley believed that by placing Locke's epistemological system on an idealistic base he had avoided the abyss of materialism.

But Berkeley could not prevent Lockean empiricism from being driven to its logical extreme of skepticism. This was masterfully done by David Hume, who denied the existence of anything behind experience. The only thing of which the mind can be positive is its perception; it cannot know the connection of these perceptions with external objects. To establish causality between perceptions and objects transcends the limits of man's understanding. Hume was not effectively confronted until Immanuel Kant reconstructed philosophy upon a different epistemological base than empirical presuppositions.

Yet a competent attempt to answer Hume was undertaken by the Scottish Common Sense philosophers in the last half of the eighteenth century. The most outstanding expositor of this philosophical position was Thomas Reid (1710–96). Reid agreed with the empiricists that sensation was subjective, but he argued that concomitant with sensation was perception, an inherent quality by which the external world is perceived. The mind possesses immediate perception (i.e., direct knowledge) instead of mediate perception. The appeal of Reid and his philosophical countrymen to common sense gave this school its name.

Where then did Witherspoon stand in this swirl of epistemological debate? First, it is evident from the *Lectures* that Witherspoon is an heir of British empiricism. During his student days at Edinburgh he had studied Locke's *Essay Concerning Human Understanding*. Fortunately, his able professor of logic and metaphysics, John Stevenson, had discarded Aristotle and used Locke as a text. Lockean influence is evident in the *Lectures* when Witherspoon mentioned sensation and reflection as the only "two ways in which we come to a knowledge of things."[89] Furthermore, in good Lockean tradition, Witherspoon prefers the inductive, rather than the deductive, approach to knowledge. He writes, "It is always safer in our reasoning to trace fact upwards, than to reason downwards, upon metaphysical principles." He even anticipates the day when the Newtonian method will be applied to moral philosophy, as well as natural philosophy.[90]

Yet Witherspoon lived in an age when epistemological study had moved beyond the conclusions of Locke. For instance, Witherspoon himself takes issue with Locke's denial of innate ideas. He specifically affirms as inherent to man a sense of beauty and a moral sense.[91] But even though Witherspoon did not follow Locke completely, he certainly did not land in either camp of Locke's leading eighteenth-century critics, Berkeley and Hume.

In Lecture II Witherspoon unleashes an attack on Berkeley and his followers, labeling them as "Immaterialists." He fails to deal substantially with Berkeley's philosophical position, largely rejecting it because it "takes away the distinction between truth and falsehood." He concludes his tirade in these words:

> The truth is, the immaterial system, is a wild and ridiculous attempt to unsettle the principles of common sense by metaphysical reasoning, which can hardly produce anything but contempt in the generality of persons who hear it, and which I verily believe, never produced conviction even on the persons who pretend to espouse it.[92]

Witherspoon's opposition to Berkeleianism was not confined to writing. When he came to Princeton, he discovered some students enamored of the metaphysical views of Bishop Berkeley. Joseph Periam, a young tutor at the college, was particularly effective in disseminating this idealistic philosophy. Even Samuel Stanhope Smith, Witherspoon's future son-in-law and successor to the Princeton presidency, had been affected. Witherspoon successfully excised the heresy by argumentation and pressure. Significantly, Joseph Periam and two other tutors, Ebenezer Pemberton and Jonathan Edwards, Jr., left Princeton after the first year of Witherspoon's administration.[93]

This intense aversion to idealism may explain partially Witherspoon's coolness to the thought of Jonathan Edwards (1703–58), America's premier theologian of the colonial period and, in the brief period before his death, Princeton's president. Witherspoon only alludes to Edwards once in the *Lectures*. In his discussion of virtue, Witherspoon writes, "We have an opinion published in this country, that virtue consists in the love of being as such."[94] Edwards's complex thought synthesized Puritan Platonism, Lockean empiricism, and Calvinist theology. His massive metaphysical system affirmed idealistic causation, for he believed that Locke's thought had mechanistic tendencies. Edwards's idealism verged on pantheism by asserting that every intelligent being is related to being in general and is part of the universal system of existence. To Witherspoon this smacked too much of the immaterialism of George Berkeley.[95]

Witherspoon also rejects the thought of David Hume as vigorously as he does that of Berkeley. In fact, on page 74 of the *Lectures*, he carelessly classifies Hume as an advocate of

Berkeley's system. An additional irritant in Hume's case was his devastating attacks on traditional religion. Witherspoon labels him an infidel writer who has "industriously endeavored to shake the certainty of our belief upon cause and effect, upon personal identity and the idea of power." To counter Hume, Witherspoon cites "the dictates of common sense" that have been advanced by "some late writers."[96]

The "late writers" to whom Witherspoon refers are obviously the Scottish Common Sense philosophers. Since this school of Scottish realism had just begun at the time of the composition of the *Lectures*, the only two writers Witherspoon could have had in mind were Thomas Reid and James Beattie.[97] Like Reid and Beattie, Witherspoon believes that the mind perceives not merely the images of external objects but the external objects themselves. Significantly, Witherspoon divides the faculty of sensation into two parts: external and internal. The internal part of sensation is that innate common sense of Scottish realism. Witherspoon admits that this innate quality cannot be proven, but he accepts it as one accepts "an axiom in mathematical science."[98]

Actually, Witherspoon's exposition of Scottish realism in the *Lectures* is sketchy and incomplete. He simply affirms the basic principles of this philosophical school but shows none of the sophisticated and careful reasoning of Reid. Yet he is confident that "these authors of Scotland" have resolved "at once all the refinements and metaphysical objections of some infidel writers."[99]

In terms of Scottish Common Sense philosophy, Witherspoon's thought is neither original nor profound. Rather, his real significance is in making Princeton a citadel of Scottish realism—a citadel that, in turn, dominated philosophical thought in American higher education for many decades. As one historian of American philosophy aptly puts it, "The Scottish common-sense philosophy introduced at the end of the eighteenth century at Princeton by President Witherspoon spread until it formed almost the sole basis of philosophic instruction."[100] Appropriately, the last great champion of Scottish realism in America was Princeton President James McCosh (1868–88), another imported Scot who arrived in America exactly one hundred years after Witherspoon.

Certain circumstances converged in America to make possible the ascendancy of Common Sense philosophy. For one, the Scotch-Irish, who looked to Princeton for spiritual guidance, led the way in the great westward movement. Many of these migrants were instrumental in establishing the denominational colleges that sprang up all over America in the first half of the eighteenth century. This, coupled with Princeton's powerful influence in higher education, assisted the dissemination of Scottish realism. But most of all, Scottish Common Sense philosophy was exactly what was needed to protect the educational and ecclesiastical orthodoxy in American colleges. This safe and sane system prevented the youth from speculative extremes. It sailed the intellectual strait between the Scylla of idealism and Charybdis of materialism. Witherspoon was instrumental in importing a philosophical system that served America's intellectual needs for almost a century.

Other than epistemology, the most controversial philosophical subject in the eighteenth century was ethics. On this topic moral philosophers of varying stripe—agnostic, Deist, orthodox Christian—crossed intellectual swords. And Scotland, Witherspoon's native country, produced its share of antagonists in this controversy.

In the *Lectures on Moral Philosophy*, Witherspoon evidences a keen awareness of the ethical discussions of his time. For instance, in Lecture IV he chronicles seven different contemporary theories on the nature of virtue.[101] Yet as Witherspoon develops his own view on morals in the *Lectures*, he borrows too freely from various thinkers. The resulting philosophy intends to be a potpourri of contemporary ethical thought, rather than an original, consistent, ethical system. An analysis of Witherspoon's thought in the context of the major ethical philosophies of his day reveals this weakness.

One ethicist, however, whose views Witherspoon has no difficulty in rejecting is Thomas Hobbes. Hobbes, the *bête noire* of orthodox religion, was suspect for many reasons: his epistemology was materialistic, his psychology was deterministic, and his political theory was absolutistic. In ethical theory Hobbes believed that all man's actions are egoistic. Man calls a thing evil when he finds it unpleasant; he calls it good when he finds it agreeable. Thus moral concepts are not a priori but are relative in terms of personal satisfaction. According to Hobbes, even an apparently altruistic emotion such as pity is selfish: "Pity is imagination or fiction of future calamity to ourselves, proceeding from the sense of another man's calamity."[102]

Witherspoon attacks "the patrons of the selfish idea" throughout the *Lectures* (for example, pp. 73, 86, 91, 118). He believes that there are "benevolent passions" as well as selfish ones. Witherspoon does not really confront this philosophical position, but simply asserts the following concerning human action: "It is certain that the direct object in view in many cases, is to promote the happiness of others; and for this many have been willing to sacrifice everything, even life itself."[103] Along with Hobbes,

Witherspoon mentions two later advocates of the egoistic view: Bernard de Mandeville (ca. 1670-1733) and Archibald Campbell (1691-1756).[104] Witherspoon considers ludicrous Mandeville's thesis that private vices produce the public good. On Campbell, he simply notes that his scheme of self-love is the best exposition of the subject. Although Witherspoon's theology led him to view man pessimistically, he refused to attribute selfishness to every human action.

Another major moral theory in the early eighteenth century was the ethical rationalism of Samuel Clarke (1675-1729). In his *Discourse Concerning the Being and Attributes of God* (1704-5), Clarke asserts that the fundamental truths of ethics are self-evident. He considers these laws of morality to be as certain and invariable as the axioms of mathematics. Using the deductive approach, Clarke is confident that he has rationally demonstrated these laws.[105]

Witherspoon expresses qualified appreciation of Clarke's work, and even organizes Lectures VI to IX along the general lines that Clarke had used in his volume: duty to God, duty to man, and duty to ourselves. But Clarke was a Cartesian and essentially structured his thought on the deductive method of Scholasticism. Witherspoon rejected this approach, choosing rather the inductive method popularized by the intellectual revolution wrought by Newton. Witherspoon may have partially approved of Clarke in order to modify another contemporary ethical theory: the moral sense school of Lord Shaftesbury and Francis Hutcheson.

The third earl of Shaftesbury, Anthony Ashley Cooper (1671-1713), expounded his ethical views in *Characteristics of Men, Manners, Opinion, Times* (1711). Central to his ethical philosophy is his theory of moral sense. This innate moral faculty is not dependent upon experience—if properly developed, it becomes an absolute standard in distinguishing right and wrong. Furthermore, Shaftesbury transferred the ethical base from reason to affection (for example, the emotional impulses that prompt to social duty). To him, the moral and aesthetic perceptions are essentially the same; only the objects differ.[106]

Hutcheson further developed the moral sense theory, structuring it in systematic philosophical fashion. He believed that the moral sense is a primitive, innate faculty given to man by God. But more fully than Shaftesbury, he emphasized that the maturation of the moral sense is dependent upon observation and is controlled by reason. It was primarily through Hutcheson's *System of Moral Philosophy* that Witherspoon received his impressions of the moral sense theory.[107]

Witherspoon's response to Shaftesbury-Hutchesonian ethical

thought is ambivalent. His deep involvement in the Moderate-Evangelical conflict within the Church of Scotland jaundiced his outlook toward their writings.[108] Thus Witherspoon repeatedly takes issue with Shaftesbury on a variety of topics. He labels him an unbeliever because of Shaftesbury's criticism of the Bible for its failure to commend private friendship and love of country. He argues at some length with Shaftesbury's contention that virtue should not be based upon future reward or punishment. (Witherspoon began this denunciation with the sentence, "Shaftesbury speaks with great bitterness against taking into view a future state of what he calls more extended self-interest.") He disagrees with the Shaftesburian doctrine of the use of ridicule as a test of truth. Significantly, even when he favorably develops a concept of Shaftesbury ("even love of beauty in man is an attachment to moral excellence"), Witherspoon fails to mention Shaftesbury's name.[109]

Although Witherspoon is not as vehement in his criticism of Hutcheson as he is of Shaftesbury, nonetheless he does not basically agree with him. Witherspoon is particularly disturbed over the utilitarian implications in Hutcheson's ethical philosophy. Indeed, Hutcheson was the first to use the utilitarian formula, "That action is best which procures the greatest happiness of the greatest numbers."[110] According to Hutcheson, the mature moral sense will make that choice that is most conducive to the public good. Aware that this principle will call occasionally for the sacrifice of private morality, Hutcheson was, nevertheless, willing to take that step:

> But, although private justice, veracity, openness of mind, compassion, are immediately approved without reference to a system; yet we must not imagine that any of these principles are destined to control or limit that regard to the most extensive good which we showed to be the noblest principle of our nature.[111]

Witherspoon strongly disagrees.

To Witherspoon, any sacrifice of private morality destroys "the perfection and immutability of the moral laws." His religious nature was too conservative and his belief in ultimate moral law too strong to follow Hutcheson at this point. For example, Witherspoon believes that a man should not lie under any circumstances. Although Hutcheson recognized the virtue of veracity, he envisions some circumstances in which a falsehood would advance the general good (for example, to save a human life, to benefit a sick person). Hutcheson labeled such actions, which are

36

normally immoral but become moral because of their intended consequence, as "extraordinary rights arising from some singular necessity." Throughout the *Lectures* Witherspoon carries on a running battle with Hutcheson on this issue, consistently choosing to follow moral laws legalistically, regardless of the situation.[112]

Despite his fundamental disagreement with Shaftesbury and Hutcheson, Witherspoon concurs with their belief that man possesses a moral sense. He asserts that "a sense of moral good and evil, is really a principle of our nature."[113] Yet Witherspoon is unhappy with Shaftesbury and Hutcheson's basing the moral sense on affection; he is convinced that such an ethical base tends to exclude reason from moral decision. In this respect he leans toward Clarke's affirmation that virtue is founded upon reason, but he cannot agree with Clarke's denial of innate ideas. Thus Witherspoon prefers an ethical theory that combines the rational element of Clarke, and the innate moral faculty of the Shaftesbury-Hutcheson tradition. One ethicist does this for Witherspoon—the great moral philosopher, Joseph Butler (1692–1752).

To Butler the key to moral behavior is the conscience. He affirmed that conscience is an innate rational faculty that determines whether man's actions are right or wrong. Although man also possesses self-love and benevolence as innate qualities, the conscience is superior to both of these and, therefore, judges them. In his famous *Fifteen Sermons Preached at Rolls Chapel*, Butler succinctly notes that "this principle in man, by which he approves or disapproves his heart, temper, and actions is conscience."[114] Butler subordinated pleasure to duty, for when man is motivated by a sense of duty, he is responding to God's great gift, the human conscience.

Witherspoon was predisposed toward Butler's thought for many reasons. For one, Butler's view of man is more guarded than the optimism characteristic of Shaftesbury and Hutcheson. Obviously this appealed to Witherspoon's Calvinistic orientation. For another, Butler maintains that punishment fulfilled an independent notion of justice regardless of the end accomplished. Hutcheson disagrees, believing that punishment is only justified if it serves the public interest. Witherspoon calls Hutcheson a loose moralist and sides with Butler on the issue, making "guilt the proper object of punishment simply in itself."[115] Additionally, Butler's inductive approach commends itself to Witherspoon. Hereby, the rationalism of Clarke could be retained without the Cartesian deductive approach of Clarke's system.

And it is clear that Witherspoon's ethical philosophy owes more to Butler than to any other thinker. Thus Witherspoon agrees with Butler in his definition of moral sense: "This moral sense is precisely the same thing with what, in scripture and common language, we call conscience. It is the law which our Maker has written upon our hearts, and both intimates and enforces duty previous to all reasoning."[116] Witherspoon is dissatisfied with the moral sense of Shaftesbury that implies "merely an approbation of a certain class of actions as beautiful, praiseworthy, or delightful." Rather he declares that "the moral sense also implies a sense of obligation."[117] Continuing in Butler's thought, Witherspoon affirms that moral actions are pleasing because of duty; not duty because they are pleasing. Repeated emphasis upon the themes of obligation, duty, and conscience mirror Butler's impact upon Witherspoon.[118]

But in the *Lectures* Witherspoon seldom relies completely on one thinker in any area of thought. So in ethical philosophy, although Witherspoon leans most heavily upon Butler, he is still reluctant to reject the systems of other contemporary moral thinkers. Witherspoon's summary of his ethical view at the end of Lecture IV makes this apparent: "The result of the whole is, that we ought to take the rule of duty and conscience enlightened by reason, experience, and every way by which we can be supposed to learn the will of our Maker, and his intention in making us."

In all of his discussion of philosophical issues, Witherspoon never strayed far from his religious moorings. The *Lectures* may not be a theological treatise, but Witherspoon's general theological stance is discernible in the ethical section. His commitment to the Reformed tradition is clear. Steeped in the Presbyterianism of Scotland, Witherspoon remained faithfully in the mainstream of Calvinism until his death. Contemporary heterodoxies such as Deism and Arminianism were resisted resolutely.

The Calvinist tendency to emphasize the Scriptures is interwoven in the *Lectures*. Witherspoon frequently alludes to the Bible in his discussions. In the very last sentence of the *Lectures*, Witherspoon refers to Paul's admonition to obey civil authorities for conscience sake (Rom. 13:4,5). Sometimes the Bible is cited as the definitive word on a matter, indicating Witherspoon's confidence in its authority. For instance, the Bible is used as the final arbiter concerning justifiable reasons for divorce.[119] Witherspoon even suggests that the Old Testament lex talionis ("an eye for an eye, a tooth for a tooth") might be appropriate punishment for certain crimes.[120]

Yet the Calvinism of Witherspoon is not the Calvinism of

Geneva. Over two centuries of development had modified Reformed theology since its classic formulation by Calvin in the *Institutes of the Christian Religion* (1536). The covenant theologians of the seventeenth century (such as William Ames in *Medulla Theologicae*) had replaced the austere, unknowable Almighty with a God who deigned to contract with man on certain terms. And eighteenth-century Calvinism was further modifying itself under the impact of the rationalist currents loosed by the Enlightenment.

This modified Calvinism is mirrored in the *Lectures*. True, the facade is orthodox Calvinism, yet some of the basic tenets of the faith have been eroded by the strong forces of intellectual change. This erosion is particularly evident in Witherspoon's exposition of his views on God and man. Witherspoon does not envision God as the arbitrary Deity portrayed by ultra-Calvinists. He makes it clear that good is not merely good because God wills it. Such an idea would destroy the basic nature of good and "unhinge all our notions of the supreme excellence of God himself." Neither will Witherspoon accept the view that God is to be obeyed merely because he is omnipotent. To Witherspoon the actions and commands of God must be partially amenable to reason; the harsh portrait of a capricious Divine Being drawn by high Calvinism is offensive to him.[121] Furthermore, Witherspoon's view of God leads to a softening of the Calvinist dogma of predestination, a notion that is clear in his discussion of prayer. Pure Calvinism was faced with the dilemma in regard to prayer: If all events are preordained, of what value is prayer? But if prayer genuinely changes matters, how then can all events be preordained? Witherspoon does not solve the difficulty, but he opts for the efficacy of prayer. He labels it a "second choice" that is powerful despite "the unchangeable purpose of God."[122]

In like manner, Witherspoon's view of man differs from that of high Calvinism—not on the matter of human depravity, but in the confidence he places in the reason of man. To some Calvinists the whole enterprise of moral philosophy was suspect. To them it smacked too much of man knowing himself apart from God. An American Puritan, Cotton Mather (1663–1728), had earlier described moral philosophy as "reducing infidelity to a system."[123] But Witherspoon had no such qualms about the study, for he is confident that reason will validate revelation. In this respect he parallels earlier Deists such as Samuel Clarke and William Wollaston who believed that reason and the Bible were complementary, never contradictory. Throughout the *Lectures* Witherspoon employs reason with a confidence atypical of earlier

Calvinism. He reflects a phenomenon of his time: rationalism had entered the house of Calvinism. This intrusion undermined the house's foundations in the eighteenth century to such an extent that the structure would collapse in the nineteenth century.

Other than rationalism, an additional factor subverting Calvinism in the eighteenth century was secularization. This process changed the essentially religious orientation of the colonies in the early eighteenth century to a primarily political and hence worldly orientation by the end of the century. Edmund S. Morgan develops this thesis in his incisive essay, "The American Revolution Considered as an Intellectual Movement:"

> In 1740 America's leading intellectuals were clergymen and thought about theology; in 1790 they were statesmen and thought about politics. A variety of forces, some of them reaching deep into the colonial past, helped to bring about the transformation, but it was so closely associated with the revolt from England that one may properly consider the American Revolution, as an intellectual movement, to mean the substitution of political for clerical leadership and of politics for religion as the most challenging area of human thought and endeavor.[124]

The Revolution is seen as the watershed in a significant transformation of America's intellectual focus. And no individual is more representative of this intellectual transition than John Witherspoon. Clergyman to the core, Witherspoon spent his first few years in America as minister and president of a religious college. But by 1776 his deep involvement in the Revolution led to the political activity that occupied the major portion of his time for the next six years. Unquestionably his thought and his example provide a kind of bridge that spans religious and political America: an earlier generation, exemplified by Jonathan Edwards, was primarily occupied with religious issues; a later generation, typified by Madison and Jefferson, would be almost totally preoccupied with political affairs. Witherspoon clings to both worlds, a trait that makes him a fascinating study.

It should not be inferred, however, that his political interest was merely a product of his American environment. The spirit of colonial liberty intensified his political concern, leading eventually to identification with the patriot cause. But Witherspoon came to America with a philosophy that was not inconsistent with his subsequent revolutionary activity. It is impossible to know exactly how much ideology motivates a person's behavior, though certainly Witherspoon's political philosophy was conducive to his participation in the American Revolution.

This political thought is fully explained in Lectures X to XVI, where the subject matter covered is extremely diverse. Today some of the material would be classified in disciplines other than political science, such as economics, jurisprudence, or sociology. For instance, Lecture XI discusses domestic society, which Witherspoon classified under the headings of the relations of marriage, of parents and children, and of master and servant. But the heart of Witherspoon's political philosophy is elucidated in Lecture X and Lecture XII. Here can be found those aspects of his thought most relevant to his political activity.

What are the sources of Witherspoon's political theory? The *Lectures* repeatedly indicate that he stands in the grand tradition of seventeenth-century English Whig thought—that tradition which triumphed in the Glorious Revolution of 1688 and whose chief political philosopher was John Locke (1632–1704). Locke's *Two Treatises of Government* (1690) best articulated the political theory that lay behind the opposition to Stuart absolutism in the seventeenth century. He continued to dominate English political thought in the eighteenth century. Significantly, Locke's *Two Treatises* was in Witherspoon's library and Witherspoon recommends Locke among writers on politics at the end of the *Lectures* (see Appendix 1). Furthermore, as annotations accompanying these lectures abundantly indicate, many of Witherspoon's political tenets are Lockean and, in some instances, are borrowed directly from Locke's writings.

Particulary apparent in Witherspoon's thought are the Calvinist roots that had nurtured this Lockean tradition. Locke's own debt to Calvinism has often been overlooked, partially because of his natural reluctance to identify himself with the discredited Cromwellian rebellion. Interestingly, Locke's father had actively participated in this Puritan revolt as a captain of the House in the Parliamentary army. Another formative Calvinist influence in Locke's life was his Oxford mentor Louis du Moulin (1606–80), whose fiery independent views lost him his teaching post at the restoration of Charles II in 1660. Almost every argument advanced by Locke can be found in earlier Calvinist thought, as, for example, in the appeal to the law of nature, the ultimate sovereignty of the people, the right of resistance, and the concept of government as a contract between the governor and the governed. Thus the wedding of Calvinist theology and Lockean political philosophy in Witherspoon's thought was entirely harmonious.[125]

Lockean political thought was a common staple for the American colonies, but in Witherspoon's case there was an additional feature: his thought had been strained through the tradition of Scottish Whiggism. After the Glorious Revolution of 1688, Tory professors were purged from the Scottish universities, where a strong Whiggish political tradition subsequently arose. As H. J. Hanham states in his book, *The Scottish Political Tradition*, "The eighteenth century Scottish universities fostered the creation of a distinctive Whig school of thought about political and economic questions, which was to dominate Scottish politics down to the First World War."[126] This was the political atmosphere in which Witherspoon was nurtured during his university years at Edinburgh (1736–39), and he continued to read the political literature of Scottish Whiggism during the years preceding his coming to America in 1768.[127]

Of all the Scottish Whigs, none influenced Witherspoon more thoroughly than Francis Hutcheson. As noted earlier, Hutcheson's *System of Moral Philosophy* was the primary source for Witherspoon's *Lectures on Moral Philosophy*. This influence is especially evident in the political section of Hutcheson's book.[128] For instance, Lecture XII has at least fourteen references by Witherspoon that can be traced directly to Hutcheson. Hutcheson was an orthodox Whig, affirming the cardinal tenets of social contract and right of rebellion, for example. So in depending upon Hutcheson's *System of Moral Philosophy* as his chief source, Witherspoon was drawing up on an accurate reflection of the Lockean tradition.

Other political writers have also been cited as significant contributors to Witherspoon's thought. Ray Forrest Harvey, in his study of Jean Jacques Burlamaqui (1694–1748), the Genevan jurist, asserted that Witherspoon relied extensively on Burlamaqui in composing the syllabus for his course on moral philosophy.[129] This is an overstatement. Witherspoon had read from Burlamaqui and occasionally borrowed from him.[130] But he evidences little dependence upon Burlamaqui and does not even mention him in the text of the *Lectures* with the exception of recommending him, along with a long list of political writers, in the section entitled "Recapitulation" at the end of the lectures.

Nevertheless, Witherspoon does rely extensively upon a source common to both him and Burlamaqui: the tradition of international law expounded by the great Dutch jurist and historian, Hugo Grotius (1586–1645), and his German disciple, Samuel von Pufendorf (1632–94). Witherspoon's library included both Grotius's and Pufendorf's *De jure belli ac pacis (On the Law of War and Peace) De officio hominis et civic (On the Duty of Man and Citizen)*. The latter book had also been used as a text in

Witherspoon's study of moral philosophy at the University of Edinburgh.[131]

Lectures XIII to XVI demonstrate a heavy obligation to Grotius and to Pufendorf. It is not easy, however, to determine whether Witherspoon borrows directly from these writers or draws upon Hutcheson, who in turn had borrowed extensively from them. In a few instances it seems clear that Witherspoon takes his material directly from Grotius or Pufendorf.[132] Yet, in most cases, it is evident that Hutcheson's *System of Moral Philosophy* is the primary source, and that through this volume Grotius and Pufendorf were refracted to Witherspoon.

In the *Lectures*, there are primarily two subjects discussed by Witherspoon that stand in the Grotius-Pufendorf tradition. The first of these is Witherspoon's exposition of the topic of war in Lecture XIII. Obviously, Witherspoon is no pacifist; rather, he believes that there are some situations in which war may be justifiably waged. The just war theory can be traced back in Christian thought to Augustine (354–430), who specified certain circumstances under which a Christian might participate in warfare. It dominated the thinking of the Christian world during the Middle Ages. Then in the sixteenth century Grotius composed the most comprehensive treatment of the just war concept in his famous volume, *On the Law of War and Peace*. Seventeenth-century students of international law, such as Pufendorf, continued to develop the rules of war essentially along the lines of Grotius. Defining the nature of a just war, in turn, became standard in eighteenth-century expositions of moral philosophy. Thus Witherspoon discusses war in a fashion typical of his day by including legitimate causes for war, proper means of carrying it on, and rights of a neutral power.

The other item in the lectures that is a part of the Grotius-Pufendorf tradition is Witherspoon's exposition on contracts and oaths.[133] Actually, Witherspoon's treatment of these juridical matters is rather prosaic and indicates no original thought. He discusses such items as the essentials of a contract, the signs of a contract, and the types of oaths, once again gleaning most of Grotius and Pufendorf through Hutcheson. However, although this material is not substantive, it does indicate the importance of international law to eighteenth-century thought. Grotius and Pufendorf, and their later intepreters—Burlamaqui, Jean Barbeyrac (1674–1744), and Emmerich de Vattel (1714–67)—were carefully read by Witherspoon's contemporaries and often found their way into the curriculum of colonial colleges.[134]

Yet another political thinker who significantly affected Witherspoon's thought was Charles Louis de Secondat Montesquieu (1689–1755). Montesquieu's *Spirit of Laws* represents a major contribution to governmental theory. Obviously Witherspoon was familiar with this work, for he borrows from it on occasion in the *Lectures*.[135] Ashbel Green states that Montesquieu was Witherspoon's favorite French author.[136] This statement should not lead to the conclusion, however, that Montesquieu was as significant to Witherspoon's political thought as Hutcheson. One subject on which Montesquieu was considered authoritative by many Americans was that of the separation of powers. In Number 47 of *The Federalist*, James Madison indicated that Montesquieu was "always consulted and cited on this subject."[137] Typically, though, in discussing this subject Witherspoon leans more heavily upon Hutcheson than Montesquieu.[138]

The one item in the *Lectures* that is most distinctly Montesquieuan is Witherspoon's assertion that a nation's polity should be forumlated to enhance the particular virtue of that nation.[139] Witherspoon even uses some of the same illustrations found in *The Spirit of Laws* (for example, sobriety as the prevailing principle in Sparta). He obviously concurs with Montesquieu's thesis, but Witherspoon's development of it is quite cursory compared to Montesquieu's incisive treatment.

Although familiar with Montesquieu, Witherspoon shows no familiarity with his countryman and important social contract theorist, Jean Jacques Rousseau (1712–78). Witherspoon does not even list Rousseau among recommended political writers at the end of the *Lectures*. Rousseau may have been omitted because of the late date of his *Contrat social* (1762), but it also could be because of his religious heterodoxy. Actually, Witherspoon's political philosophy is predominantly English with only an occasional Continental influence such as Grotius, Pufendorf, and Montesquieu. In truth, these Continental writers had become such a part of the English political tradition that Witherspoon cannot really be credited with stepping outside his intellectual heritage in a significant way.

There is one strain of the English political tradition that is not found in Witherspoon: eighteenth-century Whiggism of the anti-Walpolean variety. Witherspoon shows no acquaintance with the writings of radical publicists such as John Trenchard and Thomas Gordon. Neither is he concerned with their chief subject matter: the denunciation of mechanisms of finance, of bureaucracy, and of the standing army to increase prerogative powers.[140] Instead, Witherspoon's political philosophy was drawn from English republican theory of the seventeenth century. This thought was communicated to Witherspoon in the following way: its author was John Locke; its teacher a fellow Scot, Francis Hutcheson. This earlier Whiggish current, above all else, is the source for the political section of Witherspoon's *Lectures on Moral Philosophy*.

The central tenet of Witherspoon's political philosophy in common with those of other American revolutionists was the theory of the social contract. This theory can be traced back to Greek and Roman times, and in some form it persisted throughout the Middle Ages.[141] But the formulation that most profoundly affected Americans of the Revolutionary generation was, of course, that of John Locke in his *Essay Concerning the True Original Extent and End of Civil Government*. It was Lockean political ideology that undergirded and animated the American Revolution and that permeates every sentence of the Declaration of Independence.

The first assumption of the social contract theory was that man originally existed in a state of nature. In this state man supposedly enjoyed natural liberty apart from all governmental forms. David Hume seriously questioned the historicity of such a state, finding no evidence for it in his historical research. In reply, Witherspoon blandly affirms that the natural state must have existed, for to deny it would invalidate the voluntary compact.[142] Admittedly, the compact theory was built upon the idea of an original natural state with certain inherent rights. Chief of these was natural liberty, about which Witherspoon writes, "Reason teaches natural liberty and common utility recommends it."[143]

If this be true, how then did Witherspoon view Negro slavery in America? Obviously, the Negro's liberty had been abrogated without his consent. Philosophically, Witherspoon believed it unlawful to take away people's "liberty by no better right than superior power.[144] There is no indication, however, that he actively involved himself in any abolition movement. Rather, he tended to view slavery as an evil that time would cure. In 1790, as a member of the New Jersey legislature, he chaired a committee to study the possibility of abolishing slavery in the state. He suggested as a possible solution that New Jersey could enact a law that all slaves born after its passage should become free at a certain age (twenty-eight was proposed). He did not personally believe such a law was necessary, for his faith in the ideal of liberty in America led him to affirm that the abolition of slavery would occur naturally within twenty-eight years. Unfortunately, his intentions were better than his prophecy.[145]

If man, then, was originally free, the only legitimate reason for surrendering some of that freedom to the state was the protection that the individual would subsequently receive. For this reason man enters into a contract. As Witherspoon wrote, "Society I would define to be an association or compact of any number of persons, to deliver up or abridge some part of their natural rights, in order to have the strength of the united body, to protect the remaining, and to bestow others.[146] Obviously, such a compact implies the consent of the governed: "Society always supposes an expressed or implied contract or agreement."[147] The contract is of mutual benefit to both the governor and the governed, with mutual responsibilities by both.

But suppose the ruler fails to keep the contract and begins to abuse the populace? Is there any recourse open to the people? In such a situation Witherspoon clearly asserts the right of rebellion: "If the supreme power wherever lodged, comes to be exercised in a manifestly tyrannical manner, the subject may certainly if in their power, resist and overthrow it."[148]

Hardly any topic engendered more controversy in seventeenth- and eighteenth-century England than the subject of the right of resistance. Royalists, such as Sir Robert Filmer in *Patriarcha* (1680), denied that the subjects of a king had the right to rebel. The Anglican clergy of the seventeenth century had buttressed Stuart rule by equating resistance to the sovereign with resistance to God. Thomas Hobbes, although not subscribing to the divine right of kings, viewed any doctrine of revolution as an invitation to anarchy.

Yet is clear that many Englishmen did not subscribe to these royalist views, for the nation was convulsed by two revolutions in the seventeenth century. The first of these, the Puritan Revolution, brought about the execution of Charles I. Revulsion at this regicide by the English people was one factor in the restoration of Charles II in 1660. Witherspoon, however, was not repelled by the Puritan Revolution; rather he viewed with disdain the willingness of the English to accept a monarchy in 1660: "At last tamely submitted without resistance to that very tyranny against which they had fought with so much glory and success."[149] After all, religious discontent in Scotland had precipitated the Puritan Revolution. One of the writers who had most ably defended the right of resistance during the turbulent 1640s was the Scotch Covenanter, Samuel Rutherford (c. 1600-61). In *Lex Rex, a Dispute for the Just Prerogative of King and People*, he had countenanced rebellion by the people: "The people have a naturall throne of policies in their conscience to give warning, and materially sentence against the King as a tyrant."[150] Witherspoon identified with these sturdy Calvinist rebels in both English Puritans and Scotch Presbyterians—who had violently revolted against the rule of Charles I.

But the revolution that gave ultimate legitimacy to the right of rebellion in England was the Glorious Revolution. Without bloodshed, Parliament deposed James II and brought William and Mary to the English throne with restrictions that effectively circumscribed the power of the monarchy. What Parliament did in actuality, John Locke justified on paper.[151] Since he felt that consent by the people was the only legitimate basis for government, rebellion was a justifiable and desirable remedy for tyranny.[152]

Such a doctrine was obviously a convenient ideological tool almost a century later when the American colonists revolted against England. No political theorist was read more avidly or quoted more frequently in the colonies from 1763 to 1776 than Locke. His political thought, and sometimes his very words, animate the document that culminated the colonial revolt, the Declaration of Independence. Although recognizing that government "should not be changed for light and transient causes," the Declaration affirms mankind's right and duty to rebel when abuses occur designed " to reduce them under absolute despotism."

Colonial clergymen were particularly effective in disseminating this Lockean doctrine to the American public. Locke's words, along with the Bible, were quoted often from their pulpits. Clinton Rossiter in his study of pre-Revolutionary thought, *Seedtime of the Republic*, concludes that ministers were responsible for twenty to twenty-five percent of the total output of political thought during the decade before the Revolution. Rossiter aptly observes:

> Had ministers been the only spokesmen of the rebellion, had Jefferson, the Adamses, and Otis never appeared in print, the political thought of the Revolution would have followed almost exactly the same line with perhaps a little more mention of God, but certainly no less of John Locke.[153]

Certainly one of the preachers who most effectively articulated this religio-political creed was Witherspoon. Unhesitatingly, he asserts that the people should decide when a government ought to be resisted. Although realizing that subjects could abuse this privilege, yet he concludes, "In experience there are many instances of rulers becoming tyrants, but comparatively, very few of causeless and premature rebellions."[154]

Witherspoon, however, was no radical revolutionary—he would never justify a coup d'etat. He suggests instead that resistance by authority should occur only when "corruption becomes intolerable"; otherwise, society would be constantly disrupted.[155] For instance, Witherspoon viewed unfavorably the radical activity of John Wilkes (1727–97), contemporary English agitator for reform.[156]

A further analysis of Witherspoon's political theory validates this somewhat conservative shading to his revolutionary views. Actually, Witherspoon was no democrat but, in typical Whiggish fashion, believed in the virtue of a government based upon intellect and property. He distrusted pure democracy, for he believed "it is very subject to caprice and the madness of popular rage." Rather he preferred a mixed form of government, based on the virtues of monarchy, aristocracy, and democracy.[157] Furthermore, Witherspoon believed that property was inviolable: "Private property is every particular person's having a confessed and exclusive right to a certain portion of the goods which serve for the support and conveniency of life.[158] All in all, the picture that emerges of Witherspoon is that of a revolutionist, though an exceedingly prudent one.

But is not this picture of Witherspoon consistent with the very nature of the American Revolution? After all, the colonists were not seeking to build a new society in their resistance to Great Britain. Rather they were preserving liberties that they believed were endangered by the presumptuous acts of George III, his ministers, and Parliament. The colonists' reluctance to separate from England (independence was not declared for over a year after armed conflict began) indicates that the original quarrel was over rights, not independence. American revolutionary leaders were in the main sober, practical men, not utopians plotting revolution in the cellar. Thus the anomaly is that British subjects were fighting against, and eventually breaking with, Great Britain in order to preserve British liberties.[159]

This idea of protecting liberties is precisely how Witherspoon viewed the colonies' struggle with England. An insight into his thought on this matter is found in the "Address to the Natives of Scotland Residing in America," published in 1776.[160] In this essay Witherspoon makes clear his pride in his British political heritage. He singularly attributes the success of North American colonies to "the degree of British liberty brought from home." But since England had begun systematically to deny the Americans their "ancient rights," independence was the only course of honor. Thus Witherspoon and his fellow Americans pictured themselves as the true British; unfortunately, the nation that had fostered the finest tradition of liberty had now become the enemy of liberty in the colonies.

Despite Witherspoon's general agreement with his contemporaries, he differs from many of them in his view of the American Revolution in one significant way. In interpreting the events of the 1770s Witherspoon always insists that emphasis be placed on the Calvinist view of man. Frequently, the colonists tended to attribute their troubles to some specific source (for example, King George, a particular minister, an unfair tax measure). Witherspoon, on the other hand, believes that the difficulty between America and Great Britain could be traced to human depravity. The Calvinist tenet of original sin corrupting all men is unmistakable in these remarks of Witherspoon to his fellow Americans:

> It has been my opinion from the beginning, that we did not carry our reasoning fully home, when we complained of an arbitrary prince, or of the insolence, cruelty, and obstinacy of Lord North, Lord Bute, or Lord Mansfield. What we have to fear, and what we have to grapple with, is the ignorance, prejudice, and partiality of human nature.[161]

Throughout the *Lectures on Moral Philosophy*, Witherspoon's pessimistic view of man is evident. At the outset he suggests that man's failure to understand himself fully is because "of the depravity and corruption of our nature."[162] He speaks of "inherent vice" as well as "inherent virtue" in his discussion of ethics.[163] As he moves into the exposition of politics in the latter half of the *Lectures*, Witherspoon's belief in human depravity is still clear. For instance, he favors a system of checks and balances in government because of man's corruption: "They must be balanced, that when everyone draws to his own interest or inclination, there may be an even poise upon the whole."[164]

With respect to this view of man, Witherspoon stands in and contributes to a long tradition found in American political thought. The New England Puritans came to American shores with a healthy suspicion of men in general, and their polity mirrored that concern. Under the impact of the Enlightenment, however, eighteenth-century America began to view man more optimistically. For instance, Thomas Jefferson affirmed that man is basically good, "that morality, compassion, generosity, are elements of the human constitution."[165] Thomas Paine, another child of the Enlightenment, discredited original sin in *Common Sense* by comparing it to the dogma of the hereditary succession of kings. But cautious Calvinists such as Witherspoon objected, for they could never view man as a creature of reason and benevolence.[166]

Witherspoon directly affected his most famous pupil, James Madison, on the matter of human nature. In *The Federalist*, Madison extols the proposed Constitution on the basis that it will lessen the violence of faction. And what does he believe causes faction? It is "sown in the nature of man."[167] Madison utilized this awareness of man's inclination to self-interest in shaping the political structure of American society. For instance, this view of man was a significant factor in producing the careful distribution of power described in the Constitution.

Witherspoon is one of the thinkers who bequeathed a realistic view of man to the American political tradition. In America this political realism has been an important factor in preventing disastrous utopian experiments that often accompany undue optimism about human nature. Reinhold Niebuhr, neo-Calvinist theologian and political analyst of the twentieth century, wisely observes, "Man's capacity for justice makes democracy possible; but man's inclination to injustice makes democracy necessary."[168] Among his eighteenth-century contemporaries, Witherspoon was foremost as one who constantly articulated the inherent corruption of mankind.

Yet the broad outline of his political thought is generally consistent with the collective political mind of his era. What emerges is a thinker well versed in the Whiggish creed of his time. As such a representative thinker, Witherspoon logically and effectively expounds the doctrine characteristic of Revolutionary America: natural rights, social contract, rights of rebellion. One can perceive how effectively Witherspoon's political philosophy meshed with his revolutionary activity in the 1770s.

Furthermore, many other Americans of the period found Witherspoon's political theory in harmony with their mood. In turbulent times people can hardly afford the luxury of novel and startling ideas. Rather, most prefer traditional concepts for an anchor in the storm. A political philosophy such as Witherspoon's was precisely what was needed to justify the colonial rebellion against England. After all, was not this theory drawn from over a century of English experience and thought? The fact that Witherspoon was a clergyman lent the additional authority of religion to his words; that he was a teacher also added force to his message. And the *Lectures on Moral Philosophy* not only affected the graduates of Princeton but influenced many others as well. For instance, Madison in his extensive political activity during the early years of the American nation often echoed concepts that he had first learned from Witherspoon.

What was true of Witherspoon politically was also true philosophically. He brought Scottish Common Sense philosophy to prominence just at a time when this philosophy fitted the intellectual needs of America. Protestant religion desired a system of thought that was neither idealistic nor materialistic. Scottish realism largely dominated the American intellectual scene during the first half of the nineteenth century, and Witherspoon's *Lectures* were no small factor in the dissemination of this philosophy. In fact, the key to Witherspoon's influence was the way in which his thought coincided with the public mood of the day.

There is yet one other fortunate circumstance that explains the wide influence of the *Lectures* during the half century after their composition—the sway that the College of New Jersey enjoyed during the Witherspoon's administration. Princeton's intercolonial prestige is explained partly by its lack of provinciality, which insured the dispersal of its influence throughout America. Yet there was one particular appeal that was especially beneficial in increasing the impact of the college upon its society. Princeton had a special claim upon one rapidly growing segment of America's population in the late eighteenth century: the Scotch-Irish. Presbyterian in faith, this group looked to Princeton for their ministers and teachers. This was quite significant, for the Scotch-Irish often led the westward movement across the Appalachian Mountains into such areas as western Pennsylvania, piedmont Virginia, upland North Carolina, Kentucky, and Tennessee. Thus the opportunity existed for Princeton's influence to reach from New Jersey to the frontier communities.

And this opportunity was seized, as graduates of the College of New Jersey went to areas peopled by the Scotch-Irish and founded academies patterned after their alma mater. In 1776 Samuel Stanhope Smith, class of 1769, began Hampden-Sidney Academy near Farmville, Virginia. One hundred and ten students attended the first session as three classmates assisted Smith at the academy. One of these assistants was Witherspoon's own son, David. Thaddeus Dod, class of 1773, started the first classical school west of the Alleghenies in a log cabin in western Pennsylvania. Forced to close the school after two years, he then became principal in 1789 of the newly formed Washington Academy at Washington, Pennsylvania. In all, thirteen who graduated during Witherspoon's administration became college presidents, and a host of others were teachers in institutions of higher learning.

In fact, Witherspoon's permanent influence was probably greater in higher education than in any other sphere. Most of his contemporaries knew him through his political and church activity, but it was in higher education that he most effectively disseminated his ideas. During Witherspoon's tenure of over a quarter of a century at Princeton (1768–94), the number of American colleges more than doubled. Frequently these new colleges were either founded by Princeton graduates or influenced by Princeton's thought. John J. Walsh in his study of colonial colleges considers Witherspoon's impact during this period so significant that he concludes, "Princeton's educational influence quite literally dominated much of the thinking in educational circles all over the country."[169]

Of all the means by which Witherspoon's influence as an educator spread, none was more pervasive than his *Lectures on Moral Philosophy*. Princeton graduates who taught in colleges often used their copies of Witherspoon's lectures as the texts for teaching moral philosophy. Witherspoon's lectures were also employed by many who were not his students. Student manuscripts were copies and subsequently were used as texts in many colleges and academies. For instance, in David Caldwell's famous academy in North Carolina, "Moral Philosophy was taught from a syllabus of lectures delivered by Dr. Witherspoon in Princeton College."[170] Even as late as 1820, the University of Pennsylvania listed "Hutcheson, Paley, Smith, or Witherspoon" as textbooks for its course on "natural and political law."[171]

Yet during Witherspoon's life and for six years after his death, *Lectures on Moral Philosophy* circulated in manuscript form only.[172] These handwritten documents had been copied from Witherspoon's original manuscript or from a copy of the *Lectures* possessed by college students. The best collection of these manuscripts is in the Princeton University Library, which has three complete copies of the *Lectures* dated 1772, 1782, and 1795, and two fragmentary manuscripts dated 1774 and 1790.[173] An unsigned and undated copy is also in the collections of the Presbyterian Historical Society in Philadephia.

Popular demand led to the publication of Witherspoon's works in 1800–1801 by William W. Woodward, Philadelphia printer, under the title, *The Works of Rev'd John Witherspoon*. Edited by Ashbel Green, this four-volume work contained *Lectures on Moral Philosophy* (3:269–374). Three later editions of Witherspoon's *Works* were published, all of which contained the *Lectures* (4 vols. [Philadelphia, Pa.: William Woodward, 1802]; 9 vols. [Edinburgh: Ogle and Aikman, 1804–5]; 9 vols. [Edinburgh: J. Ritchie, 1815]. Woodward also published two editions of the lectures separately in 1810 and 1822.

The best edition of *Lectures on Moral Philosophy* is that edited by Varnum Lansing Collins for the American Philosophical Association and published in 1912 by the Princeton University Press. Collins was a careful student of Princeton history, as his long list of publications indicates.[174] Particularly significant is his two-volume biography of Witherspoon. Collins based his text of the lectures on Woodward's first edition. He made changes, however, in this text whenever comparison with the student manuscripts warranted it. His overall job of editing is excellent, indicating exacting care. Thus Collins's text is the one used in this annotated edition.[175]

The primary task of this work is not textual criticism, a task ably done by Collins. Collins did not, however, explore the roots of Witherspoon's thought in his edition of the lectures. Furthermore, his introdution is too brief and simply chronicles some details of Witherspoon's life. The thrust of this project is to move behind the *Lectures*, to discover, if possible, Witherspoon's original sources. By this means, some new insights may be gained about the intellectual life of a forceful activist and theorist in revolutionary America. And, equally important, it is hoped the intellectual terrain of that turbulent era may come into sharper focus.

NOTES

1. John Adams, *Diary and Autobiography of John Adams*, ed. L. H. Butterfield, 4 vols. (Cambridge, Mass.: Harvard University Press, 1961) Vol. 2, *Diary, 1771-1781*, p. 112.
2. Ibid., p. 121.
3. William H. Foote, *Sketches of Virginia* (Philadelphia, 1850), pp. 438-70.
4. The names "Princeton" and "College of New Jersey" will be used interchangeably. Chartered as the College of New Jersey in 1746, the name of the institution was not changed to Princeton University until 1896. However, because of its geographical location, the college was often called "Princeton" before the official change of name.
5. For an extensive biography of Witherspoon, consult Varnum Lansing Collins, *President Witherspoon*, 2 vols. (Princeton, N.J.: Princeton University Press, 1925).
6. Alexander Carlyle, *The Autobiography of Dr. Alexander Carlyle of Inveresk, 1722-1805*, ed. John Hill Burton (London: T. N. Foulis, 1910), pp. 63-64.
7. Ashbel Green, "The Life of the Rev'd John Witherspoon, D. D. LL. D., With a Brief Review of His Writings; and a Summary Estimate of His Character and Talents," MS, New Jersey Historical Society, Newark, N.J.; hereafter cited as "Life of Witherspoon." Ashbel Green (1762-1848) was closely connected with Princeton most of his life. Entering the junior class of the college in 1782, he graduated the following year with honors. He remained at Princeton for four more years: first, as tutor and after 1785 as professor of natural philosophy and mathematics. After a distinguished ministerial career, Green returned to the College of New Jersey as president for a ten-year incumbency (1812-22).

Green studied under Witherspoon and greatly admired his mentor. He edited the first edition of Witherspoon's *Works* (Philadelphia, 1800-1801). The above biography was written after 1829, for Green mentioned the October 1829 issue of the *Edinburgh Christian Instructor* in his preface. The biography was based on Green's personal recollections, unpublished manuscripts, and a collection of Witherspoon's letters. Although flawed by Green's obvious predilection to view Witherspoon favorably, the manuscript biography contains many details not found elsewhere.
8. Green, "Life of Witherspoon," p. 43.
9. John Witherspoon, *The Works of John Witherspoon*, 9 vols. (Edinburgh, 1804-5), 6: 138-222; hereafter cited as *Works*.

10. Witherspoon, *Works*, 6:222.

11. Appendix, Article 1: Hutcheson to Rev. Thomas Drennan, n.d., in James McCosh, *The Scottish Philosophy, Biographical, Expository, Critical, from Hutcheson to Hamilton* (New York: R. Carter, 1875), p. 465.

12. Carlyle, *Autobiography*, p. 55.

13. For a full discussion of Witherspoon's borrowing from Hutcheson, see pp. 27–28.

14. Witherspoon, *Works*, 6: 38–128.

15. See p. 119 and accompanying note.

16. Many of these letters have been collected and edited by L. H. Butterfield in *John Witherspoon Comes to America* (Princeton, N.J.: Princeton University Press, 1953). A majority of the letters are correspondence between Witherspoon and Benjamin Rush, Princeton graduate of 1760 and medical student in Edinburgh from 1766 to 1768. On at least one occasion Rush visited the Witherspoon home in Paisley to plead in person Princeton's cause.

17. Green, "Life of Witherspoon," p. 116.

18. Witherspoon's almanac reveals that during the brief period of October 7–December 3, 1768 he preached in six different towns: New York, Boston, Philadelphia, New Haven, Weston, Mass. and New Brunswick, N. J. "Almanac and Memorandum Book of Dr. John Witherspoon," 1768, Princeton University, General MSS, AM 18653, n.p.).

19. Thomas Jefferson Wertenbaker, *Princeton, 1746–1896* (Princeton, N.J.: Princeton University Press, 1946), pp. 53–54.

20. *Records of the Presbyterian Church in the United States of America*, (Philadephia, 1841), pp. 396–97.

21. Wertenbaker, *Princeton, 1746–1896*, p. 53.

22. Green, "Life of Witherspoon," p. 104.

23. Ibid., p. 106.

24. Ibid., pp. 105–11.

25. For more details on this transaction and the subsequent history of the orrery, consult Howard Crosby Rice, *The Rittenhouse Orrery: Princeton's Eighteenth-Century Planetarium, 1767–1954* (Princeton, N.J.: Princeton University Press, 1954).

26. John Witherspoon, "Address to the Inhabitants of Jamaica, and Other West-India Islands in Behalf of the College of New Jersey" (Philadelphia, 1772), reprinted in *American Higher Education: A Documentary History*, ed. Richard Hofstadter and Wilson Smith, 2 vols. (Chicago: University of Chicago Press, 1961), 1: 142.

27. Ibid., p. 141.

28. Witherspoon, "Almanac and Memorandum Book," n.p.

29. *Records of the Presbyterian Church*, pp. 389–548.

30. *Records of the Presbyterian Church*, pp. 392, 406, 416, 427, 440, 453, 464 and Carl Bridenbaugh, *Mitre and Sceptre: Transatlantic Faiths, Ideas, Personalities, and Politics, 1689–1775* (New York: Oxford University Press, 1962), pp. 281, 282, 328–29.

31. John Adams, *The Works of John Adams, Second President of the United States*, ed. Charles Francis Adams, 10 vols. (Boston, 1856), 10: 185.

32. Arthur Lyon Cross, *The Anglican Episcopate and the American Colonies* (New York: Longmans, Green & Co., 1902) and Bridenbaugh, *Mitre and Sceptre*.

33. Ambrose Serle to Lord Dartmouth, April 25, 1777, in Henry Stevens, *Facsimiles of Manuscripts in European Archives Relating to America, 1773 to 1783*, vol. 24, no. 2057, cited by Leonard J. Trinterud, *The Forming of an American Tradition: A Re-examination of Colonial Presbyterianism* (Philadelphia: Westminster Press, 1949), p. 250.

34. Witherspoon, *Works*, 9:85.

35. Witherspoon, *Works*, 8:304–7.

36. Witherspoon's collection of pamphlets contained one entitled *A Short Narrative of the Horrid Massacre in Boston* (Boston, 1770).

37. Witherspoon, *Works*, 8:305. "Captain P—" refers to Captain Thomas Preston, guard commander at Boston in 1770.

38. Collins, *President Witherspoon*, l: 132–33.
39. *Archives of the State of New Jersey*, ed. William A. Whitehead et al. (Newark, N.J.: 1880–present) 1st ser. 28:278.
40. See pp. 145–46.
41. Ibid.
42. Witherspoon, "Address to the Inhabitants of Jamaica," in *"American Higher Education*, ed. Hofstadter and Smith, l: 141.
43. James Hasting Nichols, "John Witherspoon on Church and State," *Journal of Presbyterian History* 42 (September 1964): 166.
44. For a thorough treatment of Madison's college days at Princeton, consult Irving Brant, *James Madison*, 6 vols. (Indianapolis, Ind.: Bobbs-Merrill Co., 1941–), 1: 72–103.
45. Varnum Lansing Collins, *Princeton* (New York: Oxford University Press, 1914), p. 96.
46. Ibid., p. 92.
47. C. C. Beatty to Enoch Green, January 31, 1774, Princeton University Library, Princeton, N.J.
48. Adams, *Diary and Autobiography*, 2:113.
49. *New Jersey Archives*, lst ser. 29: 430–32.
50. Witherspoon, *Works*, 9:73–77.
51. *New Jersey Archives*, lst ser. 29: 554–55.
52. The complete text of this letter is in *Records of The Presbyterian Church*, pp. 466–69.
53. Ibid., p. 468.
54. Ecclesiastical Records of the State of New York, 6: 4293, cited by Trinterud, *The Forming of an American Tradition*, p. 250.
55. Witherspoon, *Works*, 9: 160.
56. *New Jersey Archives*, lst ser. 31: 225.
57. Although *Plain Truth* was published anonymously (March 11), research indicates that its author was William Smith, provost of the College of Philadelphia (P. L. Ford, "The Authorship of *Plain Truth*," *Pennsylvania Magazine of History and Biography* 22 [1888–89]: 421–24).
58. Witherspoon, *Works*, 9:88–98
59. Witherspoon to Philadelphia Committee of Correspondence, February 14, 1776, New York City Public Library, Emmet Collection 5764.
60. Witherspoon to Lord Stirling, March 19, 1776, in *American Archives*, ed. Peter Force (Washington, 1844), 4th ser. 5: 414.
61. Elias Boudinot, *Journal of Historical Recollection of American Events during the Revolutionary War* (Philadelphia, 1894), pp. 4–8.
62. John Adams to James Warren, in Worthington Chauncey Ford, ed. *Warren-Adams Letters; Being Chiefly a Correspondence Among John Adams, Samuel Adams, and James Warren . . . 1743-1814*, Collections of the Massachusetts Historical Society, Vols. 72 and 73 (Boston, 1917–25), l: 249.
63. The complete text of this sermon is in *Works*, 5: 176–216.
64. Ibid., p. 198.
65. Ibid., p. 203.
66. William Warren Sweet, *Religion in the Development of American Culture, 1765-1840* (New York: Scribner, 1952), p. 8.
67. *New Jersey Archives*, 1st ser. 10: 719–28; Donald L. Kemmerer, *Path to Freedom: The Struggle for Self-Government in Colonial, New Jersey, 1703-1776* (Princeton, NJ: Princeton University Press, 1940), pp. 343–45.
68. Adams, *Diary and Autobiography*, 3: 395–97.
69. George Otto Trevelyan, *The American Revolution*, 3 vols. (New York, 1899–1907), 1: Part II, 158; *Dictionary of American Biography*, s. v. "Witherspoon, John."
70. Green, "Life of Witherspoon," p. 128.
71. *Records of Presbyterian Church*, pp. 505–48.
72. Samuel Blair, *An Account of the College* (Woodbridge, N.J., 1764), p. 25.

73. Herbert W. Schneider, *A History of American Philosophy* (New York: Columbia University Press, 1946), p. 242.

74. Carlyle, *Autobiography*, p. 55.

75. Ibid., p. 72.

76. See pp. 112, 133, 135.

77. See p. 114.

78. For an example, see Witherspoon's discussion of money in Lecture XV n. 15 containing Hutcheson's material as comparison.

79. See p. 78.

80. See pp. 122, 133.

81. See p. 104.

82. See p. 74.

83. Green, "Life of Witherspoon," p. 107.

84. In the 1822 edition of the *Lectures* the preface tells of Witherspoon's compelling a printer, who without Witherspoon's knowledge had undertaken to publish the *Lectures*, "to desist from the design, by threatening a prosecution as the consequence of persisting in it." Ashbel Green did not believe, however, that such a wish should deter the publication of the lectures after Witherspoon's death. He admits that the lectures have certain deficiencies, yet adds, "But that these imperfections are such as should have induced his friends, from a regard to his memory, to assign them to oblivion, his present memorialist is by no means prepared to admit" ("Life of Witherspooon," p. 108).

85. See p. 92.

86. Aristotle, *Politics*, trans. H. Rackham, Loeb Classical Library (Cambridge, Mass.: Harvard University Press, 1944), p. xii.

87. Samuel Eliot Morison, *The Founding of Harvard College* (Cambridge, Mass.: Harvard University Press, 1935), p. 435.

88. See pp. 71, 83–87.

89. See p. 73.

90. See p. 186.

91. See pp. 77–79. Witherspoon also mentioned a sense of honor and shame as well as a sense of ridicule, but neither is adequately developed.

92. See pp. 73–74.

93. Green, "Life of Witherspoon," n.p. A possible source of Berkeleian idealism at Princeton was *Elementica Philosophica* (1752) by Samuel Johnson (1696–1772). Johnson disseminated Berkeley's thought through his writings and from his post as president of King's College (1754–63). Bishop Berkeley profoundly affected Johnson during Berkeley's three-year sojourn (1728–31) in America and by a long correspondence between the two. For complete details concerning the life and writings of Johnson, see *Samuel Johnson, President of King's College*, ed. H. W. and C. Schneider, 4 vols. (New York: Columbia University Press, 1929).

94. See p. 85.

95. Another reason for Witherspoon's aversion to Edwards was the enthusiasm characteristic of Edwards and his contemporary disciples, the New Divinity men (e.g., Samuel Hopkins, Joseph Bellamy). Witherspoon had opposed the liberalism of the Moderate party in the Church of Scotland, but this had not led him to embrace the revivalism of men such as John Wesley and George Whitefield. Furthermore, American Presbyterianism had split over revivalism in 1741, and the union effected in 1758 was still tenuous. Witherspoon preferred to avoid identification with either side in the dispute; to side with Edwards's disciples would have immediately stamped him as a New Side (or revivalistic) minister.

Thus Edwardsean theology became unacceptable at Princeton. This is indicated in a letter from Ebenezer Bradford, Princeton student, to Joseph Bellamy. He wrote that Dr. Witherspoon was a great enemy of New Divinity and Bradford had been advised to keep his sympathies secret. Bradford continued to read Bellamy's books with the title pages cut out and he intended to advance the New Divinity cause in a private manner (cited in I. Woodbridge Riley, *American Philosophy, The Early Schools*, [New York, 1907], p. 496.

Witherspoon's antipathy toward certain facets of Edwards's thought did not prevent him from reading his works. Edwards's *Remarks on the Principles of Morality and Natural Religion* (Edinburgh, 1768) and *Life of Brainerd* (Edinburgh, 1765) were in Witherspoon's library. In a 1773 letter to Samuel Hopkins, Witherspoon requests more of Edwards's writings for his personal use: "I would therefore be obliged to you if you could make a collection for me of all Mr. Edwards works and of all the pieces published by you for though I have Several of both I would rather have the whole again than have them imperfect" (John Witherspoon to Samuel Hopkins, December 14, 1773, Pierpont Morgan Library, New York).

96. See p. 97.

97. Both Reid and Beattie are recommended by Witherspoon in his bibliography and Beattie's *Essay on Truth* is specifically mentioned on page 186.

98. See pp. 73, 97.

99. See p. 97.

100. Morris R. Cohen, *American Thought: A Critical Sketch* (Glencoe, Ill.: Free Press, 1954), p. 258. Also consult I. Woodbridge Riley, *American Thought from Puritanism to Pragmatism and Beyond* (New York: Henry Holt & Co., 1923), pp. 118-39; Joseph L. Blau, *Men and Movements in American Philosophy* (Englewood Cliffs, N. J.: Prentice-Hall, Inc., 1952), pp. 73-109; Schneider, *History of American Philosophy*, pp. 246-50.

101. See pp. 84-85.

102. Thomas Hobbes, *The English Works of Thomas Hobbes*, ed. William Molesworth, 11 vols. (London, 1839-45), vol. 6, *Human Nature*, p. 44.

103. See p. 73.

104. Information about Mandeville may be found on pp. 89 and 162; for information on Campbell, see p. 88, n. 8.

105. A brief biographical sketch of Clarke is on p. 68, n. 5, and other comments about Clarke are on p. 84. Notice that Clarke's book is in Witherspoon's library (see Appendix 2). William Wollaston (1660-1724), an ethicist with views are similar to Clarke, is also mentioned by Witherspoon (p. 84).

106. See p. 69, n. 11, for a brief biographical sketch of Shaftesbury. The best treatment of Shaftesbury's ethical thought in Stanley Green, *Shaftesbury's Philosophy of Religion and Ethics: A Study in Enthusiasm* (Athens, Ohio: Ohio University Press, 1967).

107. See pp. 27-28 for a discussion of Hutcheson's influence upon Witherspoon. An interesting monograph on Hutcheson is William T. Blackstone, *Francis Hutcheson and Contemporary Ethical Theory* (Athens, Ga.: University of Georgia Press, 1965).

108. See pp. 4-7.

109. See pp. 78-79, 92-94, 109, 134.

110. Francis Hutcheson, *Inquiry Concerning Moral Good and Evil,* sec. 3, ch. 8, cited in Leslie Stephen, *History of English Thought in the Eighteenth Century*, 2 vols. 3 ed. (New York: Peter Smith, 1949), 2: 61.

111. Francis Hutcheson, *A System of Moral Philosophy* (London, 1755), 1: 255-56. Utility is important to Hutcheson, but it becomes central to the ethical philosophy of his countryman and associate, David Hume. Hume, for instance, writes in his *Enquiry Concerning the Principles of Morals*: "Personal Merit consists altogether in the possession of mental qualities, useful or agreeable to the person himself or to others" ([London, 1751], sec. 9, p. 102.) Although in the *Lectures* Witherspoon only mentions in passing Hume's utilitarian philosophy, he clearly disagrees with it. He especially denounces Hume's basing the virtues of justice and chastity totally upon utility (see pp. 84-85, 112.

112. See pp. 86, 116, 172-73, 179-81. Hutcheson develops his thesis in ch. 16 of book 2 of the *System of Moral Philosophy* (2: 117-40). Philosophically, Hutcheson agrees with

modern advocates of situation ethics such as Joseph Fletcher, James Pike, and John A. T. Robinson.

113. See p. 78.

114. Joseph Butler, *The Works of Joseph Butler*, ed. W. D. Gladstone, 2 vols. (Oxford, 1896), 1: 42.

115. See p. 102.

116. See p. 78. Significantly, Butler also cited this Biblical passage, to which Witherspoon alludes (Rom, 2: 14-15) in building his ethical system upon the conscience.

117. See p. 80.

118. See pp. 78, 80-81, 91-94.

119. See pp. 134, 135.

120. See p. 165.

121. See pp. 85-86, 103-104.

122. See pp. 106-107.

123. See p. 64.

124. Edmund S. Morgan, "The American Revolution Considered as an Intellectual Movement," in *Paths of American Thought*, ed. Arthur M. Schlesinger, Jr. and Morton M. White (Boston: Houghton Mifflin Co., 1963), p. 11.

125. For a discussion of the centrality of the depravity of man in Witherspoon's political theory, see pp. 48-50.

126. (Edinburgh, 1964), p. 3.

127. This political tradition, which must have been influential among Scots and Scotch-Irish during the American Revolution, has been generally overlooked in the historical literature about the period. It is discussed in ch. 6, "The Interest of Scotland," in Caroline Robbins, *The Eighteenth-Century Commonwealthman: Studies in the Transmission, Development and Circumstance of English Liberal Thought from the Restoration of Charles II until the War With the Thirteen Colonies* (Cambridge, Mass.: Harvard University Press, 1959), pp. 177-220.

128. Cf. Hutcheson, *System of Moral Philosophy* (1: 252-358; 2: 1-380), which forms the basis for Lectures X-XVI of the *Lectures*.

129. Ray Forrest Harvey, *Jean Jacques Burlamaqui: A Liberal Tradition in American Constitutionalism* (Chapel Hill, N.C.: University of North Carolina Press, 1937), p. 97. Perhaps this information leads Wilson Ober Clough to conclude erroneously that Burlamaqui "was the basis for Witherspoon's lectures at Princeton from 1768 to the Revolution" (*Intellectual Origins of American National Thought* [New York: Corinth Books, 1961], p. 189.

130. See pp. 95, 146.

131. Carlyle, *Autobiography*, p. 55.

132. Witherspoon probably used some of Pufendorf's wording in his definition of an oath at the beginning of Lecture XVI.

133. Lectures XV and XVI.

134. Anna Haddow, *Political Science in American Colleges and Universities, 1636-1900* (New York: Appleton-Century, 1939), pp. 26-28.

135. See pp. 136, 161, 165.

136. Green, "Life of Witherspoon," n.p.

137. Ed. Benjmain Fletcher Wright (Cambridge, Mass.: Harvard University Press, 1961), p. 337.

138. Lecture XII, "Of the different forms of government." The example of Witherspoon tends to validate the thesis of Benjamin Wright, who disagrees with those who believe Montesquieu to be the author of separation of powers in American political thought ("Origins of Separation of Powers," in *Origins of American Political Thought*, ed. John P. Roche [New York: Harper & Row, 1967], pp. 139-62).

139. Pp. 161-162.

140. The issue of whether seventeenth- or eighteenth-century Whig tradition was more

important to Revolutionary America is debated by Jack P. Greene and Bernard Bailyn in the December 1969 issue of *The American Historical Review* (Greene, "Political Mimesis: A Consideration of the Historical and Cultural Roots of Legislative Behavior in the British Colonies in the Eighteenth Century" and Bailyn, "A Comment," 75: 337-67). Greene affirms the seventeenth-century Whig tradition to be more important; Bailyn, that of the eighteenth century. This study of the thought of Witherspoon validates Greene's assertion.

141. A critical study of the development of the social contract theory is done by J. W. Gough, *The Social Contract: A Critical Study of its Development* (Oxford: Clarendon Press, 1936).

142. See. p. 122.

143. See. p. 125.

144. See p. 125.

145. Additional information on this mater can be found in a letter of Dec. 14, 1773 from Witherspoon to Samuel Hopkins, minister of Newport, Rhode Island. In it Witherspoon mentions the proposed education of two Negroes at Princeton. He heartily favored the project and indicated that Anthony Benezet (1713-84) would be contacted for possible financial assistance. He referred to the fact that Benezet had "zealously taken up the controversy against Mankeeping and caused himself to be introduced to me last Summer with the view of interesting me in the Matter." However, Witherspoon does not add that he shared Benezet's zeal for the anti-slavery cause (John Witherspoon to the Reverend Mr. Samuel Hopkins, Dec. 14, 1773, Pierpont Morgan Library, New York).

146. See pp. 123.

147. See p. 140.

148. See p. 145.

149. Witherspoon, *Works*, 5:227.

150. Cited by George L. Hunt, ed., *Calvinism and the Political Order* (Philadelphia: Westminster Press, 1965), p. 77.

151. However, from this it should not be inferred that Locke wrote his *Two Treatises of Government* after 1688. In his critical edition of this work, Peter Laslett successfully established that Locke composed the substantial portion of the *Two Treatises* before the Glorious Revolution (Cambridge: at the University Press, pp. 45-66).

152. John Locke, *Essay Concerning the True Original Extent and End of Civil Government in The Works of John Locke*, 9 vols. 12th ed. (London, 1824), ch. 19, "Of the Dissolution of Government," 5: 464-85.

153. Clinton Rossiter, *Seedtime of the Republic* (New York: Harcourt, Brace & Co., 1953), p. 328.

154. See p. 146.

155. See pp. 145.

156. Witherspoon, *Works*, 9:86. Wilkes's anti-Scotism may have also contributed to Witherspoon's animus toward Wilkes.

157. See pp. 142-44.

158. See p. 126.

159. The issue of how revolutionary the American Revolution was is hotly debated by historians. Jack P. Greene analyzes these differing interpretations in his essay, "The Reappraisal of the American Revolution in Recent Historical Literature" (*The Reinterpretation of the American Revolution, 1763-1789*, ed. Jack P. Greene [New York: Harper & Row, 1968], pp. 2-74). The Progressive conception of the Revolution emphasized the internal divisions in the colonies. The American Revolution, much like the French Revolution, was pictured as truly revolutionary. Representative of this general view are Arthur M. Schlesinger, *The Colonial Merchants and the American Revolution, 1763-1776* (New York: Columbia University Press, 1918); Carl L. Becker, *The Declaration of Independence* (New York: Peter Smith, 1922); J. Franklin Jameson, *The American Revolution Considered as a Social Movement* (Princeton, N.J.: Princeton University Press, 1926); and Merrill Jensen, *The Articles of Confederation* (Madison, Wis.: University of Wisconsin Press, 1948).

Since World War II this interpretation of the internal revolution has been sharply reassessed. It is argued that colonial society was remarkably democratic and that the Revolution was fought to protect already existing rights. Furthermore, the political and social changes wrought by the American Revolution were rather moderate. Among those who developed this general thesis are Robert E. Brown, *Middle-Class Democracy and the Revolution in Massachusetts, 1671-1780* (Ithaca, N.Y.: Cornell University Press, 1955); Edmund S. Morgan, *The Birth of the Republic, 1763-1789* (Chicago: University of Chicago Press, 1956); Clinton Rossiter, *Seedtime of the Republic*; and Bernard Bailyn, *The Ideological Origins of the American Revolution* (Cambridge, Mass.: Harvard University Press, 1967). As indicated above, Witherspoon was a conservative revolutionist and his thought and actions during the Revolutionary era clearly support the neo-Bancroftian interpretation.

160. This address was added to the publication of the famous sermon, "The Dominion of Providence over the Passions of Men," preached by Witherspoon on May 17, 1776. The addendum was intended to encourage Americans of Scottish descent to participate in the Revolution (Witherspoon, *Works*, 5: 217-6).

161. Ibid., 9: 80.

162. See p. 66.

163. See p. 87.

164. See p. 144.

165. Edward Boykin, ed., *The Wisdom of Thomas Jefferson*, (New York: Doubleday & Co., 1941), p. 40.

166. Despite Witherspoon's general approval of *Common Sense*, he disputes it under-cutting of original sin (*Works*, 5: 184). The generalization, however, that thinkers of the Enlightenment viewed man as 'natively good,' (e.g., Carl Becker, *The Heavenly City of the Eighteenth Century Philosophers* [New Haven, Conn.: Yale University Press, 1932]) is open to serious question. A. O. Lovejoy in his study of the Enlightenment labels this a "radical historical error" and documents his conclusion with extensive citations from such eighteenth-century writers as Voltaire, Alexander Pope, Jonathan Swift, Bernard de Mandeville, and John Adams (*Reflections on Human Nature* [Baltimore, Md.: Johns Hopkins Press, 1961], pp. 37-65). Yet Witherspoon was still less confident of human nature than his contemporaries.

167. James Madison, *The Federalist*, 2 vols. (New York, 1788), No. 10, 1: 54. An excellent treatment of the theological impact of Witherspoon upon Madison is James H. Smylie, "Madison and Witherspoon: Theological Roots of American Political Thought," *The Princeton University Library Chronicle* 22 (Spring 1961): 118-32.

168. Reinhold Niebuhr, *The Children of Light and the Children of Darkness* (New York: Charles Scribner's Sons, 1944), p. xi.

169. John J. Walsh, *Education of the Founding Fathers of the Republic: Scholasticism in the Colonial Colleges* (New York: Fordham University Press, 1935), p. 162.

170. Alice M. Baldwin, "Sowers of Sedition: The Political Theories of Some of the New Light Presbyterian Clergy of Virginia and North Carolina," *William and Mary Quarterly*, 3 ser. 5 (January 1948): 62.

171. Haddow, *Political Science in American Colleges*, p. 44. The mention of Smith is significant, for Samuel Stanhope Smith patterned his lectures after Witherspoon, his mentor and father-in-law (*The Lectures corrected and improved, which have been delivered for a series of years in the College of New Jersey, on the subject of moral and political Philosophy* [Trenton, N.J., 1812]). This use of his lectures was yet another way by which Witherspoon's influence was spread.

172. Witherspoon first composed his lectures on moral philosophy during the period from 1770 to 1772. The fact that on page 186 he mentions Beatties's *Essay on the Nature and Immutability*, first published in 1770, places the writing no earlier than that date. The other determining factor is the earliest date (1772) for one of the extant student

manuscripts. Therefore, from 1772 until his death in 1794, Witherspoon resisted any effort to publish the lectures (for details, see pp. 56, n. 84).

173. Three of these copies bear the names of Princeton students on their covers: Andrew Hunter, Jr.—1772; John Ewing Colhoun—1774; and James Agnew—1795. The other two are unsigned.

174. Varnum Lansing Collins (1870–1936) was a professor of French and later secretary of the university at Princeton. His works include *The Continental Congress at Princeton* (Princeton, N.J.: Princeton University Press, 1908); *Early Princeton Printing* (Princeton, N.J.: Princeton University Press, 1911); *Princeton*, American University and College Series (New York, 1914); *President Witherspoon: A Biography*, 2 vols. (Princeton, N.J.: Princeton University Press, 1925); and *Princeton, Past and Present* (Princeton, N.J.: Princeton University Press, 1931).

175. In this annotated edition occasional changes were from Collins's text if textual evidence and improved sense required it. For instance, *hand-maids* is substituted for *hard words* (Collins's text) on page 186. Also, textual variants are noted in the footnotes when considered significant. In these footnotes the student manuscripts dated 1772, 1782, and 1795 are identified as MSS A, B, and C, respectively.

Lectures on Moral Philosophy

LECTURE I

Moral Philosophy is that branch of Science which treats of the principles and laws of Duty or Morals. It is called *Philosophy*, because it is an inquiry into the nature and grounds of moral obligation by reason, as distinct from revelation.

Hence arises a question, is it lawful, and is it safe or useful, to separate moral philosophy from religion? It will be said, it is either the same or different from revealed truth; if the same, unnecessary—if different, false and dangerous.

An author of New England, says, moral philosophy is just reducing infidelity to a system.[1] But however specious the objections, they will be found at bottom not solid. If the Scripture is true, the discoveries of reason cannot be contrary to it; and therefore, it has nothing to fear from that quarter. And as we are certain it can do no evil, so there is a probability that it may do much good. There may be an illustration and confirmation of the inspired writings, from reason and observation, which will greatly add to their beauty and force.[2]

The noble and eminent improvements in natural philosophy, which have been made since the end of the last century, have been far from hurting the interest of religion; on the contrary, they have greatly promoted it. Why should it not be the same with moral philosophy, which is indeed nothing else but the knowledge of human nature? It is true that infidels do commonly proceed upon pretended principles of reason. But as it is impossible to hinder them from reasoning upon this subject, the best way is to meet them upon their own ground, and to show from reason itself, the fallacy of their principles. I do not know any thing that serves more for the support of religion than to see from the different and opposite systems of philosophers, that there is nothing certain in their schemes, but what is coincident[3] with the word of God.

Some there are, and perhaps more in the present than any former age, who deny the law of nature, and say, that all such sentiments as have been usually ascribed to the law of nature, are from revelation and tradition.

We must distinguish here between the light of nature and the law of nature: by the first is to be understood what we can or do discover by our own powers, without revelation or tradition: by the second, that which, when discovered, can be made appear to be agreeable to reason and nature.

There have been some very shrewd and able writers of late, viz. Dr. Willson, of New Castle, and Mr. Ricalton of Scotland, who have written against the light of nature, shewing that the first principles of knowledge are taken from information.[4] That nothing can be supposed more rude and ignorant, than man without instruction. That when men have been brought up so, they have scarcely been superior to brutes. It is very difficult to precise upon this subject, and to distinguish the discoveries of reason from the exercise of it. Yet I think, admitting all, or the greatest part, of what such contend for, we may, notwithstanding, consider how far any thing is consonant to reason, or may be proven by reason; though perhaps reason, if left to itself, would never have discovered it.

Dr. Clark was one of the greatest champions for the law of nature; but it is only since his time that the shrewd opposers of it have appeared.[5] The Hutchinsonians (so called from Hutchinson of England) insist that not only all moral, but also all natural knowledge comes from revelation, the true system of the world, true chronology, all human arts, &c.[6] In this, as is usual with most other classes of men, they carry their favourite notion to extravagance. I am of opinion that the whole Scripture is perfectly agreeable to sound philosophy; yet certainly it was never intended to teach us every thing. The political law of the Jews contains many noble principles of equity, and excellent examples to future lawgivers; yet it was so local and peculiar, that certainly it was never intended to be immutable and universal.

It would be more just and useful to say that all simple and original discoveries have been the production of Providence, and not the invention of man. On the whole, it seems reasonable to make moral philosophy, in the sense above explained, a subject of study. And indeed let men think what they will of it, they ought to acquaint themselves with it. They must know what it is, if they mean ever to show that it is false.

The Division of the Subject.

Moral philosophy is divided into two great branches, Ethics and Politics, to this some add Jurisprudence, though this may be considered as a part of politics.[7]

Ethics relate to personal duties, Politics to the constitution,

65

government, and rights of societies, and Jurisprudence, to the administration of justice in constituted states.

It seems a point agreed upon, that the principles of duty and obligation must be drawn from the nature of man. That is to say, if we can discover how his Maker formed him, or for what he intended him, that certainly is what it ought to be.

The knowledge of human nature, however, is either perplexed and difficult of itself, or hath been made so, by the manner in which writers in all ages have treated it. Perhaps this circumstance itself, is a strong presumption of the truth of the Scripture doctrine of the depravity and corruption of our nature. Supposing this depravity, it must be one great cause of difficulty and confusion in giving an account of human nature as the work of God.[8]

This I take to be indeed the case with the greatest part of our moral and theological knowledge.

Those who deny this depravity, will be apt to plead for every thing, or for many things as dictates of nature, which are in reality propensities of nature in its present state, but at the same time the fruit and evidence of its departure from its original purity. It is by the remaining power of natural conscience that we must endeavor to detect and oppose these errors.

(1) We may consider man very generally in his species as distinct from and superior to the other creatures, and what it is, in which the different truly consists.[9] (2) As an individual, what are the parts which constitute his nature.

I. Philosophers have generally attempted to assign the precise distinction between men and the other animals; but when endeavoring to bring it to one peculiar incommunicable characteristic, they have generally contradicted one another and sometimes disputed with violence and rendered the thing more uncertain.

The difficulty of fixing upon a precise criterion only serves to show that in man we have an example of what we see also every where else, viz. a beautiful and insensible gradation from one thing to another, so that the highest of the inferior is, as it were, connected and blended with the lowest of the superior class. Birds and beasts are connected by some species so that you will find it hard to say whether they belong to the one or the other—So indeed it is in the whole vegetable as well as animal kingdom.

(1) Some say *men* are distinguished from brutes by reason, and certainly this, either in kind or degree, is the most honorable of our distinctions. (2) Others say that many brutes give strong signs of reason, as dogs, horses and elephants. But that man is distinguished by memory and foresight: but I apprehend that these

are upon the same footing with reason, if there are some glimmerings of reason in the brute creation, there are also manifest proofs of memory and some of foresight. (3) Some have though it proper to distinguish man from the inferior creatures by the use of speech, no other creatures having an articulate language. Here again, we are obliged to acknowledge that our distinction is chiefly the excellence and fullness of articulate discourse; for brutes have certainly the art of making one another understand many things by sound. (4) Some have said that man is not completely distinguished by any of these, but by a sense of religion. And I think it must be admitted that of piety or a sense of a Supreme Being, there is not any trace to be seen in the inferior creatures. The stories handed about by weak-minded persons, or retailed by credulous authors, of respect in them to churches, or sacred persons, are to be disdained as wholly fabulous and visionary.[10] (5) There have been some who have said that man is distinguished from the brutes by a sense of *ridicule*.

The whole creation (says a certain author) is grave except man, no one laughs but himself.[11] There is something whimsical in fixing upon this as the criterion, and it does not seem to set us in a very respectable light. Perhaps it is not improper to smile upon the occasion, and to say, that if this sentiment is embraced, we shall be obliged to confess kindred with the apes, who are certainly themselves possessed of a risible faculty, as well as qualified to excite laughter in us. On the whole there seems no necessity of fixing upon some one criterion to the exclusion of others.

There is great and apparant distinction between man and the inferior animals, not only in the beauty of his form, which the poet takes notice of, Os homini sublime dedit, &c.[12] But also in reason, memory reflection, and the knowledge of God and a future state.

A general distinction, which deserves particularly to be taken notice of in moral disquisitions, is that man is evidently made to be guided, and protected from dangers, and supplied with what is useful more by reason, and brutes more by instinct.

It is not very easy and perhaps not necessary to explain instinct. It is something previous to reason and choice. When we say the birds build their nests by instinct, and man builds his habitation by reflection, experience or instruction, we understand the thing well enough, but if we attempt to give a logical definition of either the one or the other, it will immediately be assaulted by a thousand arguments.

Though man is evidently governed by something else than instinct, he also has several instinctive propensities, some of them independent of, and some of them intermixed with his moral disposition. Of the first are hunger, thirst, and some others; of the last is the *storge*,[13] or parental tenderness toward offspring.

On instinct we shall only say farther, that it leads more immediately to the appointment of the Creator, and whether in man, or in other creatures, operates more early and more uniformly than reason.

NOTES

1. The "author of New England" is Cotton Mather (1663–1728). A Boston minister, Cotton Mather was of distinguished Puritan lineage. Both his grandfathers, Richard Mather and John Cotton, were Puritan divines of the Bay Colony and his father, Increase Mather, was also a leading minister and president of Harvard College (1685–1701). Cotton Mather was a learned man and prolific writer whose scholarly and scientific achievements led to his election to the Royal Society in 1714.

The quotation, critical of moral philosophy, is taken from Mather's *Manuductio ad Ministerium: Directions for a Candidate of the Ministry* (Boston, 1726). In this volume he carefully instructed ministerial students on the areas of studies that were most profitable. He was skeptical of "Ethics" (or moral philosophy) and described it as a "Vile Thing; and no other than what honest Vockerodus has justly called it: Impietas in Artis formam redacta" (ibid., p. 37). Vockerodus is probably Gottfried Vockerodt (1665–1727), German savant and author, who sometimes Latinized his name to read "Gothofredus Vockerodtius."

Interestingly enough, Mather's antipathy was only toward moral philosophy, not natural philosophy. "What we call Natural Philosophy, is what I must encourage you to spend much more Time in the Study of" (ibid., p. 47). He enthusiastically described Isaac Newton as being incomparable. Thus Cotton Mather took a Puritan half-step toward rationalism; fifty years later, Witherspoon moved more boldly in that direction.

2. Witherspoon is confident that reason will validate revelation. Although generally opposed to Deism, in this respect Witherspoon is influenced by one of its tenets.

3. MS C: consistent.

4. Andrew Wilson (1718–92), philosophical and medical writer, was born in Scotland and educated at the University of Edinburgh. However, he practiced medicine in England at Newcastle and London and wrote tracts attacking natural religion. I. Woodbridge Riley incorrectly identified this reference to "Dr. Willson" as Matthew Wilson of Delaware, a writer with whom Witherspoon corresponded (*American Philosophy, The Early Schools* [New York, 1907], p. 489).

Robert Riccaltoun (1691–1769) served as minister of Hopekirk, Scotland. He, too, inveighed against advocates of natural religion such as Samuel Clarke. Riccaltoun's *An Inquiry into Letters on Theron and Aspasio* (Glasgrow, 1762) was in Witherspoon's library (see Appendix 2).

5. Samuel Clarke (1675–1729) was an Anglican clergyman whose intellectual achievements eventually led to his promotion in 1709 to chaplain for Queen Anne. He argued that no article of the Christian faith was opposed to right reason. He employed the Cartesian method of postulating a priori truths (or deductive method). From these intuitive truths, Clarke aspired to construct a work that would be to Christianity what Newton's *Principia* was to astronomy. His *Discourse Concerning the Being and Attributes of God* (4th ed. [London, 1716]) was also in Witherspoon's library.

6. John Hutchinson (1674–1737), not to be confused with the Scottish philosopher Francis Hutcheson (1694–1746), attacked the Newtonian system and viewed the natural religion of

Samuel Clarke as satanic. *Moses Principia* (1724) by Hutchinson set forth a pseudo-science based upon a modification of the early chapters of Genesis. His fanciful scriptural symbolism attracted followers and his denial of natural knowledge appealed to many of the orthodox. Andrew Wilson and Robert Riccaltoun, mentioned above, were Hutchinsonian in their philosophical views.

7. In this work Witherspoon divides his lectures accordingly: Ethics (VI–IX), Politics (X–XIII), and Jurisprudence (XIV–XVI).

8. The Calvinist doctrine of human depravity is central in the thought of Witherspoon. For a full discussion of his view of human nature, see Introduction, pp. 148-50.

9. The comparison of the faculties of men and animals was typical of seventeenth-and eighteenth-century philosophers (see John Locke, *An Essay Concerning Human Understanding*, 4th ed. [London, 1700], bk. 2, ch. II, secs. 10-11, pp. 76-77; David Hume, *An Enquiry Concerning Human Understanding*, 2d ed. [Oxford, 1902]. sec. 9, pp. 104-8; Francis Hutcheson, *A System of Moral Philosophy*, 2 vols. [London, 1755], 1: 2-3).

10. This is a probable reference to the alleged miracles of Francis of Assisi. For instance, according to the *Little Flowers of Francis* (trans. Thomas Okey [London, 1934], pp. 38-41), he once tamed a fierce wolf who had been terrorizing the neighborhood. Subsequently, the wolf lowered its head and kneeled before Francis. Another story from the same source claimed that Anthony of Padua, a later Franciscan, called upon the fishes to praise God. The fish ascended above the water, opened their mouths, and bowed their heads (pp. 70-72).

11. Here Witherspoon is referring to Anthony Ashley Cooper, third earl of Shaftesbury (1671-1713). Lord Shaftesbury was the grandson of the first earl of Shaftesbury (1621-83), lord high chancellor of England. At his grandfather's suggestion he was tutored by John Locke, yet he broke later with Locke's denial of innate ideas. Shaftesbury contended that man has an innate sense of both beauty and morality. The best collection of his writings is *Characteristics of Men, Manners, Opinions, Times*, 3 vols. (London, 1711), the popularity of which led to eleven editions by 1790.

Shaftesbury viewed ridicule as the best method to test the truth of any claim, including religion. He ably developed this thesis in *Sensus Communis, An Essay on the Freedom of Wit and Humour* (London, 1709), which was later incorporated in *Characteristics* (1: 59-150). For a thorough treatment of Shaftesbury's doctrine of ridicule, see ch. 7 of *The Third Earl of Shaftesbury: A Study in Eighteenth-Century Literary Theory* by R. L. Brett ([London: Hutchinson's University Library, 1951], pp. 165-86). Also see Introduction (pp. 35-37) for a discussion of Shaftesbury's influence on Witherspoon.

12. The full quotation is "Pronaque cum spectant animalia cetera terram. Os homini sublime dedit caelumque videre iussit et erectos ad sidera tollere oultus" (Ovid *Metamorphoses* 1. 84-85). Translated, it reads, "And, though all other animals are prone, and fix their gaze upon the earth, he gave to man an uplifted face and bade him stand erect and turn his eyes to heaven."

13. ὅτοργπ, π—a Classical Greek word meaning "love, affection, particularly in reference to parents and children."

LECTURE II

Considering man as an individual, we discover the most obvious and remarkable circumstances of his nature, that he is a compound of body and spirit. I take this for granted here, because we are only explaining the nature of man. When we come to his sentiments and principles of action, it will be more proper, to take notice of the spirituality and immortality of the soul, and how they are proved.

The body and spirit have a great reciprocal influence one upon another. The body on the temper and disposition of the soul, and the soul on the state and habit of the body. The body is properly the minister of the soul, the means of conveying perceptions to it, but nothing without it.

It is needless to enlarge upon the structure of the body; this is sufficiently known to all, except we descend to anatomical exactness, and then like all the other parts of nature it shows the infinite wisdom of the Creator.[1]

With regard to morals, the influence of the body in a certain view may be very great in enslaving men to appetite, and yet there does not seem any such connection with morals as to require a particular description.

I think there is little reason to doubt that there are great and essential differences between man and man, as to the spirit and its proper powers; but it seems plain that such are the laws of union between the body and spirit, that many faculties are weakened and some rendered altogether incapable of exercise, merely by an alteration of the state of the body. Memory is frequently lost and judgment weakened by old age and disease. Sometimes by a confusion of the brain in a fall the judgment is wholly disordered.

The instinctive appetites of hunger and thirst seem to reside directly in the body, and the soul to have little more than a passive perception. Some passions, particularly fear and rage, seem also to have their seat in the body, immediately producing a certain modification of the blood and spirits. This indeed is perhaps the case in some degree with all passions whenever they are indulged, they give a modification to the blood and spirits, which make them easily rekindled, but there are none which do so instantaneously arise from the body, and prevent deliberation, will and choice, as these now named. To consider the evil passions to which we are liable, we may say those that depend most upon the body, are fear, anger, voluptuousness; and those that depend least upon it, are ambition, envy, covetousness.

The faculties of the mind are commonly divided into these three kinds, the understanding, the will, and the affections;[2] though perhaps it is proper to observe, that these are not three qualities wholly distinct, as if they were three different beings, but different ways of exerting the same simple principle. It is the soul or mind that understands, wills, or is affected with pleasure and pain.

The understanding seems to have truth for its object, the discovering things as they really are in themselves, and in their relations one to another.

It has been disputed whether good be in any degree the object of the understanding. On the other hand it seems as if truth and that only belonged to the understanding; because we can easily suppose persons of equal intellectual powers and opposite moral characters. Nay, we can suppose malignity joined to a high degree of understanding and virtue or true goodness to a much lower. On the other hand, the choice made by the will seems to have the judgment or deliberation of the understanding as its very foundation. How can this be, it will be said if the understanding has nothing to do with good or evil. A considerable opposition of sentiments among philosophers, has arisen from this question. Dr. Clark, and some others make understanding or reason the immediate principle of virtue. Shaftsbury, Hutchinson, and others, make affection the principle of it. Perhaps neither the one nor the other is wholly right. Probably both are necessary.[3]

The connection between truth and goodness, between the understanding and the heart, is a subject of great moment, but also of great difficulty. I think we may say with certainty that infinite perfection, intellectual and moral, are united and inseparable in the Supreme being. There is not however in inferior natures an exact proportion between the one and the other; yet I apprehend that truth naturally and necessarily promotes goodness, and falsehood the contrary; but as the influence is reciprocal, malignity of disposition, even with the greatest natural powers, blinds the understanding, and prevents the perception of truth itself.

Of the will it is usual to enumerate four acts; desire, aversion, joy and sorrow. The two last, Hutchinson says are superfluous, in which he seems to be right.[4] All the acts of the will may be reduced to the two great heads of desire and aversion, or in other words, chusing and refusing.

The affections are called also passions because often excited by external objects. In as far as they differ from a calm deliberate decision of the judgment, or determination of the will, they may be called strong propensities, implanted in our nature, which of themselves contribute not a little to bias the judgment, or incline the will.

The affections cannot be better understood than by observing the difference between a calm deliberate general inclination, whether of the selfish or benevolent kind, and particular violent inclinations. Every man deliberately wishes his own happiness, but this differs considerably from a passionate attachment to particular gratifications, as a love of riches, honors, pleasures. A good man will have a deliberate fixed desire of the welfare of mankind; but this differs from the love of children, relations, friends, country.

The passions are very numerous and may be greatly diversified, because every thing, however modified, that is the object of desire or aversion, may grow by accident or indulgence, to such a size as to be called, and deserved to be called, a passion. Accordingly we express ourselves thus in the English language—A passion for horses, dogs, play, &c.

However all the passions may be ranged under the two great heads of *love* and *hatred*. To the first belong esteem, admiration, good-will, and every species of approbation, delight and desire; to the other, all kinds of aversion, and ways of expressing it, envy, malice, rage, revenge, to whatever objects they may be directed.

Hope and fear, joy and sorrow, though frequently ranked among the passions, seem rather to be states or modifications of the mind, attending the exercise of every passion, according as its object is probable or improbable, possest or lost.

Jealousy seems to be a passion of a middle nature, which it is not easy to say whether it should be ranked under the head of love or hatred. It is often said of jealousy between the sexes, that it springs from love; yet, it seems plainly impossible, that it can have place without forming an ill opinion of its object, at least in some degree. The same thing may be said of jealousy and suspicion in friendship.

The passions may be ranged in two classes in a different way, viz. as they are selfish or benevolent, public or private.[5] There will be great occasion to consider this distinction afterwards, in explaining the nature of virtue, and the motives that lead to it. What is observed now, is only to illustrate our nature as it really is.

There is a great and real distinction between passions, selfish and benevolent. The first point directly, and immediately at our own interest in the gratification; the others point immediately at the happiness of others. Of the first kind, is the love of fame, power, property, pleasure. And of the second, is family and domestic affection, friendship and patriotism. It is to no purpose to say, that ultimately, it is to please ourselves, or because we feel a satisfaction in seeking the good of others; for it is certain, that the direct object in view in many cases, is to promote the happiness of others; and for this many have been willing to sacrifice every thing, even life itself.[6]

After this brief survey of human nature, in one light, or in one point of view, which may be called its capacity, it will be necessary to return back, and take a survey of the way, in which we become acquainted with the objects about which we are to be conversant, or upon which the above faculties are to be exercised.

On this it is proper to observe in general, that there are but two ways in which we come to the knowledge of things, viz. 1st, Sensation, 2nd, Reflection.[7]

The first of these must be divided again into two parts, external and internal.[8]

External arises from the immediate impression of objects from without. The external senses in number are five; seeing, hearing, feeling, tasting and smelling.

In these are observable the impression itself, or the sensation we feel, and the supposition inseparable from it, that it is produced by an external object. That our senses are to be trusted in the information they give us, seems to me a first principle, because they are the foundation of all our after reasonings. The few exceptions of accidental irregularity in the senses, can found no just objection to this, as there are so many plain and obvious ways of discovering and correcting it.

The reality of the material system I think, may be easily established, except upon such principles as are subversive of all certainty, and lead to universal scepticism; and persons who would maintain such principles, do not deserve to be reasoned with, because they do not pretend to communicate knowledge, but to take all knowledge from us.

The Immaterialists[9] say, that we are conscious of nothing, but the impression or feeling of our own mind; but they do not observe that the impression itself, implies and supposes something external, that communicates it, and cannot be separated from that supposition. Sometimes such reasoners tell us, that we cannot shew the substance separate from its sensible qualities; no more can any man shew me a sensible quality separate from a particular subject. If any man will shew me whiteness, without shewing me any thing that is white, or roundness without any thing that is round, I will shew him the substance without either color or shape.

Immaterialism takes away the distinction between truth and falsehood. I have an idea of a house or tree in a certain place, and I call this true, that is, I am of opinion, there is really a house or tree in that place. Again, I form an idea of a house or tree, as what may be in that place; I ask what is the difference, if after all, you tell me, there is neither tree, house nor place any where existing. An advocate for that system says, that truth consists in the liveliness of the idea, than which nothing can be more manifestly false.[10] I can form as distinct an idea of any thing that is not, as any thing that is, when it is absent from my sight. I have a much more lively idea of Jupiter and Juno, and many of their actions, from Homer and Virgil, though I do not believe that any of them ever existed, than I have of many things that I know happened within these few months.

The truth is, the immaterial system, is a wild and ridiculous attempt to unsettle the principles of common sense by metaphysical reasoning, which can hardly produce any thing but contempt in the generality of persons who hear it, and which I verily believe, never produced conviction even on the persons who pretend to espouse it.

NOTES

1. This was a standard argument of eighteenth-century apologetics for the existence of God. It was asserted that the evidence of design in nature, and especially of the human organism, pointed to a divine Designer. The first important blow against this argument was struck by David Hume (1711-76), Scottish philosopher and advocate of skepticism. He cited the chaos and disharmony present in the universe, questioning its unity and perfection. Thus in his *Dialogues Concerning Natural Religion* (ed. N. Kemp Smith [Oxford: Clarendon Press, 1935], p. 260, Hume described life, "The whole presents nothing but the idea of a blind nature, impregnated by a great vivifying principle, and pouring forth from her lap, without discernment or parental care, her maimed and abortive children." The coup-de-grace to the design argument was delivered by Charles Darwin (1809-82) in the mid-nineteenth century. His principle of natural selection as set forth in *Origin of the Species* (1859) made the presuppositions of the design argument untenable.

2. These three distinctions were significant in epistemological theory of the eighteenth century. Affection was identified with emotion, or as Samuel Johnson defined it, "passion of any kind" (*A Dictionary of the English Language* [London, 1755], 1: n.p.). In philosophical usage, affection was frequently contrasted with reason.

The distinction between understanding and will current in this period can be illustrated by a quote from John Locke (1632-1704), father of English empiricism. Locke defined the two qualities accordingly: "The power of thinking is called the Understanding, and the power of volition is called the Will; and these two powers or abilities in the mind are denominated qualities" (*Concerning Human Understanding*, bk. 2, ch. 6, sec. 2, p. 56).

3. The greatest expositor and systematizer of Shaftesbury's thought was Francis Hutcheson. Hutcheson held the chair of moral philosophy at the University of Glasglow from 1730 until his death sixteen years later. His philosophical thought was seminal to the Scottish Common Sense philosophers; among his successors to the chair of moral philosophy at Glasglow were Adam Smith (1752-64) and Thomas Reid (1764-80). His significant philosophical works were *An Inquiry into the Original of our Ideas of Beauty and Virtue* (1725) and *A System of Moral Philosophy* (1755), the latter of which is Witherspoon's central source in *Lectures on Moral Philosophy* (see pp. 27-28 of Introduction).

Both Shaftesbury and Hutcheson disputed Samuel Clarke's assertion that reason was the principle of virtue. Clarke had ascribed to man "those excellent faculties of reason and will, whereby they are enabled to distinguish good and evil" (*A Discourse Concerning the Being and Attributes of God*, 8th ed. [London, 1732], 2:187).

Shaftesbury moved away from this rationalistic stance, affirming that moral judgments proceed from an inner sentiment that is not subject to empirical analysis. He defined the nature of virtue as "a certain just Disposition, or proportionate Affection of a rational creature toward the Moral Objects of Right and Wrong" (*Characteristics*, 2: 40). In a similar vein, Hutcheson wrote that virtue "consists primarily in the affections" (*System of Moral Philosophy*, 1: 228). To Shaftesbury and Hutcheson, emotion was more central to the moral nature of man than reason. Thus they presaged Romanticism's glorification of emotion in the following century.

4. Hutcheson, *System of Moral Philosophy*, 1:8.

5. This division of passions (or affections) was described as "selfish and benevolent" by Hutcheson (ibid., 1:17) and "public and private" by Shaftesbury (*Characteristics*, 2:86-87).

6. This is Witherspoon's first reference to one of the most hotly debated questions of the eighteenth century: Is all human action selfish? Most moral philosophers answered the question negatively (e.g., Samuel Clarke, Lord Shaftesbury, David Hume), and the chief antagonist at which they fired their shots was Thomas Hobbes (1588-1679). Hobbes's philosophical thought, conceived in the turbulence of seventeenth-century England, was seminal in the diverse fields of psychology, ethics, politics, and natural science. Although attracting more opponents than disciples, his genius could not be ignored.

To Hobbes every motive and action of man is egoistic. Even those deeds that appear benevolent, in reality, are motivated by self interest. For instance, he defined pity as "imagination or fiction of future calamity to ourselves, proceeding from another man's calamity" (*The English Works of Thomas Hobbes*, ed. William Molesworth, 11 vols. [London, 1839-45], Vol. 2, *Human Nature*, p. 44). He rejected the view that the condition of pre-civilized man was a state of peace and superior virtue. Rather he asserted, "During the time men live without a common power to keep them all in awe, they are in that condition which is called war; and such a war as is of every man, against every man" (ibid., vol. 3, *Leviathan*, pp. 112-13).

Witherspoon refuses to take such a dim view of mankind and argues that altruistic action is possible. However, he has some discomfort in siding with opponents of Hobbes such as Lord Shaftesbury and Francis Hutcheson. Their view of man as essentially benevolent could not be completely reconciled with Witherspoon's Calvinist doctrine of the depravity of man (see Introduction, pp. 48-50). Hence he tends to take the middle ground between the pessimism of Hobbes and the optimism of Enlightenment thinkers such as Shaftesbury.

7. This distinction between sensation and reflection is Lockean. Sensation is defined in Johnson's *Dictionary* as "perception by means of the senses" (2: n.p.). John Locke em-

phasized its importance: "This great source of most of the ideas we have, depending wholly upon our senses, and derived by them to the understanding, I call sensation" (*Concerning Human Understanding*, bk. 2, Ch. 1, sec. 3, p. 41). Reflection then was subsequent to sensation and was defined by Locke as "that notice which the mind takes of its own operations" (ibid., sec. 4, p. 42). He believed that these two sources, sensation and reflection, begot all ideas and that both arose solely from experience.

8. Locke also used this division of the external and internal, but he identified sensation with the external sense and reflection with the internal sense. Witherspoon, on the other hand, follows the lead of the Scottish Common Sense philosophers in dividing sensation itself into external and internal parts. According to this view, the internal sensation was an innate common sense, existing prior to any experience. For a fuller discussion of Witherspoon's epistemological approach, see pp. 30–34 of Introduction.

9. This refers primarily to those who subscribed to the philosophical system of George Berkeley (1685–1753). The greatest philosopher of idealism in the eighteenth century, Berkeley was an Anglican clergyman who became a bishop in Ireland for the last two decades of his life. He viewed the empiricism of Locke as implicitly mechanistic and atheistic. Hence, he affirmed that all reality was spiritual; this continuous spiritual activity began first in the mind of God and secondly in the mind of his creature, man.

Witherspoon does not seem to grasp the subtleties of Berkeley's philosophy and confuses it with popular notions of immateriality. However, this did not prevent him from unleashing a frontal attack against Berkeleyan thought in the College of New Jersey. He successfully excised idealism from the college shortly after his arrival and made Princeton the American citadel of Scottish realism for many decades (See Introduction, pp. 32–34, 50–52.

10. The advocate is David Hume. In *A Treatise on Human Nature* ([London, 1874], bk. 1, ch. 3, sec. 7, p. 396), Hume wrote: "So that as belief does nothing but vary the manner, in which we conceive any object, it can only bestow on our ideas an additional force and vivacity. An opinion, therefore, or belief may be most accurately defined, a lively idea related to or associated with a present impression."

A careful reading of this section makes it evident that Witherspoon does not fully understand Hume's skeptical reasoning. He couples Hume, the philosopher who drew out the negative implictions of empiricism, with Berkeley, whose rigorous empiricism led him to a thoroughgoing idealism. Samuel Stanhope Smith, Witherspoon's son-in-law and successor at Princeton, followed Witherspoon's reasoning and accused Berkeley and Hume of denying "the existence of the material subject altogether, as being wholly unnecessary." He also asserted that Hume believed that the "vivacity of an idea" (Witherspoon used the word "liveliness") was its only criterion of truth (*The Lectures . . . on the Subjects of Moral and Political Philosophy*, 2 vols. [Trenton, N.J., 1812], 1:20).

LECTURE III

Internal sensation is what Mr. Hutchinson calls the finer powers of perception.[1] It takes its rise from external objects, but by abstraction, considers something farther than merely the sensible qualities—

1. Thus with respect to many objects there is a sense of beauty in the appearance, structure or composition, which is altogether distinct from mere color, shape and extention. How then is this beauty perceived? It enters by the eye, but it is perceived and relished by what may be well enough called an internal sense, quality or capacity of the mind.

2. There is a sense of pleasure in imitation, whence the arts of painting, sculpture, poetry, are often called the imitative arts. It is easy to see that the imitation itself gives the pleasure, for we receive much pleasure from a lively description of what would be painful to behold.

3. A sense of harmony.

4. A sense of order or proportion.

Perhaps after all, the whole of these senses may be considered as belonging to one class, and to be the particulars which either singly, or by the union of several of them, or of the whole, produce what is called the pleasures of the imagination. If so, we may extend these senses to every thing that enters into the principles of beauty and gracefulness.—Order, proportion, simplicity, intricacy, uniformity, variety—especially as these principles have any thing in common that is equally applicable to all the fine arts, painting, statuary, architecture, music, poetry, oratory.

The various theories upon the principles of beauty, or what it is that properly constitutes it, are of much importance on the subject of taste and criticism, but of very little in point of morals. Whether it be a simple perception that cannot be analysed, or a Je ne scai quoi,[2] as the French call it, that cannot be discovered; it is the same thing to our present purpose, since it cannot be denied, that there is a perception of beauty, and that this is very different from the mere color or dimensions of the object. This beauty extends to the form and shape of visible, or to the grace and motion of living objects; indeed, to all works of arts, and productions of genius.

These are called the reflex senses sometimes, and it is of moment to observe both that they really belong to our nature, and that they are very different from the grosser perceptions of external sense.

It must also be observed, that several distinguished writers have added as an internal sense, that of morality, a sense and perception of moral excellence, and our obligation to conform ourselves to it in our conduct.

Though there is no occasion to join Mr. Hutchinson or any other, in their opposition to such as make reason the principle of virtuous conduct, yet I think it must be admitted, that a sense of moral good and evil, is as really a principle of our nature, as either the gross external or reflex senses, and as truly distinct from both, as they are from each other.[3]

This moral sense is precisely the same thing with what, in scripture and common language, we call conscience. It is the law which our Maker has written upon our hearts, and both intimates and enforces duty, previous to all reasoning.[4]

The opposers of innate ideas, and of the law of nature, are unwilling to admit the reality of a moral sense, yet their objections are wholly frivolous. The necessity of education and information to the production and exercise of the reflex senses or powers of the imagination, is every whit as great as to the application of the moral sense. If therefore any one should say, as is often done by Mr. Locke, if there are any innate principles, what are they? enumerate to me, if they are essential to man they must be in every man; let me take any artless clown and examine him, and see if he can tell me what they are.[5]—I would say, if the principles of taste are natural, they must be universal. Let me try the clown then, and see whether he will agree with us, either in discovering the beauty of a poem or picture, or being able to assign the reasons of his approbation.

These are two senses which are not easily reducible to any of the two kinds of internal senses, and yet certainly belong to our nature. They are allied to one another.—A sense of ridicule, and a sense of honor and shame. A sense of the ridiculous is something peculiar; for though it be admitted that everything that is ridiculous is at the same time unreasonable and absurd; yet it is as certain the terms are not convertible, or any thing that is absurd is not ridiculous. There are a hundred falsehoods in mathematics and other sciences, that do not tempt any body to laugh.

Shaftsbury has, through his whole writings, endeavored to establish this principle that ridicule is the test of truth; but the falsehood of that opinion appears from the above remark, for there is something really distinct from reasoning in ridicule. It seems to be putting imagination in the place of reason.—See Brown's Essays on the Characteristics.[6]

A sense of honor and shame seems, in a certain view, to subject us to the opinions of others, as they depend upon the sentiments of our fellow-creatures. Yet, perhaps we may consider this sentiment as intended to be an assistant or guard to virtue, by making us apprehend reproach from others for what is in itself worthy of blame. This sense is very strong and powerful in its effects, whether it be guided by true or false principles.[7]

After this survey of human nature, let us consider how we derive either the nature of obligation of duty from it.

One way is to consider what indications we have from our nature of the way that leads to the truest happiness. This must be done by a careful attention to the several classes of perceptions and affections, to see which of them are most excellent, delightful, or desirable.

They will then soon appear to be of three great classes, as mentioned above, easily distinguishable from one another, and gradually rising above one another.[8]

1. The gratification of the external senses. This affords some pleasure. We are led to desire what is pleasing, and to avoid what is disgustful to them.

2. The finer powers of perception give a delight which is evidently more excellent, and which we must necessarily pronounce more noble. Poetry, painting, music, &c. the exertion of genius, and exercise of the mental powers in general, give a pleasure, though not so tumultuous, much more refined, and which does not so soon satiate.

3. Superior to both these, is a sense of moral excellence, and a pleasure arising from doing what is dictated by the moral sense.

It must doubtless be admitted that this representation is agreeable to truth, and that to those who would calmly and fairly weigh the delight of moral action, it must appear superior to any other gratification, being most *noble, pure* and *durable*. Therefore we might conclude that it is to be preferred before all other sources of pleasure—that they are to give way to it when opposite, and to be no otherwise embraced than in subserviency to it.

But though we cannot say there is any thing false in this theory, there are certainly very essential defects.—As for example, it wholly confounds, or leaves entirely undistinguished, acting virtuously from seeking happiness: so that promoting our own happiness will in that case be the essence or definition of virtue, and a view to our own interest will be the sole and complete obligation to virtue. Now there is good ground to believe not only that reason teaches us, but that the moral sense dictates to us, something more on both heads, viz. that there are disinterested affections that point directly at the good of others, and that these are so far from meriting to be excluded from the notion of virtue altogether, that they rather seem to claim a preference to the selfish affections. I know the friends of the scheme of self interest have a way of coloring or solving this. They say, men only approve and delight in benevolent affections, as pleasing and delightful to themselves. But this is not satisfying, for it seems to weaken the force of public affection very much, to refer it all to self interest, and when nature seems to be carrying you out of yourself, by strong instinctive propensities or implanted affections, to turn the current and direction of these into the stream of self interest in which experience tells us we are most apt to run to a vicious excess.

Besides it is affirmed, and I think with good reason, that the moral sense carries a good deal more in it than merely an approbation of a certain class of actions as beautiful, praise worthy, or delightful, and therefore finding our interest in them as the most noble gratification. The moral sense implies also a sense of obligation, that such and such things are right and others wrong; that we are bound in duty to do the one, and that our conduct is hateful, blameable, and deserving of punishment, if we do the contrary; and there is also in the moral sense or conscience, an apprehension or belief that reward and punishment will follow, according as we shall act in the one way, or in the other.[9]

It is so far from being true, that there is no more in virtuous action than a superior degree of beauty, or a more noble pleasure, that indeed the beauty and sweetness of virtuous action arises from this very circumstance—that it is a compliance with duty or supposed obligation. Take away this, and the beauty vanishes, as well as the pleasure. Why is it more pleasant to do a just or charitable action than to satisfy my palate with delightful meat, or to walk in a beautiful garden, or read an exquisite poem? Only because I feel myself under an obligation to do it, as a thing useful and important in itself. It is not duty because pleasing, but pleasing because duty.—The same thing may be said of beauty and approbation. I do not approve of the conduct of a plain, honest, industrious, pious man, because it is more beautiful than that of an idle profligate, but I say it is more beautiful and amiable, because he keeps within the bounds of duty. I see a higher species of beauty in moral action; but it arises from a sense of obligation. It may be said, that my interest and duty are the same, because they are inseparable, and the one arises from the other; but there is a real distinction and priority of order. A thing is not my duty, because it is my interest, but it is a wise appointment of nature, that I shall forfeit my interest, if I neglect my duty.

Several other remarks might be made to confirm this. When any person has by experience found that in seeking pleasure he embraced a less pleasing enjoyment, in place of one more delightful, he may be sensible of mistake or misfortune, but he has nothing at all of the feeling of blame or self-condemnation; but when he hath done an immoral action, he has an inward remorse, and feels that he has broken a law, and that he ought to have done otherwise.

NOTES

1. The enumeration of these finer powers of perception follows the outline of Francis Hutcheson in *A System of Moral Philosophy* (1:15-16). The four qualities listed above are the same as Hutcheson's list, although Witherspoon chooses to label the last quality as "order or proportion" rather than "design." Hutcheson had also used the expression "pleasures of the imagination" to sum up these finer powers of perception.

Hutcheson elaborated this internal sense of beauty in much greater depth and detail than does Witherspoon. Hutcheson was indebted to Lord Shaftesbury for his philosophy of aesthetics. Shaftesbury held that man's sense of beauty was intuitive, both preceding and going beyond human reason. Hutcheson's most thorough development of this Shaftesburian concept was in an earlier volume, *Inquiry into the Original of our Ideas of Beauty and Virtue*.

2. "Scai" should be spelled "sais" (from the verb, "savoir"—to know). It is probable that this error was in the students' manuscripts, for Witherspoon knew French well. The phrase is literally translated as "I know not what." In this context it refers to an indefinable something that definitely exists, although it cannot be empirically verified or specifically explained. Witherspoon chooses to use the common French expression in his discussion of man's innate sense of beauty.

3. Notice Witherspoon's hesitancy to enlist on the side of Francis Hutcheson in his dispute with Samuel Clarke concerning reason as the basis of virtue. This, no doubt, was because of Hutcheson's identification with the Moderate party in the Church of Scotland (see Introduction, pp. 4-7).

Yet Witherspoon follows the lead of Lord Shaftesbury, Hutcheson, and Joseph Butler in affirming an innate moral sense. This topic was the subject of fierce philosophical debate in the eighteenth century. An innate moral sense had been denied by premier seventeenth-century philosophers such as Hobbes and Locke and by the contemporary Scottish thinker Hume.

4. "For when the Gentiles, which have not the law, do by nature the things contained in the law, these, having not the law, are a law unto themselves: which shew the work of the law written in their hearts, their conscience also bearing witness, and their thoughts the meanwhile accusing or else excusing one another" (Romans 2:14, 15).

5. The existence of any innate principles was categorically denied in book 1 ("Of Innate Ideas") of Locke's famous *Essay Concerning Human Understanding* (pp. 1-39).

6. As noted in Lecture I, n. 11, Shaftesbury expounded this principle in his "Essay on the Freedom of Wit and Humour" (*Characteristics*, 1: 59-150). Although Witherspoon tends to agree that the sense of ridicule was an internal sense, he refuses to give it the prominence Shaftesbury had. His argument against Shaftesbury is probably taken from John Brown's *Essays on the Characteristics* (London, 1752). The first essay in Brown's extended refutation of Shaftesbury's thought was entitled "On Ridicule, considered as a Test of Truth" (pp. 1-107). Although contained in this first edition of Witherspoon's *Lectures*, the above notation ("See Brown's Essay on the Characteristics") was not in any of the students' manuscript copies. Thus it must have been added by Ashbel Green when he prepared these lectures for publication.

7. Francis Hutcheson discussed "the sense of honour and shame" in book 1, chapter 5 of his *System of Moral Philosophy* (1: 79-99). Obviously Witherspoon treats this innate sense much more briefly than Hutcheson did. Furthermore, he has more reservations about its unqualified virtue, for he suggests that on occasions it can be guided by false principles.

8. This list of the ways to truest happiness with emphasis on the sense of moral excellence is from the Shaftesbury-Hutchesonian ethical system (see Shaftesbury, *Characteristics*, "An Inquiry Concering Virtue or Merit," 2: 1-176). However, despite general agreement with this system of thought, Witherspoon has some reservations. He questions its hedonistic thrust—"It wholly confounds, or leaves entirely undistinguished, acting virtuously from seeking happiness" (p. 29)—thereby taking issue with Shaftesbury and Hutcheson's tendency to identify virtue with happiness.

9. In this continuing critique of the ethical thought of Shaftesbury and Hutcheson, Witherspoon borrows heavily from the thought of Joseph Butler (1692-1752). An Anglican clergyman, Butler began his career at Rolls Chapel. Here he preached his famous sermons on human nature, *Fifteen Sermons Preached at Rolls Chapel (London, 1726)*, the second edition of which (1729) was in Witherspoon's library. This work contained the essence of Butler's ethical thought. He argued that conscience is a principle of reflection superior to either self-love or benevolence. Later he wrote the *Analogy of Religion* (London, 1736), the most famous and carefully reasoned defense of revealed religion in the eighteenth century. In 1738 Butler was appointed Bishop of Bristol and in 1750 he was promoted to Bishop of Durham, the position he held at his death.

Witherspoon sides with the ethical thinking of Bishop Butler as it opposed the view of virtue espoused by Shaftesbury and Hutcheson. Duty precedes interest; all must be subordinate to the sense of obligation. (See Butler's Sermon II and III entitled "Upon the Natural Supremacy of Conscience" in his *Fifteen Sermons—The Works of Joseph Butler*, ed. W. E. Gladstone, 2 vols. [Oxford, 1896], 2: 51-76.) Witherspoon resists the Shaftesbury-Hutchesonian definitions of the moral sense as "an approbation of a certain class of actions as beautiful, praise worthy, or delightful." Rather, as Joseph Butler had, Witherspoon believed the sense of obligation to be the integral part of the moral sense of man.

LECTURE IV

This therefore lays us under the necessity[1] of searching a little further for the principle of moral action. In order to do this with the greater accuracy, and give you a view of the chief controversies on this subject, observe, that there are really three questions upon it, which must be inquired into, and distinguished. I am sensible, they are so intimately connected, that they are sometimes necessarily intermixed; but at others, not distinguishing, leads into error. The questions relate to

1. The nature of virtue.
2. The foundation of virtue.
3. The obligation of virtue.

When we inquire into the nature of virtue, we do enough, when we point out what it is, or show how we may come to the knowledge of every particular duty, and be able to distinguish it from the opposite vice. When we speak of the foundation of virtue, we ask or answer the question. Why is it so? Why is this course of action preferable to the contrary? What is its excellence? When we speak of the obligation of virtue, we ask by what law we are bound, or from what principles we ought to be obedient to the precepts which it contains or prescribes?

After speaking something to each of these—to the controversies that have been raised upon them—and the propriety or importance of entering far into these controversies, or a particular decision of them, I shall proceed to a detail of the moral laws or the several branches of duty according to the division first laid down.

1. As to the nature of virtue, or what it is; or, in other words, what is the rule by which I must try every disputed practice—that I may keep clear of the next question, you may observe, that upon all the systems they must have recourse to one or more of the following, viz. Conscience, reason, experience.

All who found virtue upon affection, particularly Hutchinson,

Shaftesbury and their followers, make the moral sense the rule of duty, and very often attempt to exclude the use of reason on this subject. These authors seem also to make benevolence and public affection the standard of virtue, in distinction from all private and selfish passions.[2]

Doctor Clark, and most English writers of the last age, make reason the standard of virtue, particularly as opposed to inward sentiment or affection. They have this to say particularly in support of their opinion, that reason does in fact often control and alter sentiment; whereas sentiment cannot alter the clear decisions of reason. Suppose my heart dictates to me anything to be my duty, as for example, to have compassion on a person detected in the commission of crimes; yet if, upon cool reflection, I perceive that suffering him to go unpunished will be hurtful to the community, I counteract the sentiment from the deductions of reason.[3]

Again: Some take in the air of experience, and chiefly act upon it. All particularly who are upon the selfish scheme, find it necessary to make experience the guide, to show them what things are really conducive to happiness and what not.[4]

We shall proceed to consider the opinions upon the nature of virtue, the chief of which are as follow:

1. Some say that virtue consists in acting agreeably to the nature and reason of things. And that we are to abstract from all affection, public and private, in determining any question upon it. Clark.[5]

2. Some say that benevolence or public affection is virtue, and that a regard to the good of the whole is the standard of virtue. What is most remarkable in this scheme is, that it makes the sense of obligation in particular instances give way to a supposed greater good. Hutchinson.[6]

3. One author (Wollaston Rel. of Nat. delineated) makes truth the foundation of virtue, and he reduces the good or evil of any action to the truth or falsehood of a proposition. This opinion differs not in substance, but in words only, from Dr. Clark's.[7]

4. Others place virtue in self-love, and make a well regulated self-love the standard and foundation of it. This scheme is best defended by Dr. Campbell, of St. Andrews.[8]

5. Some of late have made sympathy the standard of virtue, particularly Smith in his Theory of Moral Sentiments. He says we have a certain feeling, by which we sympathize, and as he calls it, go along with what appears to be right. This is but a new phraseology for the moral sense.[9]

6. David Hume has a scheme of morals that is peculiar to himself. He makes every thing that is *agreeable* and *useful* vir-

tuous, and vice versa, by which he entirely annihilates the difference between natural and moral qualities, making health, strength, cleanliness, as really virtues as integrity and truth.[10]

7. We have an opinion published in this country, that virtue consists in the love of being as such.[11]

Several of these authors do easily and naturally incorporate piety with their system, particularly Clark, Hutchinson, Campbell and Edwards.

And there are some who begin by establishing natural religion, and then found virtue upon piety. This amounts to the same thing in substance; for reasoners upon the nature of virtue only mean to show what the Author of nature has pointed out as duty. And after natural religion is established on general proofs, it will remain to point out what are its laws, which, not taking in revelation, must bring us back to consider our own nature, and the rational deductions from it.

2. The opinions on the foundation of virtue may be summed up in the four following:

1. The will of God. 2. The reason and nature of things. 3. The public interest. 4. Private interest.

1. The will of God. By this is not meant what was mentioned above, that the intimations of the divine will point out what is our duty; but that the reason of the difference between virtue and vice is to be sought no where else than in the good pleasure of God. That there is no intrinsic excellence in anything but as he commands or forbids it. They pretend that if it were otherwise there would be something above the Supreme Being; something in the nature of things that would lay him under the law of necessity or fate. But notwithstanding the difficulty of our forming clear conceptions on this subject, it seems very harsh and unreasonable to say that the difference between virtue and vice is no other than the divine will. This would be taking away the moral character even of God himself. It would not have any meaning then to say, he is infinitely holy and infinitely perfect. But probably those who have asserted this, did not mean any more than that the divine will is so perfect and excellent, that all virtue is reduced to conformity to it—and that we ought not to judge of good and evil by any other rule. This is as true as that the divine conduct is the standard of wisdom.[12]

2. Some found it in the reason and nature of things. This may be said to be true, but not sufficiently precise and explicit. Those who embrace this principle succeed best in their reasoning when endeavoring to show that there is an essential difference between virtue and vice. But when they attempt to show wherein this dif-

ference doth or can consist, other than public or private happiness, they speak with very little meaning.[13]

3. Public happiness. This opinion is that the foundation of virtue, or that which makes the distinction between it and vice, is its tendency to promote the general good; so that utility at bottom is the principle of virtue, even with the great patrons of disinterested affection.[14]

4. Private happiness. Those who choose to place the foundation of virtue here, would have us to consider no other excellence in it than what immediately conduces to our own gratification.[15]

Upon these opinions I would observe, that there is something true in every one of them, but that they may be easily pushed to an error by excess.

The nature and will of God is so perfect as to be the true standard of all excellence, natural and moral: and if we are sure of what he is or commands, it would be presumption and folly to reason against it, or put our views of fitness in the room of his pleasure; but to say that God, by his will, might have made the same temper and conduct virtuous and excellent, which we now call vicious, seems to unhinge all our notions of the supreme excellence even of God himself.

Again, there seems to be in the nature of things an intrinsic excellence in moral worth, and an indelible impression of it upon the conscience, distinct from producing or receiving happiness, and yet we cannot easily illustrate its excellence, but by comparing one kind of happiness with another.

Again, promoting the public or general good seems to be so nearly connected with virtue, that we must necessarily suppose that universal virtue could be of universal utility. Yet there are two excesses to which this has sometimes led.—One the fatalist and necessitarian schemes, to which there are so many objections,[16] and the other, the making the general good the ultimate practical rule to every particular person, so that he may violate particular obligations with a view to a more general benefit.[17]

Once more, it is certain that virtue is as really connected with private as with public happiness, and yet to make the interest of the agent the only foundation of it, seems so to narrow the mind, and to be so destructive to the public and generous affections as to produce the most hurtful effects.

If I were to lay down a few propositions on the foundation of virtue, as a philosopher, they should be the following:

1. From reason, contemplation, sentiment and tradition, the Being and infinite perfection and excellence of God may be deduced; and therefore what he is, and commands, is virtue and duty.

Whatever he has implanted in uncorrupted nature as a principle, is to be received as his will. Propensities resisted and contradicted by the inward principle of conscience, are to be considered as inherent or contracted vice.[18]

2. True virtue certainly promotes the general good, and this may be made use of as an argument in doubtful cases, to determine whether a particular principle is right or wrong, but to make the good of the whole our immediate principle of action, is putting ourselves in God's place, and actually superseding the necessity and use of the particular principles of duty which he hath impressed upon the conscience. As to the whole, I believe the universe is faultless and perfect, but I am unwilling to say it is the *best* possible system, because I am not able to understand such an argument, and because it seems to me absurd that infinite perfection should exhaust or limit itself by a created production.

3. There is in the nature of things a difference between virtue and vice, and however much virtue and happiness are connected by the divine law, and in the event of things, we are made so as to feel towards them, and conceive of them, as distinct. We have the simple perceptions of duty and interest.

4. Private and public interest may be promoted by the same means, but they are distinct views; they should be made to assist, and not destroy each other.

The result of the whole is, that we ought to take the rule of duty from conscience enlightened by reason, experience, and every way by which we can be supposed to learn the will of our Maker, and his intention in creating us such as we are. And we ought to believe that it is as deeply founded as the nature of God himself, being a transcript of his moral excellence, and that it is productive of the greatest good.

NOTES

1. MS C: "This scheme being found defective leaves under a necessity," etc.
2. See Lecture II, n. 3.
3. Ibid.
4. Illustrating this position was the ethical teaching of David Hume. Sanctioning the experimental (or inductive) method in natural philosophy, Hume suggested that men "should attempt a like reformation in all moral disquisitions; and reject every system of ethics, however subtle or ingenious, which is not founded on fact and observation" (*An Enquiry Concerning the Principles of Morals* [London, 1751], sec. 1, p. 9).
5. Comparing intellectual and moral truth, Samuel Clarke wrote: "The only difference is that assent to a plain speculative truth, is not in a man's power to withhold; but to act according to the plain right and reason of things, this he may, by the natural liberty of his

will, forbear. But the one he ought to do; and 'tis as much his plain and indispensable duty; as the other he cannot but do, and 'tis the necessity of his nature to do it" (*Discourse Concerning God*, 2: 188). Also see Lecture II, n. 3.

6. A representative quotation from Francis Hutcheson that verifies Witherspoon's summation of his view is this: "He [God] plainly intended the universal happiness, and that of each individual, as far as it is consistent with it; and that this intention should be our rule; that we should therefore restrain and control, not only all selfish affections, but even all generous affections, within such bounds as the universal interest requires" (*System of Moral Philosophy*, 1: 51).

7. Wiliam Wollaston (1660-1724) tended toward an intellectual theory of morality similar to that of Samuel Clarke. As Clarke did, Wollaston employed deductive reasoning rather than the inductive method that typified eighteenth-century Deism. He argued that vice was a lie and all virtues were deduced from truth: "I lay this down as a fundamental maxim, that whoever acts as if things were so, or not so, doth by his acts declare they are so or not so; as plainly as he could by words, and with more reality" (*The Religion of Nature Delineated*, 8th ed. [London, 1759], p. 16). Witherspoon recommends this volume by Wollaston in the section entitled "Recapitulation" at the end of these lectures (see also Appendix 1).

8. Archibald Campbell (1691-1756), Scottish divine and professor of ecclesiastical history at St. Andrews, advocated self-love in the boldest of terms. Hutcheson, whom Campbell attacked, labeled him a disciple of Epicurus. Campbell's best known work was *Enquiry in the Original of Moral Virtue* (Edinburgh, 1733). In this book he described self-love as "the great Cause, or the first Spring of all our several Motions and Actions, which way soever they may happen to be directed" (p. 4).

9. Adam Smith is best known for his economic thought contained in the celebrated volume, *The Wealth of Nations* (1776). He was also a noted philosopher, having succeeded Hutcheson to the chair of moral philosophy at the University of Glasgow. Here he wrote his central ethical volume, *The Theory of Moral Sentiments* (London, 1759). Evidence of his thesis that sympathy is the basis of all moral sentiments were the opening words of his book: "How selfish soever man may be supposed, there are evidently some principles in his nature, which interest him in the fortune of others, and render their happiness necessary to him, though he derives nothing from it except the pleasure of seeing it. Of this kind is pity or compassion, the emotion which we feel for the misery of others" (pp. 1-2).

10. Illustrating the utilitarian thrust of Hume's ethics is this sentence: "Personal Merit consists altogether in the possession of mental qualities, useful or agreeable to the person himself or to others" (*Enquiry Concerning Morals*, sec. 9, p. 102).

11. Witherspoon is referring to Jonathan Edwards (1703-58), America's leading theologian and philosopher of the eighteenth century. Edwards was also a leading revivalist, initiating the New England phase of the Great Awakening from his parish ministry in Northampton, Massachusetts. In later life he was called to the presidency of the College of New Jersey but in 1758 succumbed to an inoculation for smallpox after a tenure of only two months.

In his work, *The Nature of True Virtue*, Edwards defined true virtue as that which "most essentially consists in benevolence to being in general" (*The Works of President Edwards*, ed. Sereno E. Dwight, 10 vols. [New York, 1830], 3: 94.) For a discussion of Edwards's philosophical system and Witherspoon's relationship to it, see p. 32 of Introduction.

12. Witherspoon tackles a thorny theological problem in this paragraph. Is goodness good because God wills it, or does God will the good because it is good? High Calvinism had opted for the former position. This is evident from the following statement by Amandus Polanus von Polansdorf, Reformed dogmatician: "The supreme rule of divine righteousness is His most perfect and infallible will. God is law to Himself. Whatever He wishes done, it is right by the very fact that He wills it" (*Syntagma Theologiae Christianiae* [Hanover, 1624], 2: 26). René Descartes (1596-1650), the father of modern philosophy, concurred with this view; to believe otherwise would subject God to something above himself, he averred.

Later Calvinists began to modify this position. The Cambridge Platonists particularly objected to resting virtue merely upon the arbitrary will of God. Their most distinguished member, Ralph Cudworth (1617–88), effectively argued that good and evil were determined not by will but by their very nature. God could not make white or black without whiteness or blackness, neither could he capriciously determine the composition of morality. The second edition (London, 1743) of Cudworth's grand work, *The True Intellectual System of the Universe*, was in Witherspoon's library and the comments in this lecture indicate familiarity with its contents.

By agreeing with those who asserted that God wills the good because of its very nature, Witherspoon hints of the hybrid nature of his own Calvinism, which had been considerably diluted by the rationalism of the eighteenth century. Yet he does soften his criticism of those who founded virtue merely upon the will of God and writes a reconciling word for the two positions.

13. Samuel Clarke and William Wollaston were two proponents of the belief that virtue is founded upon the nature of things. For example, Wollaston declared, "And indeed it is true, that whatever will bear to be tried by right reason, is right; and that which is condemned by it, wrong" (*Religion of Nature Delineated*, p. 9).

14. This utilitarian thrust was typical of Shaftesbury and Hutcheson. Shaftesbury concluded his treatise on virtue in this manner: "That single Quality, thus beneficial to all Society, and to Mankind in general, is found equally a Happiness and Good to each creature in particular; and is that by which alone Man can be Happy and without which he must be miserable" (*Characteristics*, 2: 176).

15. In attacking egoism as the basis of virtue, Witherspoon may be referring to several sources of this tenet. The chief protagonist was Hobbes, who viewed all human action as stemming from self-love interest (see Lecture II, n.6). Another advocate of self-love as the basic human motivation was Archibald Campbell, to whom Witherspoon refers earlier in this lecture (see Note 8). A third devotee of this view and a frequent target of contemporary orthodoxy was Bernard Mandeville (ca. 1670–1733).

Mandeville was born and educated in Holland but settled in London after graduation from the University of Leiden. His *The Fable of the Bees; or, Private Vices, Public Benefits* (1714) stirred up great controversy by asserting that private evils such as envy, vanity, and the love of luxury actually contributed to the economic good of society. He severely ridiculed Shaftesbury's estimate of man as essentially virtuous.

16. It is not easy to discern the deterministic philosophies to which Witherspoon refers. He may be following the lead of Samuel Clarke in his *Discourse* (in Witherspoon's library). Clarke's flyleaf for the first volume of this work clearly stated his opponents: "More Particularly in Answer to Mr. Hobbs, Spinoza, and their Followers. Wherein the Notion of Liberty is Stated, and the Possibility and Certainty of it Proved, in Opposition to Necessity and Fate." Thus Witherspoon may be taking a swipe at Thomas Hobbes and Baruch Spinoza (1632–77), the great Dutch philosopher.

On the other hand, Witherspoon may have in mind the thought of Henry Home, Lord Kames (1696–1782). His *Essays on the Principles of Morality* (3d ed. [Ediburgh, 1751]) was also in Witherspoon's library. Here Kames asserted that though the sense of free will existed in the human mind, in reality it was deceitful. In referring to Lord Kames, Dugald Stewart said, "Perhaps no opinion on the subject of Necessity was ever offered to the public which excited more general opposition than this hypothesis of a deceitful sense" (Henry Laurie, *Scottish Philosophy in its National Development* [Glasgow, 1902], p. 106).

17. Witherspoon fears that the Shaftesbury-Hutcheson emphasis upon the public good may lead to the occasional sacrifice of private morality, an eighteenth-century version of situation ethics. That this was the thrust of Hutcheson's philosophy is evident from this quotation: "But, although private justice, veracity, openness of mind, compassion, are immediately approved, without reference to a system; yet we must not imagine that any of these principles are destined to control or limit that regard to the most extensive good which we showed to be the noblest principle of our nature" (*System of Moral Philosophy*, 1: 256).

18. Witherspoon believed man possesses an innate conscience as eighteenth-century moralists such as Butler also assumed. However, unlike Butler, Witherspoon's theology was Calvinistic rather than Arminian. Thus Witherspoon affirms the doctrine of original sin. Inherent virtue was originally implanted in man's "uncorrupted nature"; "inherent vice" now also exists in man's nature because of the fall of man. This inherited depravity of man must be compounded with his innate moral sense in order to understand his true nature.

LECTURE V

3. It remains only that we speak of the obligation of virtue, or what is the law that binds us to the performance, and from what motives or principles we ought to follow its dictates.

The sentiments upon the subject differ, as men have different views of the nature and foundation of virtue, yet they may be reduced within narrower bounds.

The obligation of virtue may be easily reduced to two general kinds, duty and interest. The first, if real, implies that we are under some law, or subject to some superior, to whom we are accountable. The other only implies that nature points it out to us as our own greatest happiness, and that there is no other reason why we ought to obey.[1]

Now I think it is very plain that there is more in the obligation of virtue, than merely our greatest happiness. The moral sentiment itself implies that it is duty independent of happiness. This produces remorse and disapprobation as having done what is blameable and of ill desert. We have two ideas very distinct, when we see a man mistaking his own interest and not obtaining so much happiness as he might, and when we seek him breaking through every moral obligation. In the first case we consider him as only accountable to himself, in the second, we consider him as accountable to some superior, and to the public. This sense of duty is the primary notion of law and of rights taken in their most extensive signification, as including every thing we think we are entitled to expect from others, and the neglect or violation of which we consider as wrong, unjust, vicious, and therefore blameable. It is also affirmed with great apparent reason by man, particularly Butler in his Analogy and his sermons, that we have a natural feeling of ill desert, and merited punishment in vice. The patrons of the selfish ideas, alone, are those who confine the obligation of virtue to happiness.

But of those who are, or would be thought of the opposite sentiment, there are some who differ very considerably from others.
Some who profess great opposition to the selfish scheme, declare
also great aversion to founding the obligation of virtue in any
degree on the will of a superior, or looking for any sanction of
punishment, to corroborate the moral laws. This they especially
treat with contempt, when it is supposed to be from the Deity.
Shaftsbury speaks with great bitterness against taking into view a
future state of what he calls more extended self-interest. He says
men should love virtue for its own sake, without regard to reward
or punishment. In this he has been followed by many reasoners, as
far as their regard to religion would permit them.[2]

If, however, we attend to the dictates of conscience, we shall
find evidently, a sense of duty, of self-approbation and remorse, which plainly show us to be under a law, and that law to
have a sanction: what else is the meaning of the fear and terror,
and apprehension of guilty persons? Quorum mentes si recludantur, &c, says Cicero.[3]

Nor is this all, but we have all certainly a natural sense of
dependence. The belief of a Divine Being is certainly either innate
and necessary, or has been handed down from the first man, and
can now be well supported by the clearest reason. And our relation
to him not only lays the foundation of many moral sentiments and
duties, but completes the idea of morality and law, by subjecting
us to him, and teaching us to conceive of him, not only as our
Maker, preserver and benefactor, but as our righteous governor
and supreme judge. As the being and perfections of God are ir-
refragably established, the obligation of duty must ultimately rest
here.

It ought not to be forgotten, that the belief or apprehension of a
future state of rewards and punishments, has been as universal as
the belief of a Diety, and seems inseparable from it, and therefore
must be considered as the sanction of the moral law. Shaftsbury
inveighs severely against this as making man virtuous from a
mercenary view; but there are two ways in which we may consider
this matter, and in either light his objections have little force. (1).
We may consider the primary obligations of virtue as founded
upon a sense of its own excellence, joined with a sense of duty and
dependence on the supreme being, and rewards and punishments
as a secondary motive, which is found in fact, to be absolutely
necessary to restrain or reclaim men from vice and impiety. Or (2).
We may consider that by the light of nature as well as by revelation, the future reward of virtue is considered as a state of perfect
virtue, and the happiness is represented as arising from this cir-

cumstance. Here there is nothing at all of a mercenary principle, but only an expectation that true goodness, which is here in a state of imperfection and liable to much opposition, shall then be improved to the highest degree, and put beyond any possibility of change.

We may add to these obligations the manifest tendency of a virtuous conduct to promote even our present happiness: this, in ordinary cases, it does, and when joined with the steady hope of futurity, does in all cases produce a happiness superior to what can be enjoyed in the practice of vice. Yet perhaps, the stoics of old, who denied pain to be any evil, and made the wise man superior to all the vicissitudes of fortune, carried things to a romantic and extravagant height. And so do some persons in modern times, who setting aside the consideration of a future state, teach that virtue is its own reward. There are many situations in which, if you deprive a good man of the hope of future happiness, his state seems very undesirable. On the contrary, sometimes the worst of men enjoy prosperity and success to a great degree, nor do they seem to have any such remorse, as to be an adequate punishment of their crimes. If any should insist, that a good man has always some comfort from within and a bad man a self-disapprobation and inward disquiet, suited to their characters; I would say that this arises from the expectation of a future state, and a hope on the one side, and fear on the other, of their condition there.

Those who declaim so highly of virtue being its own reward in this life, take away one of the most considerable arguments, which, from the dawn of philosophy, has always been made use of, as a proof of a future state, viz. the unequal distribution of good and evil in this life. Besides they do not seem to view the state of bad men properly. When they talk of remorse of conscience, as a sufficient punishment, they forget that this is seldom to a high degree, but in the case of some gross crimes. Cruelty and murder, frequent acts of gross injustice, are sometimes followed with deep horror of conscience; and a course of intemperance or lust is often attended with such dismal effects upon the body, fame and fortune, that those who survive it a few years, are a melancholy spectacle, and a burden to themselves and others. But it would be very loose morality, to suppose none to be bad men, but those who were under the habitual condemnation of conscience. On the contrary, the far greater part are blinded in their understandings, as well as corrupt in their practice—They deceive themselves, and are at peace. Ignorance and inattention keep the multitude at peace. And false principles often produce self-justification and ill-founded peace, even in atrocious crimes. Even common robbers are sometimes found to justify themselves, and say—I must live—I have a right to my share of provision, as well as that proud fellow that rolls in his chariot.[4]

The result of the whole is that the obligation to virtue ought to take in all the following particulars: A sense of its own intrinsic excellence—of its happy consequences in the present life—a sense of duty and subjection to the Supreme Being—and a hope of future happiness, and fear of future misery from his decision.

Having considered the reasonings on the nature, foundation and obligation of virtue, I now proceed to a more particular detail of the moral laws, and shall take them under the three heads formerly mentioned, Ethics, Politics and Jurisprudence.

NOTES

1. Witherspoon contrasts ethical systems based upon a sense of duty or upon self-interest. The first of these refers to the thought of Butler, the most able exponent of ethics founded upon conscience (see Lecture III, n. 9). This is made explicit in the subsequent paragraph.

On the other hand, the best-known advocate of self-interest was Hobbes (see Lecture IV, n. 15). Witherspoon asserts that Shaftesbury, despite his professed opposition to the "selfish scheme," has affinity with the advocates of egoistic virtue. This is because of his facile identification of virtue and happiness and his unwillingness to connect virtue and vice with reward and punishment (see subsequent paragraphs).

2. This thesis was central in all of Shaftesbury's moral writings. For instance, he declared, "By building a future State on the Ruins of Virtue, Religion, in general, and the Cause of a Diety is betray'd; and by making Rewards and Punishments the Principal Motives to Duty, the Christian Religion in particular is overthrown, and its greatest Principle, that of Love, rejected and expos'd" (*Characteristics*, 2: 279).

3. This quotation is wrongly attributed to Cicero. It appears in none of the standard lexicons of Cicero's works. Furthermore, the Latin verb "recludo" was used only in poetry and post-Augustan prose.

Witherspoon quotes rather from Tacitus *Annals* 6.6: "Neque frustra praestantissimus sapientiae firmare solitus est, si recludantur tyrannorum mentes, posse aspici laniatus et ictus, quande ut corpora verberibus, ita saevitia, libidine, malis consultis animus dilaceretur," Translated this sentence reads, "Nor was it in vain that the first of sages was accustomed to affirm that, could the souls of tyrants be laid open, lacerations and wounds would meet the view; since, as the body is torn by the lash, so is the spirit of man by cruelty and lust and evil purposes." Tacitus's reference to the first of sages is to Socrates, to whom Plato attributed the above statement (Plato *Gorgias* 524. E).

The quotation from Tacitus fits in nicely with the development of Witherspoon's thought in this section. It is probably a quotation from memory and Witherspoon inadvertently confuses its source. Volumes by both Cicero and Tacitus were in his private collection.

4. Witherspoon draws upon his Biblical knowledge in expounding the themes of self-deceit and undisturbed conscience (e.g., "But evil man and seducers shall wax worse and worse, deceiving, and being deceived"—II Timothy 3:12). In Butler's famous *Fifteen Sermons*, the tenth in this series was entitled "Upon Self-Deceit" (*Works of Joseph Butler*, 2: 168–84).

LECTURE VI

As to the first we must begin with what is usually called the states of man, or several lights or relations in which he may be considered, as laying a foundation for duty. These states may be divided into two kinds—(1.) Natural. (2.) Adventitious.[1]

The natural states may be enumerated thus: (1.) His state with regard to God, or natural relation to him. (2.) To his fellow-creatures. (3.) Solitude or society. (4.) Peace or war. Perhaps we may add to these (5.) His outward provision, plenty or want.[2]

These are called natural states, because they are necessary and universal. All men, and at all times, are related to God. They were made by him, and live by his providence. We must also necessarily know our fellow-creatures, and their state to be similar to ours in this respect and many others. A man must at all times be independent or connected with society—at peace with others, or at war—well provided, or in want.

The other states are called adventitious, because they are the effect of choice and the fruit of industry, as marriage—family—master and servant—particular voluntary societies—callings or professions—characters or abilities, natural and acquired—offices in a constituted society—property, and many particular modifications of each of these.

In prosecuting the subject farther, and giving an analysis of the moral duties founded upon these states, I shall first take notice of our relation to God, with the proofs of his being and perfections, and then consider the moral laws under three heads: our duty to God, to our neighbor, and to ourselves.

1. Our duty to God. To this place I have reserved what was to be said upon the proof of the being of God, the great foundation of all natural religion; without which the moral sense would be weak and insufficient.

The proofs of the being of God are generally divided into two kinds. (1.) *A priori*. (2.) *A posteriori*.[3] The first is, properly speaking, metaphysical reasoning downward from the first principles of science or truth, and inferring by just consequence the being and perfections of God. Clark's Demonstration, &c. (if there be any thing that should be called *a priori*, and if this is a conclusive method of reasoning) is as complete as any thing ever published, perhaps he has carried the principle as far as it will go.

This way of arguing begins by establishing our own existence from consciousness. That we are not necessarily existent, therefore must have a cause; that something must have existed from all eternity, or nothing ever could have existed; that this being must exist by an internal necessity of nature; that what exists necessarily must exist alike every where; must be perfect; act every where; be independent, omnipotent, omniscient, infinitely good, just, true— Because as all these are evidently perfections or excellencies, that which exists by a necessity of nature must be possessed of every perfection. And the contrary of these virtues implying weakness or insufficiency, cannot be found in the infinite Being.

The other medium of proof, commonly called *a posteriori*, begins with contemplating the universe in all its parts, observing that it contains many irresistible proofs that it could not be eternal, could not be without a cause; that this cause must be intelligent; and from the astonishing greatness, the wonderful adjustment and complication of things, concludes that we can set no bounds to the perfection of the Maker, because we can never exhaust the power, intelligence and benignity that we see in his works. In this way of arguing we deduce the moral perfections of the Deity from the faint resemblances of them that we see in ourselves. As we necessarily conceive justice, goodness, truth, &c. to be perfections or excellencies, we are warranted by the plainest reason to ascribe them to the Divine Being in an infinite degree.

There is perhaps at bottom no difference between these ways of reasoning, because they must in some degree, rest upon a common principle, viz. that every thing that exists must have a cause. This is equally necessary to both the chains of reasoning, and must itself be taken for an original sentiment of nature, or an impression necessarily made upon us, from all that we see and are conversant with.

About this and some other ideas great stir has been made by some infidel writers, particularly David Hume, who seems to have industriously endeavored to shake the certainty of our belief upon cause and effect, upon personal identity and the idea of power. It is easy to raise metaphysical subtleties, and confound the understanding on such subjects. In opposition to this, some late writers have advanced with great apparent reason, that there are certain first principles or dictates of common sense, which are either simple perceptions, or seen with intuitive evidence. These are the foundation of all reasoning, and without them, to reason is a word without a meaning. They can no more be proved than you can prove an axiom in mathematical science. These authors of Scotland have lately produced and supported this opinion, to resolve at once all the refinements and metaphysical objections of some infidel writers.[4]

There is a different sort of argument often made use of, or brought in aid of the others for the being of God, viz. the consent of all nations, and the universal prevalence of that belief. I know not whether we must say that this argument rests also upon the principle that nothing can exist without a cause, or upon the plan just now mentioned. If it is a universal dictate of our nature, we must take it as true immediately, without further examination.[5]

The author I formerly mentioned has set this argument in a peculiar light (Dr. Wilson of New Castle).[6] He says that we receive all our knowledge, as philosophers admit, by sensation and reflection. Now, from all that we see, and all the reflection and abstraction upon it we are capable of, he affirms it is impossible we could ever form the idea of a spirit or a future state. They have, however, been early and universal, and therefore must have been communicated at first, and handed down by information and instruction from age to age. So that unless upon the supposition of the existence of God, and his imparting the knowledge of himself to men, it is impossible that any idea of him could ever have entered into the human mind. There is something ingenious and a good deal of probability in this way of reasoning.

As to the nature of God, the first thing to be observed is the unity of God. This is sufficiently established upon the reasonings both *a priori* and *posteriori*. If these reasonings are just for the being of God, they are strictly conclusive for the unity of God. There is a necessity for the existence of one supreme Being, the first cause, but no necessity for more; nay, one supreme independent Being does not admit any more. And when we view the harmony, order and unity of design in the created system, we must be led to the belief of the unity of God.

Perhaps it may be thought an objection to this (especially if we lay any stress on the universal sentiments of mankind,) that all nations have been so prone to the belief and worship of a plurality of gods. But this argument is rather specious than solid; as however prone men were to worship local inferior deities, they seem to have considered them only as intermediate divinities and intercessors between them and the Supreme God.

The perfections of God may be divided into two kinds, *Natural* and *Moral*.

1. The natural perfections of God are spirituality, immensity, wisdom and power.

We call these natural perfections, because they can be easily distinguished, and in idea at least separated, from goodness of disposition. It is highly probable indeed that supreme excellence, natural and moral, must always reside in the same subject, and are truly inseparable; yet we distinguish them not only because the ideas are distinct, but because they are by no means in proportion to one another in inferior natures. Great powers of mind and perfection of body are often joined to malignity of disposition. It is not so, however, in God; for as his natural perfections are founded on reason, so his moral excellence is evidently founded in the moral sense or conscience which he hath implanted in us.

Spirituality is what we may call the very *nature* of God. It must be admitted that we cannot at present form any complete or adequate idea of a spirit. And some, as you have heard formerly, insist that without revelation we could never have acquired the idea of it that we have.[7] Yet there are many who have reasoned in a very strong and seemingly conclusive manner to show that mind or intelligence must be a substance altogether distinct from matter. That all the known properties of matter are incapable of producing thought, as being wholly of a different kind—that matter as such and universally is inert and divisible; thought or intelligence, active and uncompounded. See the best reasoning on this subject in Baxter's Immateriality of the Soul.[8]

Immensity in the Divine Being is that by which he is every where, and equally present. Metaphysicians, however, differ greatly upon this subject. The Cartesians will not admit that place is at all applicable to spirits. They say it is an idea wholly arising from extension, which is one of the peculiar and essential qualities of matter. The Newtonians, however, who make so much use of the idea of infinite space, consider place as essential to all substance, spirit as well as matter. The difficulties are great on both sides. It is hard to conceive of spirit at all, separating from it the qualities of matter; and after we have attempted to do so, it seems to be bringing them back to talk of place. And yet it seems not only hard, but impossible, to conceive of any real being without supposing it in some place, and particularly upon the immensity of the Deity; it seems to be putting created spirits too much on a level with the infinite spirit to deny his immensity. It is I think certain they are either confined to a place, or so limited in their operations as is no way so well expressed as by saying we are here and no where else. And in this sense both parties must admit the divine immensity—that his agency is equal, universal and irresistible.[9]

Wisdom is another natural attribute of God, implying infinite knowledge—that all things in all their relations, all things existing, and all things possible, are the objects of the divine knowledge. Wisdom is usually considered as respecting some end to be attained, and it implies the clear discovery of the best and most effectual means of attaining it.

Power is the being able to do all things without limit or restraint. The omnipotence of God is always considered as an essential perfection, and seems to arise immediately from creation and providence. It is common to say that God can do all things, except such as imply a contradiction—such as to make a thing to be and not to be at the same time; but this is unnecessary and foolish in the way of an exception, for such things are not the objects of power at all. They are mere absurdities in our conception, and indeed we may say, of our own creation. All things are possible with God—nothing can withstand his power.

NOTES

1. This was a common method of division in eighteenth-century philosophy (e.g., Francis Hutcheson in book 2 of *A System of Moral Philosophy* discussed natural rights in chapter 5 and adventitious rights in chapter 6: 1: 293-324). The meaning of *adventitious* at this time was "That which advenes; accidental; supervenient; extrinsically added, not essentially inherent" (Johnson, *Dictionary*, 1: n.p.).

2. This list of natural states apparently is taken from *Principes du droit naturel* (*The Principles of Natural Law*; 1747) by Jean Jacques Burlamaqui. Burlamaqui had enumerated the following five "primitive and original" states, as summarized in the marginal notations:
   1. State of man with regard to God
   2. State of society
   3. State of solitude
   4. Peace; war.
   5. State of man with regard to the goods of the earth
The similarity between the two lists is striking, even to the same number (*The Principles of Natural and Politic Law*, trans. Mr. Nugent, 2d ed. [London, 1763], 1: 37-39).

Burlamaqui (1694-1748) was professor of ethics and the law of nature at the University of Geneva. His principal works, *Principa du droit natural* (1747) and *Principa du droit politique* (1751), were often combined into one two-volume work, as indicated above. Burlamaqui wrote with clarity and organized his material well. His work is largely based on Hugo Grotius and Samuel Pufendorf (see pp. 42-43).

Witherspoon shows knowledge of Burlamaqui but does not borrow extensively from him. For a discussion of Burlamaqui and other sources for these lectures, see pp. 42-43 of Introduction.

3. Witherspoon categorizes Christian apologetics according to two approaches—deductive or inductive. Butler in his preface to his *Sermons* had mentioned these "two ways in which

the subject of morals may be treated (*Works of Joseph Butler*, 2: 5). Witherspoon is convinced that Samuel Clarke is the finest example of the a priori method. By metaphysical rationalism Clarke believed that he had proved the existence of God.

The second approach, a posteriori, was used by Butler. Although Shaftesbury and Hutcheson had also used the empirical method, it was Butler who most effectively built a grand apologetic system upon the inductive method (e.g., analogies from nature indicated the existence of God).

It is clear that Witherspoon prefers the latter approach. In his "Recapitulation" at the conclusion of these lectures, he writes, "It is always safer in our reasonings to trace facts *upwards*, than to reason *downwards*, upon metaphysical principles."

4. Hume had logically forced Lockean empiricism to the extreme of skepticism. If ideas are but representative of external reality, then one must be skeptical concerning the true knowledge of these realities. His damaging arguments against traditional verities, such as cause and effect, are fully developed in his *An Enquiry Concerning Human Understanding*.

In opposition to Hume there arose the Scottish school of Common Sense philosophy (see Introduction, pp. 33-34). Most able of its expositors was Thomas Reid. He asserted that our belief in an external world in intuitive, based upon an innate common sense; that our perceptions are not constructed from sensations, but rather from the external objects themselves.

It appears that Witherspoon's reference to "certain first principles or dictates of common sense" is taken from James Beattie rather than Reid. Beattie (1735-1803), professor of moral philosophy at Aberdeen, had a contemporary reputation larger than Reid's, although he was not as profound. His *Essay on the Nature and Immutability of Truth* (1770) went through five large editions in four years. Indicative of his popularity is Witherspoon's comment in the Recapitulation: "An attempt has been lately made by Beatty, in his Essay on Truth, to establish certain impressions of common sense as axioms and first principles of all our reasonings on moral subjects."

5. That the universal belief in deity indicated the existence of God was a central tenet of eighteenth-century apologetics. First, it was asserted that all men have worshipped a divine being from the beginning: "That it is certain historical Fact, so far as we can trace things up, that this whole System of Belief, that there is one God the Creator and moral Governor of the world, and that Mankind is in a State of Religion, was believed in the first Age" (Joseph Butler, *The Analogy of Religion* [London, 1736], p. 116).

How this belief in deity originated was disputed. Some believed that primitive man had concluded that there was a god through his own reason. John Locke, who denied that man had any innate ideas, held to this position. Others affirmed that God himself had placed the belief in a divine sovereign in the mind of man. This was the conclusion of John Leland (1691-1766), nonconformist divine and antagonist of the Deists, in *The Advantage and Necessity of the Christian Revelation in the Ancient Heathen World* (2 vols. [London, 1764], 1: 43-68), a book in Witherspoon's library. Thus Cotton Mather, Witherspoon's own countryman, also wrote, "Whence is this impression of a God on the Souls of Men? 'Tis none but a God, that could Imprint it" (*Reasonable Religion* [London, 1713], p. 12).

6. See Lecture I, n. 4.

7. Here Witherspoon refers back to the Hutchinsonians previously discussed (Lecture I, n. 6). This school of thought believed that moral knowledge could only come to man through the medium of divine revelation.

8. Andrew Baxter (1686-1750) was a Scottish philosopher who wrote *Enquiry into the Nature of the Human Soul*. The first edition, published in London in 1730, was in Witherspoon's library. Baxter argued that all matter is inert, that all changes imply the constant action of an immaterial principle. Consequently, the universal superintendence of a divine power is required.

9. Descartes's dualistic distinction between extended substance and thinking substance was disputed by Isaac Newton (1642-1727), England's great mathematician and natural

philosopher. Newton argued that God is extended and that materiality literally exists in the divine mind. This deification of infinite space was followed by America's great Calvinist theologian, Jonathan Edwards. Edwards wrote, "It is self-evident I believe to every man, that Space is necessary, eternal, infinite, and omnipresent. But I had as good speak plain: I have already said as much as, that Space is God" (*Works of President Edwards*, 1: 706). A discussion of the relationship between Edwards and Witherspoon is on pp. 00-00 of the Introduction.

Witherspoon tentatively sides with the Newtonians in this philosophical dispute, although his reasoning is obtuse. Furthermore, there is a confusing use of pronouns in this paragraph; their antecedents are not always clear.

LECTURE VII

2d. The moral perfections of God are holiness, justice, truth, goodness and mercy.

Holiness is sometimes taken in a general and comprehensive sense, as being the aggregate, implying the presence of all moral excellence; yet it is sometimes used, and that both in the Scripture revelation and by heathen writers, as a peculiar attribute.[1] In this limited sense it is extremely difficult to define or explain. Holiness is that character of God to which veneration, or the most profound reverence in us, is the correspondent affection. It is sometimes also expressed by purity, and when we go to form an idea of it, perhaps we can scarce say any thing better than that it is being removed at an infinite distance from the grossness of material indulgence.

Justice is an invariable determination to render to all their due. Justice seems to be founded on the strong and unalterable perception we have of right and wrong, good and evil, and particularly that the one deserves reward, the other punishment. The internal sanction, or the external and providential sanction of natural laws, point out to us the justice of God. The chief thing that merits attention upon this subject is the controversy about what is called the vindictive justice of God. That is to say, is there in God, or have we a natural sense of the propriety of, a disposition to inflict punishment independent of the consequences, viz. the reformation of the offender, or the example of others. This loose moralists often declaim against.[2] Yet it seems plain, that the sense in our minds of good and ill desert, makes guilt the proper object of punishment simply in itself. This may have a relation to general order and the good of the whole, which however is out of our reach.

The truth of God is one of his perfections, greatly insisted upon in Scripture, and an essential part of natural religion. It is inseparable from infinite perfection; for any departure from truth must be considered as arising from weakness or necessity. What end could be served to a self sufficient and all sufficient being by falsehood or deception?

Goodness in God is a disposition to communicate happiness to others. This is easily understood. The creation is a proof of it—Natural and moral evil no just objection to it, because of the preponderancy of happiness.

Mercy, as distinguished from goodness or benignity, is his being of a placable nature—Ready to forgive the guilty, or to remit deserved punishment. It has been disputed how far mercy or placability is discoverable by reason. It is not mercy or forgiveness, unless it would have been just at the same time to have punished. There are but two ways by which men from reason may infer the attribute of mercy to belong to the Deity. (1) Because we ourselves are sensible of this disposition, and see in it a peculiar beauty. (2) From the forbearance of Providence that sinners are not immediately overtaken with punishment, but have space given them to repent.—Yet as all the conclusions drawn from these principles must be vague and general, the expectations of the guilty founded upon them, must be very uncertain. We must conclude therefore, that however stable a foundation there is for the other attributes of God in nature and reason, the way in which and the terms on which, he will show mercy, can be learned from Revelation only.[3]

Having considered the being and perfections of God, we proceed to our duty to him. This may be considered in two views, as general and special.

1. By the first I understand our duty to obey him and submit to him in all things. This you see includes every branch of moral duty to our neighbor and ourselves, as well as to God, and so the particular parts of it will be considered afterwards. But in this place, considering every good action as an act of obedience to God, we will a little attend to the divine sovereignty and the foundation of it.

In speaking of the foundation of virtue, I took in a sense of dependence and subjection to God.—But as men are not to be deterred from bold inquiries, a further question is raised by some—what is properly the foundation of the divine dominion? (1) Some found it directly upon Omnipotence. It is impossible to resist his power. This seems to lay us under a necessity, rather than to convince us of duty. We ought, however, to think and speak of this subject with reverence; and certainly Omnipotence seems to oblige us to actual, if it should not bring us to willing obedience. It

103

is somewhat remarkable, that in the Book of Job, composed on purpose to resolve some difficulties in providence, where God is brought in as speaking himself out of the whirlwind, he makes use of no other argument than his tremendous majesty and irresistible power.[4] Yet to rest the matter wholly upon this, seems much the same as founding virtue on mere will;[5]—therefore (2) some found the divine dominion on his infinite excellence, they say it is the law of reason that the wisest should rule, and therefore that infinite perfection is entitled to universal sway. Even this, taken separate and alone, does not seem wholly to satisfy the mind. If one person is wiser than another, it seems reasonable that the other should learn of him and imitate him; but it scarcely seems a sufficient reason that the first should have absolute authority. But perhaps the weakness of the argument, taken in this view, may arise from the inconsiderable difference between man and man, when compared to the superiority of universal and unchangeable perfection. (3) Some found it upon creation. They say, that God has an absolute property in all his creatures; he may therefore do what he will with his own. This no doubt, goes a good way, and carries considerable force with it to the mind, the rather that, as you will afterwards see, it is something similar to this in us, that lays the foundation of our most perfect rights, viz. That the product of our own industry is properly at our own disposal.

As upon the foundation of virtue I thought it necessary to unite the principles of different writers, so upon this subject, I think that all the three particulars mentioned, ought to be admitted, as the grounds of the divine dominion. Omnipotence, infinite excellence, and the original production and continual preservation of all creatures.[6]

2. Our duty to God may be considered more specially, as it points out the duties we owe immediately to himself. These may be divided into internal and external.

1st. The internal are all included under the three following, love, fear, and trust.

The love of God, which is the first and great duty both of natural and revealed religion, may be explained in a larger and more popular, or in a more precise and stricter way.[7]

In the first, love may be resolved into the four following acts, (1) esteem, (2) gratitude, (3) benevolence, (4) desire.

These four will be found inseparable from true love; and it is pretty much in the same order, that the acts succeed one another.

Love is founded on esteem, on the real or supposed good qualities of the object. You can no more love that which you despise, than that which you hate. Gratitude is also inseparable

104

from it, to have a lively sense of favors received, and to esteem them for the sake of the person from whom they came. Benevolence or rejoicing in the happiness and wishing well to the object. And lastly, a desire of a place in his esteem. Whatever we love, we desire to possess, as far as it is suited to our faculties.

The stricter, and more precise method of considering the love of God, is to divide it into two branches, benevolence and desire. And indeed our affections to God seem to be capable of the same division as our affection to our fellow-creatures, benevolent and selfish. I think it undeniable, that there is a disinterested love of God, which terminates directly upon himself, without any immediate view to our own happiness—as well as a discovery of our great interest in his favor.

The second great duty to God is fear; but here we must carefully distinguish this affection from one which bears the name, and is different from it—at least in a moral view it is altogether opposite.—Dutiful fear is what may be otherwise called veneration, and hath for its object the infinity of the divine perfection in general, but particularly his majesty and greatness. The other is merely a fear of evil or punishment from him: these are called sometimes a filial and a servile fear. The first increases, as men improve in moral excellence, and the other is destroyed. Perfect love casteth out fear.[8] Perhaps, however opposite, as they have the same name, they may be said to be the same natural affection, only as it takes place in innocent or holy, and in guilty creatures. The same majesty of God, which produces veneration in the upright, produces horror and apprehension of punishment in the guilty.

The third great duty is trust. This is a continual dependence on God for every thing we need, together with and approbation of, and absolute resignation to his providence.

2. The external duties to God I shall briefly pass over, being only, all proper and natural expressions of the internal sentiments.

It may be proper, however, to take notice in general of the worship due to God, that whether we consider the nature of things, or the universal practice of mankind, in all ages, worship, and that not only private, but public and social worship is a duty of natural religion.

Some of the enemies of revealed religion, have spoken with great virulence against this, as unreasonable, and even dishonorable to the Divine Being. The substance of what they say, is this, is that as it would be no part of the character of an eminent and good man, to desire and take pleasure in others praising him and recounting his good qualities, so it is absurd to suppose, that the Supreme Being is pleased with incense, sacrifices and praises. But it ought to be observed, that he does not require these acts and exercises as any gratification to himself, but as in themselves just and necessary and suited to the revelation we stand in to him, and useful for forming our temper and universal practice.[9]

We ought also to remember, that we must not immediately and without discrimination, reason from what would be praise and blameworthy among men, to what would be just or unjust in God, because the circumstances are very different. Besides, though for any man to desire the applause of his fellow-creatures, or be pleased with adulation, would be a mean and contemptible character, because indeed there is such unspeakable imperfection in the best of men, yet when any duty or sentiment is fully and manifestly due from man to man, there is nothing improper or dishonorable in requiring or expecting it. Thus a parent requires respect and submission from his children, a master from his servants; and though the injury is merely personal, he thinks himself entitled to punish every expression of contempt or disregard. Again, every man who has bestowed signal favors upon another, expects to see evidence of a grateful and sensible mind, and severely condemns every sentiment or action that indicates a contrary disposition.

On the whole, then, we see that if the worship of God be what is due from us to him in consequence of the relation we stand in to him, it is proper and necessary that he should require it. To honor God is to honor supreme excellence; for him not to expect and demand it, would be to deny himself.

One other difficulty I shall touch upon a little. It respects the duty of prayer; and the objections lie equally against it on the footing of natural religion and revealed. The objections are two. (1.) Why does God, who perfectly knows all our wants, require and expect prayer before he will supply them? To this I would answer that he supplies great multitudes of our wants without asking it; and as to his requiring the duty of prayer, I say the same thing as of worship in general; it is reasonable and necessary to express, and to increase upon our minds, a sense of dependence, and thereby lay us under an obligation of properly improving what we receive.

(2.) The other objection is with regard to the force of efficacy of prayer. Why, it is said, should we pray when the whole system of divine providence is fixed and unalterable? Can we possibly suppose that God will change his purposes, from a regard to our cries or tears? To this some answer no otherwise than as before, that without having any effect upon the event, it has only an effect upon our minds, in bringing us to a right temper. Dr. Leechman of

Glasgow, in his discourse on prayer, makes no other answer to this difficulty.[10] But I think to rest it here, and admit that it has no influence in the way of causality upon the event, would in a great measure break the force and fervency of prayer. I would therefore say further, that prayer has a real efficacy on the event, and just as much as any other second cause. The objection arises from going beyond our depth, and reasoning from the unchangeable purpose of God to human actions, which is always unjust and fallacious.— However unable we may be to explain it, notwithstanding the fixed plan of providence, there is a real influence of second causes, both natural and moral, and I apprehend the connection between cause and effect is similar in both cases. If it is fixed from eternity that there shall be a plentiful crop upon a certain field, I know that nothing whatsoever can prevent it; if otherside, the efforts of the whole creation cannot product it; yet I know as certainly that, hypothetically, if it is not ploughed and sown there will be no grain upon it, and that if it be properly manured and dressed, it will probably be fruitful. Thus in moral matters, prayer has as real an influence in procuring the blessing, as ploughing and sowing has in procuring the crop; and it is as consistent with the established order of nature and the certainty of events in the one case, as in the other: for this reason the stoical fate of old, was called the *ignava ratio* of the stoics, as they sometimes made use of the above fallacious reasoning.[11]

NOTES

1. These two definitions of holiness in relation to God were elucidated by Samuel Endemann, a German Reformed theologian contemporary with Witherspoon. In *Institutiones Theologicae Dogmaticae* (Hanover, 1777–78), he defined the twofold *sanctitas* of God: "essential holiness—according as God's essence, nature and attributes are so perfect as to render any imperfection in God impossible," and "moral holiness, which separates moral imperfection from actions and purifies them, so that they are right and just" (p. 28).
2. One philosopher toward whom Witherspoon undoubtedly hurls this epithet is Francis Hutcheson. In developing his thesis that all should be subordinated to the public good, Hutcheson argued that punishment was justified only as it served the public interest. He specifically took issue with Bishop Butler, who had asserted that there was an independent notion of justice involved in punishment (Joseph Butler, *Works*, vol. 2, *The Analogy of Religion*, pp. 47–62). Witherspoon clearly sides with Butler in this dispute, making "guilt the proper object of punishment simply in itself."
3. Here and at other points in these lectures Witherspoon takes issue with the Deist creed that all religious knowledge may be discovered naturally. Certain truths may be discerned via natural religion, but revelation is essential in order to know all the will of God. Mercy is one attribute of God that can only be understood fully through the Scriptures.
   John Leland, in his book emphasizing the superiority of Christianity to paganism, had

cited the Christian quality of mercy. Although praising the Stoics as eminent moralists, he indicated their ethical inadequacy at this point by quoting Seneca: "Mercy, says he, is the vice or fault of souls that are too favourable to misery, which if any one requireth of a wise man, he may also require lamentations and groans" (*Advantage and Necessity of Revelation*, 2: 204). Witherspoon was probably familiar with Leland's argument, for he owned a copy of the book.

4. Job 38:1–42:6.

5. This theological issue is discussed on page 88, n. 12. Once again, it is evident that Witherspoon's Calvinism is a rationalistic modification of the austere Reformed doctrine that emanated from Geneva in the sixteenth century (see Introduction, pp. 38–40).

6. Again Witherspoon shows his proclivity to synthesize varying theological views. Rather than choose one factor as the basis of divine dominion, he is willing to grant the significance of God's omnipotence, excellence, and creative power, and combines all three as the foundation of God's authority.

7. Jesus declared the love of God to be the primary duty of man: "Thou shalt love the Lord thy God with all thy heart, and with all thy soul, and with all thy mind. This is the first and great commandment" (Matthew 22:37–38).

8. "There is no fear in love; but perfect love casteth out fear: because fear hath torment. He that feareth is not made perfect in love" (I John 4:18).

9. It is probable that one of "the enemies of revealed religion" is Henry St. John, Lord Bolingbroke (1678–1751). Noted for his political activity as Tory leader, Walpole critic, and Jacobite intriguer, Bolingbroke was also a severe critic of religious orthodoxy. His writings on this matter were not philosophically substantial, but their rhetorical style, coupled with their author's reputation, demanded contemporary attention. For instance, the writings of Bolingbroke and Hume were the chief occasion for John Leland issuing a second volume of his *View of the Principal Deistical Writers* (London, 1756).

Bolingbroke recognized the need for inward worship, which he defined in terms of resignation to God's providence. But he questioned the propriety of external worship: "Bare reason cannot discover how any external service that man can pay should be acceptable to the Supreme and All-perfect Being" (*The Works of Lord Bolingbroke*, ed. David Mallet, 5 vols. [Longer, 1754], 5: 208).

10. William Leechman (1706–85) had been Witherspoon's predecessor at the church of Beith. After a close election occasioned by charges of heresy, Leechman became professor of divinity at the University of Glasgow. Along with his university colleague Francis Hutcheson, he was identified with the Moderate party—Witherspoon's ecclesiastical opponents in Scotland (see pp. 4–7). Leechman's celebrated sermon, *The Nature, Reasonableness and Advantages of Prayer*, had been published in Glasgow in 1743.

11. In this paragraph Witherspoon reacts against both Old Calvinism and Deism. Each theological system lessened or completely negated the effect man could have upon God: hyper-Calvinism, by asserting that every event is predestined, and Deism, by viewing the universe as governed by immutable laws. Witherspoon argues for the possibility of human influence upon divine purpose, particularly through the agency of prayer. For details on Witherspoon's relationship to Calvinism and Deism, see Introduction (pp. 38–40).

His reference to the *ignava ratio* means essentially the "idle argument" (or the Stoic view that all events are determined by fate). Cicero had denounced this fatalistic philosophy of the Stoics: "Nor shall we for our part be hampered by what is called the 'idle argument'—for one argument is named by the philosophers the *Argus Logos*, because if we yielded to it we should love a life of absolute inaction" (*De Fato*, trans. H. Rackham, Loeb Classical Library [Cambridge, 1942], pp. 224–25). Witherspoon may have been familiar with this specific statement, since some of Cicero's works were in his library.

LECTURE VIII[1]

We come now to our duty to man. This may be reduced to a short sum, by ascending to its principle. Love to others, sincere and active, is the sum of our duty.[2]

Benevolence, I formerly observed, ought not to be considered as the whole of virtue, but it certainly is the principle and sum of that branch of duty which regards others.[3]

We may distinguish between (1) particular kind affection, and (2) a calm and deliberate good will to all.—The particular kind affections, as to family, friends, country, seem to be implanted by nature, to strengthen the general principle; for it is only or chiefly by doing good to those we are particularly related to, that we can promote the general happiness.

Particular kind affections should be restrained and directed by a calm good will to all. Wherever our attachments to private persons prevents a greater good, they become irregular and excessive.

Some think that a calm and settled good will to others, is an improvement of the particular affections, and arises from the more narrow to the more extensive; from family, friend, country, to all our fellow creatures. But it seems more reasonable to say, that the general affection is a dictate of our conscience of a superior kind. If it were only an increase and extension of the private affection, it would grow more weak, as the distance from ourselves increased, whereas in fact the more enlarged affections are intended to be more powerful than the confined.[4]

When we are speaking of kind affections, it will not be improper to observe that some unbelievers have objected against the gospel, that it does not recommend private friendship and the love of our country.[5] But if fairly considered, as the Scripture, both by example and precept, recommends all particular affections, so it is to its honor that it sets the love of mankind above them every one, and by so much insisting on the forgiveness of injuries and the love of enemies, it has carried benevolence to its greatest perfection. The parable of the Samaritan in answer to the question, who is my neighbor? is one of the greatest beauties in moral painting any where to be seen.[6]

The love of our country to be sure, is a noble and enlarged affection, and those who have sacrificed private ease and family relations to it, have become illustrious, yet the love of mankind is still greatly superior. Sometimes attachment to country appears[7] in a littleness of mind, thinking all other nations inferior, and foolishly believing that knowledge, virtue and valor are all confined to themselves. As the Romans long ago made the *Punica fides*[8] to mean deceit, so there are not wanting among us those who think that all the French are interested, treacherous and cowardly.

On the great law of love to others, I shall only say further that it ought to have for its object their greatest and best interest, and therefore implies wishing and doing them good in soul and body.

It is necessary now to descend to the application of this principle to particular duties, and to examine what are the rights or claims that one man has upon another.

Rights and obligations are correlative terms. Whatever others have a just right or title to claim from me, that is my duty, or what I am obliged to do to them.

Right in general may be reduced, as to its source, to the supreme law of moral duty; for whatever men are in duty obliged to do, that they have a claim to, and other men are considered as under an obligation to permit them. Again, as our own happiness is a lawful object or end, we are supposed to have each a right to prosecute this; but as our prosecutions may interfere, we limit each others rights; and a man is said to have a right or power to promote his own happiness by those means which are not in themselves criminal or injurious to others.

Rights may be divided or classed in several different ways; an attention to all of which is of use on this subject.[9] Rights may be (1) natural or acquired. Natural rights are such as are essential to man, and universal—acquired are those that are the fruits of industry, the effects of accident or conquest. A man has a natural right to act for his own preservation and to defend himself from injury, but not a natural right to domineer, to riches (comparatively speaking) or to any particular office in a constituted state.

(2.) Rights are considered as perfect and imperfect. Those are called perfect rights which can be clearly ascertained in their circumstances, and which we may make use of force to obtain when they are denied us. Imperfect rights are such as we may demand, and others ought to give us, yet we have no title to compel them. Self-preservation is a perfect right, but to have a grateful return for a favor is not a perfect right. All the duties of justice are founded on the perfect rights; those of mercy generally on the imperfect rights.

The violation of an imperfect right is often as great an act of immorality as that of a perfect right. It is often as immoral, or more so, to refuse to supply the necessitous, or to do it too sparingly, as to commit a small injury against a man's person or fortune. Yet the last is the breach of perfect right, and the other of an imperfect.

Human laws reach only, in ordinary cases, to the perfect rights. Sometimes imperfect rights, by being carried far, become perfect, as humanity and gentleness in a parent to a child may be so grossly violated as to warrant the interposition of human authority.

(3.) Rights are alienable and unalienable. The first we may, according to justice and prudence, surrender or give up by our own act; the others we may not. A man may give away his own goods, lands, money. There are several things which he cannot give away, as a right over his own knowledge, thoughts, &c. Others which he ought not, as a right to judge for himself in all matters of religion, his right to self-preservation, provision, &c. Some say that liberty is unalienable, and that those who have even given it away may lawfully resume it.[10]

The distinction between rights as alienable and unalienable is very different from that of natural and acquired. Many of the rights which are strictly natural and universal may be alienated in a state of society for the good of the whole as well as of private persons; as for example, the right of self defense; this is in a great measure given up in a state of civil government into the hands of the public—and the right of doing justice to ourselves or to others in matters of property is wholly given up.

(4.) Rights may be considered as they differ with regard to their object. 1. Rights we have over our own persons and actions. This class is called liberty. 2. Rights over things or goods which belong to us. This is called property. 3. Rights over the persons and actions of other men. This is called authority. 4. Rights in the things which are the property of others, which are of several sorts.

When we come to the second great division of moral philosophy, politics, the above distinctions will be more fully explained—at present it is sufficient to point at them in order to show that are the great lines of duty from man to man.

Our duty to others, therefore, may be all comprehended in these two particulars, justice and mercy.

Justice consists in giving or permitting others to enjoy whatever they have a perfect right to—and making such an use of our own rights as not to encroach upon the rights of others. There is one writer, David Hume, who has derided the duty of justice, resolving it wholly into power and conveniency, and has affirmed that property is common, than which nothing can be more contrary to reason; for if there is anything clear as a dictate of reason, it is, that there are many rights which men severally possess, which others ought not to violate.[11] The foundation of property in goods, I will afterwards show you, is plainly laid in the social state.[12]

Another virtue which this author ridicules is chastity. This however will be found to be included in justice, and to be found in the sentiments of all nations, and to have the clearest foundation both in nature and public utility.[13]

Mercy is the other great branch of our duty to man, and is the exercise of the benevolent principle in general, and of the several particular kind affections. Its acts, generally speaking, belong to the class of imperfect rights, which are strongly binding upon the conscience, and absolutely necessary to the subsistence of human society; yet such as cannot be enforced with rigor and precision by human laws.

Mercy may be generally explained by a readiness to do all the good offices to others that they stand in need of, and are in our power, unless they are opposed to some perfect right, or an imperfect one of greater moment.

NOTES

1. The thoughts and the structure of this lecture owe a great deal to Hutcheson's *System of Moral Philosophy*. Witherspoon, however, does not always follow Hutcheson's order and adds some material not found in Hutcheson. Furthermore, Witherspoon often condenses the material and in some instances expounds the thought with greater clarity than Hutcheson. Yet the influence of Hutcheson on this chapter is unmistakable.

For instance, in discussing a man's duty to his fellowman, Hutcheson wrote of these two distinctions: "particular kind affections and passions pursuing the good of societies, or individuals" and "calm and fixed principle of good-will to the greatest system" (1:228). Compare the divisions used by Witherspoon above in writing about the same matter: "particular kind affections" and "a calm and deliberate good-will to all." Witherspoon's dependence upon Hutcheson is discussed in the Introduction.

2. After Jesus had enjoined the love of God as the first commandment, he added the injunction, "The second is like unto it, Thou shalt love thy neighbor as thyself" (Matthew 22:39).

3. See p. 84 and p. 88, n. 6.

4. Witherspoon demurs from Hutcheson at this point. Hutcheson had stated the possibility of extending "all our calm particular kind affections to the general extensive benevolence" (*System of Moral Philosophy*, 1:11). In like manner, Shaftesbury declared the oneness of

self-interest and public interest, for he said they are "not only consistent, but inseparable" (*Characteristics*, 2:81). Witherspoon desires a sharper distinction between the types of affection; to him, general affection for all creatures was not only superior but actually different from affection for family and friends.

5. The unbeliever referred to is undoubtedly Lord Shaftesbury. His criticism of Christianity is not as virulent as Witherspoon represents, but he was disappointed over the fact that these qualities were not included among Christian virtues: "Private Friendship, and Zeal for the Publick, and our Country, are Virtues purely Voluntary in a Christian." To substantiate his point, Shaftesbury had cited A *Discourse on Friendship* (1657) by Bishop Jeremy Taylor (1613–67), who had also written that friendship is not enjoined by the New Testament (ibid., 2:98–99).

To Shaftesbury, who considered patriotism the noblest affection (ibid., 3:143), this omission must have been disturbing. He went on to suggest that perhaps the love of country and friendship were not mentioned so that one may pursue these excellent virtues with no thought of reward.

6. Luke 10:29–37.

7. MS C inserts "to have its foundation."

8. As Witherspoon indicates, this epithet ("Punic faith") was used by the Romans to describe perfidy. For instance, Sallust (Gaius Sallustius Crispur) labeled an act of treachery by Bocchus as "Punica fide" (*The War with Jugurtha* 108.3).

9. Hutcheson's influence on Witherspoon is especially noticeable in this discussion of rights. Hutcheson used the following divisions of rights in his *System*: natural and adventitious (1:293–324); perfect and imperfect (1:257–61); and alienable and unalienable (1:261–62). With some additions and modifications, Witherspoon follows the same outline. Hutcheson's discussion had been more detailed, but some of Witherspoon's elucidation of rights is reserved for his lectures on politics (Lectures X–XIII).

10. Hutcheson believed that liberty is unalienable. On the state of natural liberty, he wrote, "Tis no fictitious state; it always existed and must exist among men, unless the whole earth should become one empire" (*System of Moral Philosophy*, 1:283). Furthermore, this state of liberty may be defended by force, if necessary (ibid., 2:92). Although Witherspoon gives only hesitant affirmation here, his conviction on this matter became obvious by 1776, for he proudly signed the Declaration of Independence, which affirmed that among man's inalienable rights were "life, liberty, and the pursuit of happiness."

It is interesting to note that John Adams's rough draft of the Declaration of Independence had the word 'unalienable" rather than "inalienable." This was also true of the Continental Congress's parchment copy, but the wording was changed to "inalienable" (the original choice of Thomas Jefferson) when the text was printed. "Unalienable" was the customary form of this word in eighteenth-century usage (Carl Becker, *The Declaration of Independence* [New York: Harcourt, Brace & Co., 1922], p. 175).

11. Hume developed this thesis in section 3 ("Of Justice") in *An Enquiry Concerning the Principles of Morals*: "Thus, the rules of equity or justice depend entirely on the particular state and condition in which men are placed and owe their origin and existence to that utility, which results to the public from their strict and regular observance" (p. 41).

Witherspoon's reference to "common property" fails to do justice to Hume. Rather, Hume argued that if property were absolutely abundant, then the "cautious, jealous Virtue of Justice would never once have been dreamt of" (ibid, p. 34). Perhaps Witherspoon's zeal to defend a metaphysical sense of justice apart from utility led him to miss Hume's argument.

12. See pp. 126–28.

13. Again Hume argued that a particular virtue (such as chastity) arose because of its utilitarian purpose. Hume believed that chastity was needed in order to maintain the family for the rearing of the young. Otherwise, "such a virtue would never have been thought of" (ibid., sec. 4, p. 66). Witherspoon insists that chastity also had its origin "in nature."

LECTURE IX

3. The third class of moral duties is what contains our duty to ourselves.[1]

This branch of duty is as real and as much founded in the moral principle, as any of the former—Conscience as clearly testifies the evil of neglecting it—and vicious conduct in this respect does and generally lead us directly not only to misery, but to shame.

We may, I think, divide our duties to ourselves into two heads, which will be both distinct and comprehensive, (1.) Self-government. (2.) Self-interest.

The first of these is to keep our thoughts, desires and affections, in due moderation. If it be asked, what is due moderation? I answer it may be discovered three ways. (1.) When the indulgence interferes with our duty to God, (2.) To ourselves, and, (3.) To our neighbor.[2]

When our thoughts or desires are such as to be contrary to the love, fear, or trust we owe to God, then they are to be restrained and brought into subjection—Thus are generated the virtues of *humility, contentment, patience,* and such as are allied to them.

When our thoughts and inward temper are such as to be any way injurious to others, they must be governed and restrained; hence arises the obligation to guard against all the immoral passions, which will produce meekness and composure of spirit.

And when we have got but a little experience we shall speedily find that an excessive indulgence of any passion, *love, hatred, anger, fear,* discomposes us exceedingly, and is an evil instead of a blessing. We shall therefore perceive the necessity of continence, self-denial, fortitude, restraint, and moderation in every thing how good soever.

(2.)The other general branch of duty of ourselves may be called self-interest. This, taking in natural religion, includes our relation to the Divine Being, and attending particularly to that of procuring his favor. Therefore it is a prime part of our duty to ourselves, to guard against any thing that may be hurtful to our moral character, or religious hopes.

We ought to be active and diligent in acquiring every thing necessary for life and comfort. Most of our duties to ourselves resemble the duties of justice and mercy to others. If there are certain offices due to them, and if they have rights and claims in consequence of their state and relations, the same is the case with ourselves. We are therefore to take all proper methods to preserve and acquire the goods both of mind and body. To acquire knowledge, to preserve health, reputation, possessions.[3]

The whole must be kept within some limits; chiefly we must guard against interfering with the rights of others.

It will be proper before concluding this part of the subject, to take notice of the opinions of the ancients, particularly their enumeration of what are called the cardinal virtues.[4]

Their cardinal virtues were *justice, temperance, prudence,* and *fortitude.* Justice included the whole of our duty to our neighbor. Humanity or benevolence, you see, is kept out of view, though a virtue of the first class; but all its exercises are with them ranked under the head of justice. Temperance was by them considered as much more extensive, than being moderate in the use of meats and drink, to which the English work is chiefly confined. The *Egkrateia*[5] of the Greeks signified, not only abstinence in meats and drink, but continence or purity, and a moderation of all our desires of whatever kind, of fame and riches, as well as pleasures. Prudence, even in the way they generally explain it, seems scarcely to be a moral, or so much as a natural quality. Prudence, they say, is taking the wisest course to obtain some good end. The placing this among the cardinal virtues will show how matters stood among them. Great parts or talents were in high esteem among them. They did not very fully distinguish between a good man, and a great man. Prudence seems rather an embellishment of an illustrious character, than a moral virtue. Another reason why prudence seems to have held such a place among the ancients was, that their chief foundation for virtue was interest, or what will produce happiness. The inquiry upon this subject was, what is the *summum bonum.* Now to this, prudence is very necessary. Agreeably to all this they commonly called the virtuous man, the *wise man,* and he was always an hero.

Fortitude is easily understood, and may be considered in two lights, as active and passive, which gives the two great virtues of patience and valor.

One of the most remarkable qualities in morals among the ancients, was the debate upon the Stoical position, that pain is no evil, nor pleasure any good. This arises from comparing external things with the temper of the mind, when it appears without doubt that the latter is of much more consequence to happiness than the former. They used to reason thus,—Outward possessions, when bestowed upon a bad man, make him no better, but worse, and finally more miserable. How then can these be goods in themselves which become good or evil, according to the state of him that uses them. They were therefore called the things indifferent. There was something strained and extravagant in some of their writings, and perhaps ostentatious, yet a great deal of true and just reasoning. The most beautiful piece of antiquity in the moral way, is the Tablature of Cebes.[6]

Let us now recapitulate what we have gone through, and then add some observation or corrolaries on the morality of actions. We have considered,

1. The nature of man.
2. The nature, foundation, and obligation of virtue.
3. Have given a sort of general analysis of the moral laws as pointing out our duty to God, to our neighbor, and ourselves.

We must now consider all morality in general as conformity to a law. We have seen above whence this law is collected, and derives its authority. Men may differ, not only as to the foundation but as to the import or meaning of the law in some particulars, but it is always supposed that the law exists.[7]

The morality of actions may be considered in two different lights but these very nearly related to each other. (1.) As they are ranked and disposed of by the law itself. (2.) In the conformity or opposition of the actions to the law.

Under the first view an action is either commanded, forbidden, or permitted.

Commanded duties oblige absolutely, and as casuists used to say, *semper non vero ad semper*;[8] that is to say, they are obligatory upon all persons, at the seasons that are proper for them, but not upon every person at every time; because then there could be but one moral duty, all men are obliged to worship God, but this only at certain times, other duties have also their place and season.

Prohibitions oblige *semper ad semper*, all persons at all times.—We must not lie—this obliges every man at every moment, because no time or circumstances can make it lawful.

On permission we may observe several things.

1. There is (as some say,) a two-fold permission, the one full and absolute, which not only gives us a right to certain things with impunity, but implies a positive approbation of the legislator; and

the other implies only that the action is left at large, being neither commanded nor forbidden.

2. Permission in natural laws always implies the approbation of the legislator, and whatever is done in consequence of it, is innocently done, for God and conscience does not permit, or pass uncondemned, any bad action.

3. It is otherwise in human laws. If they leave any action open, it may be done with impunity, and yet by no means with approbation. I may have a right by human laws to say things in a covered or couched manner, which yet may carry in them the highest degree of malignity.

4. The truth is, when we consider the morality of action in a strict or proper manner, the whole class of permitted actions vanishes. They become by their intention and application either good or bad.

Considering actions in their conformity to the laws, a distinction arises similar to the former, into *good* or just, *bad* or indifferent.

A good action must be wholly conformable to the law in its substance, and in all its circumstances. It is not enough that it be materially good, the time must be proper, and the intention laudable.

A bad action is that which, either in substance or in any circumstance, is contrary to the law.

In consequence of this, strictly and properly speaking, all truly good or just actions are equally so, arising from a perfect conformity to the law, as all straight lines are equally straight; but all bad actions are not equally bad, as lines may be bent in a different degree from the straight direction.

Indifferent actions, if there are any truly such, are those that are permitted, and neither commanded nor forbidden by the law. But when we consider the spirit and principles of true morality, we shall find no actions wholly indifferent, because we are under an obligation to promote the happiness of ourselves and others, to which every action may be applied immediately or remotely; and subjection to the Divine will may make a part of our design in doing or forbearing any thing whatever.

In estimating the morality of actions several circumstances must be considered, (1) the good done (2) the principle from which it flows,—self-interest of the contracted kind, benevolence, or hope of reward. (3) The hindrances or opposition that must be surmounted, as interest, inclination, difficulty. An objection seems to arise from this, not easily solved. If an action is the more virtuous, the more opposition, internal and external, that is overcome, then the longer man has had the habit of virtue, and the more completely it is formed, the less merit in his actions. It seems also to take away all moral excellence from the Deity, who cannot be supposed to have the least opposition to encounter either from within or without. This objection cannot be easily removed, but by saying, that the opposition is in no other respect an evidence of the good moral temper, but as it shows the strength of the inclination that overcomes it, and therefore, when a moral habit is so strong as to overcome and annihilate all opposition, it is so much the more excellent.

An action good in itself, may be made criminal by an evil intention.

A man is obliged to follow the dictates of conscience; yet a mistaken conscience does not wholly absolve from guilt, because he ought to have been at more pains to obtain information.

An action is not virtuous in proportion to its opposite being vicious. It is no high degree of virtue to love our offspring, or provide for a family; but to neglect either is exceedingly vicious.

One phenomenon in human nature, nearly connected with the moral feelings, has been particularly considered by some writers, viz. that there is such a disposition in the generality of men to crowd to see objects of distress, as an extraordinary public execution. What is the desire that prompts to it? Is the sight of misery a pleasant feeling? Some resolve it merely into curiosity, which they consider as a natural and original impression. But there seems to be something in it different from novelty. Others say it arises from benevolence, and is an exercise of compassion, and that we have a strong natural impulse to the affection of pity, and really feel a pleasure in indulging it. But though every well disposed mind is highly susceptible of pity, at least of all the benevolence and help that pity suggests when the object presents itself, we can scarcely say that the feeling is pleasant, or that we have a desire after such objects, in order to the gratification.

They who reason on the selfish scheme, as usual, resolve all into private interest; they say we delight to see objects of distress, because it gives a secret satisfaction in reflecting upon our own different situation. I believe there is such a satisfaction in narrow and contracted minds; but to those tolerably disposed it has an opposite effect; it makes them rather consider the calamities which they themselves are subject to, than those from which they are free.[9]

Perhaps it would be best to take more than one principle to account for this effect—curiosity must make a part, and probably humanity and compassion also contribute to it. It seems to be thought some little alleviation to the sufferer's misery when others pity him—Yet prudent persons knowing how unavailing this pity is, often choose to be absent.

Sympathy is a particular affection in aid of benevolence—Yet like all other private affections, when it is not moderated, it prevents its own effect—One deeply affected with the view of an object in distress, is often thereby incapacitated to assist him.

Another question is sometimes subjoined to the above, why men have pleasure in seeing Tragedy, which is a striking representation of a melancholy catastrophe. As far as the subject differs from Comedy, it may be accounted for on the same principles with the desire to see objects of distress—But one powerful principle leads both to Comedy and Tragedy—a pleasure in the imitative arts, an exact portrait of any object whatever gives the highest pleasure, even though the object itself were originally terrible or disgusting.

We see plainly, that an indulgence of the pleasure given by a fine performance is what crowds the theatre. Unhappily, to give greater pleasure to a corrupt mind, they often invent such scenes, and conduct the matter so, as to make the stage the greatest enemy to virtue and good mortals.[10]

NOTES

1. In this discussion of "our duty to ourselves," Witherspoon is probably using the thought of Joseph Butler as his central source. Butler asserted that self-love and virtue are not contradictory: "Self-love, then, though confined to the interest of the present world, does in general perfectly coincide withe virtue; and lead us to one and the same course of life" (Joseph Butler, *Works* 2:75.)

To Butler self-love was an inward principle of man's nature that should dominate his passions. If, however, the passions occasionally gained mastery of self-love, then the highest principle of man (conscience) would testify to this unfortunate state and make man uncomfortable (ibid., 2:38–43). This reasoning is followed by Witherspoon in this lecture.

2. This emphasis on moderation was typical of ethical thought in the Graeco-Roman world. For instance, Aristotle almost deified moderation in his famous *Nicomachean Ethics*. He defined virtue as "a mean state between two vices, one of excess and one of defect." Illustrating this is Aristotle's definition of courage as the middle ground between the opposite vices of cowardice and rashness (*The Nicomachean Ethics* 2.6.16; 2.7.2).

However, moderation is hardly a central virtue in the New Testament. One does find an occasional prudential word: "And every man that striveth for the mastery is temperate in all things." (I Corinthians 9:25). But the quality of life taught by Jesus—love of enemies, absolute purity of life, non-resistance—is scarcely compatible with the pagan ideal of moderation.

3. Again there seems to be an underlying conflict between Witherspoon's prudential admonitions and certain strands of Christian teaching. His advice on the preservation of "health, reputation, possessions" is quite foreign to Jesus' words: "Therefore take no thought, saying, What shall we eat? or, What shall we drink? or, Wherewithal shall we be clothed?. . . But seek ye first the kingdom of God, and his righteousness; and all these

things shall be added unto you" (Matthew 6:31,33). Jesus' own poverty and the life of his disciple Paul (cf. II Corinthians 11:23–33) indicate that this teaching was taken seriously. In borrowing from classical and contemporary sources apparently Witherspoon was not fully conscious of the clash between Christianity and paganism at this point. He is more aware of the variance between the two ethical systems in his later discussion of prudence in this lecture.

4. The enumeration of the four cardinal virtues may be traced back to Plato, although his list of principal virtues differed from the list given by Witherspoon: wisdom, self-control, justice, and courage (*The Republic* 4. 427E).

Other ancient writers such as Cicero continued this discussion of the four cardinal virtues (see *De Finibus Bonorum et Malorum* 2. 14). Cicero first subsumed benevolence under the category of justice, a procedure mentioned by Witherspoon. It was also Cicero's writings that led to the later discussion of these virtues by Christian authors such as Origen, Ambrose, and Augustine.

Of course, Christian theologians modified these four cardinal virtues with their own doctrines. By the time of Thomas Aquinas, the list was the same as the one used by Witherspoon: prudence, temperance, fortitude, and justice (Aquinas, *Summa Theologica*, trans. Fathers of the English Dominican Province, 2d ed. [London, 1927], vol. 7, part 2 (first part, question 61: "Of the Cardinal Virtues," pp. 135-46).

An excellent discussion of the long history of the cardinal virtues may be found in *Moral Values in the Ancient World* by John Ferguson ([London: Barnes & Noble, 1958], pp. 24–52).

5. This is not the original Greek word used by Plato and Aristotle in their discussion of the cardinal virtue of temperance. Rather, they chose the word *sophrosune*, which meant "moderation in sensual desires, self-control, temperance"(Henry George Liddell and Robert Scott, *A Greek-English Lexicon*, rev. ed. Henry Stuart Jones [Oxford: Clarendon Press, 1940], 2:1751.) In Plato's writing, *egkrateia* had its original meaning of "mastery over," and only meant self-control when joined with a reflexive pronoun. It is true that *egkrateia* came to mean "temperance" in later Greek writing (ibid., 1:473). Since the cardinal virtues had been carried down through the ages in several linguistic forms, Witherspoon probably surmised that the original word for temperance was *egkrateia*.

6. This book, widely circulated in the eighteenth century, was in Witherspoon's library. Cebes was a Greek philosopher and disciple of Socrates. He composed three dialogues but only the Tablature is extant. In this didactic dialogue written in a readable style, Cebes affirmed that happiness consists in the practice of virtue. Many allurements entice men to vice, but by patience and endurance they may attain happiness and virtue.

Witherspoon seems to consider the *Tablature of Cebes* a Stoic work. Cebes preceded the advent of Stoicism, although his work has some affinity with this later philosophy. For this reason some classical scholars suggest that the *Tablature* contained Stoic accretions; however, there is no textual evidence to support this conjecture.

7. The discussion of the morality of actions that follows was common in the ethical writings of this era. For instance, Hutcheson had two chapters in his *System of Moral Philosophy* on this theme (ch. 1, bk. 2: "The Circumstances which increase or diminish the Moral Good or Evil of Actions" and ch. 2, bk. 2: "General Rules of Judging about the Morality of Actions, from the Affections exciting to them, or opposing them"—1:227-51).

Witherspoon seems familiar with Hutcheson at this point, although again he is much briefer in his discussion. To illustrate their similarity, note that Hutcheson asserted that ignorance and error do not always remove culpability, since "prior diligence might have prevented them" (ibid., 1: 233). In like manner, Witherspoon points out that a "mistaken conscience does not wholly absolve from guilt, because he ought to have been at more pains to obtain information" (p. 118).

8. Literally, this phrase would be translated   always, but in fact, not at all times." On the other hand, the phrase in the subsequent paragraph, *semper et ad semper*, means "always,

120

and indeed, at all times." Witherspoon's use of the term *casuists* indicates that this was a formulation of medieval Catholic theology.

9. This eighteenth-century debate had been largely precipitated by Hobbes. The philosopher of Malmesbury considered pity to be selfishly motivated. Thus he wrote: "Pity is imagination or fiction of future calamity to ourselves, proceeding from the sense of another man's calamity. But when it lighteth on such as we think have not deserved the same, the compassion is greater, because then there appeareth more probability that the same may happen to us: for, the evil that happeneth to every man. But when we see a man suffer for great crimes, which we cannot easily think will fall upon ourselves, the pity is less" (Hobbes, *Works*, vol. 4, *Human Nature*, ch. 9, p. 44).

Other philosophers of this period discussed the emotional response of man when he saw one of his fellow human beings in distress. Most disagreed with Hobbes, believing man's basic reaction under these circumstances to be altruistic. Representative of this school was Lord Shaftesbury, who realized that self-love motivated by anger, revenge, or fear might cause one to delight in torture or pain visited upon an enemy. But the natural state of man was to react with compassion to the distress of his fellow creatures and any other response was "horrid and miserable" (*Characteristics*, 2:164). Witherspoon's view tends to parallel that of Shaftesbury rather than that of Hobbes.

10. Witherspoon's animus toward the stage no doubt stemmed from his strict religious up-bringing. It was further heightened by an incident that occurred during his Scottish years. In 1756, *Douglas*, a play written by John Home, a clergyman, was presented on the stage in Edinburgh. Witherspoon, along with other conservative clergymen, was indignant and wrote a pamphlet entitled *A Serious Enquiry into the Nature and Effects of the Stage* (a more detailed account of this event is given in the Introduction, p. 61).

That Witherspoon's opposition to the stage did not lessen through the years is evidenced by a piece written by him only one year before his death (1793). A French article that defended the theater was reprinted in the *National Gazette*, a Philadelphia newspaper published by Philip Freneau (1752–1832), staunch Jeffersonian and Princeton alumnus of the class of 1771. Witherspoon wrote a stinging letter in reply to the French article. Freneau chose not to publish his old mentor's letter and it did not appear until its inclusion under the title "Letter Respecting Play-actors" in the posthumous publication of *The Works of The Rev. John Witherspoon*, 4 vols., 1st ed. (Philadelphia, Pa. 1800–1801).

LECTURE X

OF POLITICS

Politics contain the principles of social union, and the rules of duty in a state of society.—This is but another and more complete view of the same things drawn out more fully, and applied to particular cases. Political law is the authority of any society, stampt upon moral duty.

The first thing to be considered, in order to see upon what principles society is formed, is the state immediately previous to the social state. This is called the state of nature—Violent and unnecessary controversies have been made on that subject. Some have denied that any such thing ever existed, that since there were men, they have always been in a social state. And to be sure, this is so far true, that in no example or fact could it ever last long. Yet it is impossible to consider society as a voluntary union of particular persons, without supposing those persons in a state somewhat different, before this union took place—There are rights therefore belonging to a state of nature, different from those of a social state.[1]

And distinct societies or states independent, are at this moment in a state of nature, or natural liberty, with regard to each other.[2]

Another famous question has been, Is the state of nature a state of war or peace? Hobbes, an author of considerable note, but of very illiberal sentiments in politics, is a strenuous advocate for a state of nature being a state of war. Hutchinson and Shaftsbury plead strongly, that a state of nature is a state of society. However opposite and hostile their opinions seem to be with regard to each other, it seems no hard matter to reconcile them. That the principles of our nature lead to society—that our happiness and the improvement of our powers are only to be had in society, is of the most undoubted certainty—and that in our nature, as it is the work of God, there is a real good-will and benevolence to others:

but on the other hand, that our nature as it is now, when free and independent, is prone to injury, and consequently to war, is equally manifest, and that in a state of natural liberty, there is no other way but force, for preserving security and repelling injury. The inconveniences of the natural state are very many.[3]

One class of the above-mentioned writers say, that nature prompts to society, and the other, that necessity and interest obliges to it—both are equally true.

Supposing then the state of natural liberty antecedent to society to be a reality, let us consider the perfect and imperfect rights belonging to that state, that we may see more distinctly how, and why, they differ in a social state.

The perfect rights in a state of natural liberty, are (1.) a right to life. (2.) A right to employ his faculties and industry for his own use. (3.) A right to things that are common and necessary, as air, water, earth. (4.) A right to personal liberty. (5.) A power over his own life, not to throw it away unnecessarily, but for a good reason. (6.) A right of private judgment in matters of opinion. (7.) A right to associate, if he so incline, with any person or persons, whom he can persuade (not force)—under this is contained the right to marriage. (8.) A right to character, that is to say, innocence (not fame)—It is easy to perceive that all these rights belong to a state of natural liberty, and that it would be unjust and unequal for any individual to hinder or abridge another in any one of them, without consent, or unless it be in just retaliation for injury received.[4]

The imperfect natural rights are very numerous, but they are nearly the same in a state of nature as in a state of society, as gratitude, compassion, mutual good offices—if they will be no injury to the person performing them—Indeed they must be the same in a natural and in a social state, because the very definition of an imperfect right is such as you cannot use force to obtain. Now, what you ought not to use force to obtain in a state of natural liberty, human laws in a well constituted state will not give you.

Society I would define to be an association or compact of any number of persons, to deliver up or abridge some part of their natural rights, in order to have the strength of the united body, to protect the remaining, and to bestow others.[5]

Hobbes and some other writers of the former age, treat with great contempt, this which is generally called the social compact.—He insists that monarchy is the law of nature. Few are of his sentiments now, at least in Britain, yet it is proper to trace them to the foundation.[6]

123

It is to be admitted, that society began first insensibly by families, and almost necessarily. Hence parental authority was the first law, and perhaps it extended for two or three generations in the early ages. Though the patrons of monarchy use this as an argument, it does not favor their scheme—This which they call the patriarchal government, could not extend far; or supposing it could, there would be but one rightful king in all the earth, the lineal descendant of Adam's eldest son; not to mention that the very order of succession in hereditary right, has never been uniform, and is but of late, settled in the European nations.

The truth is, though man for wise reasons, afterwards to be noticed, continues longer in a family dependence, than other animals, yet in time he becomes sui juris,[7] and when their numbers are increased, when they either continue together or remove and form distinct societies, it is plain that there must be supposed an expressed or implied contract.

Some say there is no trace or record of any such contract in the beginning of any society. But this is no argument at all, for things inseparable from, and essential to any state, commonly take place so insensibly, that their beginning is not observed.

When persons believe themselves, upon the whole, rather oppressed than protected in any society, they think they are at liberty, either to rebel against it, or fly from it; which plainly implies that their being subject to it arose from a tacit consent.

Besides, in migrations and planting of colonies, in all ages, we see evident traces of an original contract and consent taken to the principles of union.[8]

From this view of society as a voluntary compact, results this principle, that men are originally and by nature equal, and consequently free.[9]

Liberty either cannot, or ought not to be given up in the social state—The end of the union should be the protection of liberty, as far as it is a blessing. The definition of liberty in a constituted government, will be afterwards explained.

Some observe, that few nations or societies in the world have had their constitutions formed on the principles of liberty: perhaps not one twentieth of the states that have been established since the beginning of the world have been settled upon principles altogether favorable to liberty. This is no just argument against natural liberty and the rights of mankind; for it is certain, that the public good has always been the real aim of the people in general, in forming and entering into any society. It has also constantly been at least the professed aim of legislators. Therefore the principle seems to have been admitted, only they have failed or been disappointed in practice, by mistake or deceit. Though perhaps not one twentieth part of mankind have any tolerable skill in the fine arts, it does not follow that there are no such arts, or that the principles of them are not founded in nature.

Reason teaches natural liberty, and common utility recommends it. Some nations have seen this more clearly than others, or have more happily found the means of establishing it.

Here perhaps we should consider a little the question, whether it is lawful to make men or to keep them slaves, without their consent? This will fall afterwards to be considered more fully: in the mean time, observe that in every state there must be some superior and other inferior, and it is hard to fix the degree of subjection that may fall to the lot of particular persons. Men may become slaves, or their persons and labor be put wholly in the power of others, by consent. They may also sometimes, in a constituted state, be made slaves by force, as a punishment for the commission of crimes. But it is certainly unlawful to make inroads upon others, unprovoked, and take away their liberty by no better right than superior power.[10]

It has sometimes been doubted, whether it is lawful to take away the liberty of others for life, even on account of crimes committed. There can be no strong reason given against this, except that which is supposed to operate in Great Britain against making malefactors slaves, that it would be unfavorable to rational liberty to see any rank of men in chains. But setting this aside, it seems plain that if men may forfeit their lives to the society, they may also forfeit their liberty, which is a less precious blessing.

It seems also more agreeable both to equity and public utility to punish some sorts of crimes, with hard labor, than death. Imprisonment for life has been admitted and practised by all nations[11]—Some have pleaded for making slaves of the barbarous nations, that they are actually brought into a more eligible state, and have more of the comforts of life, than they would have had in their own country. This argument may alleviate, but does not justify the practice. It cannot be called a more eligible state, if less agreeable to themselves.[13]

Upon the whole, there are many unlawful ways of making slaves, but also some that are lawful—And the practice seems to be countenanced in the law of Moses, where rules are laid down for their treatment, and an estimation of injuries done to them, different from that of free men.[13] I do not think there lies any necessity on those who found men in a state of slavery, to make them free to their own ruin. But it is very doubtful whether any original cause of servitude can be defended, but legal punishment for the commission of crimes. Humanity in the manner of treating them is manifestly a dictate of reason and nature, and I think also of private and public utility, as much as of either.

The next step in opening the principles of the social state, is to consider the foundation, establishment and extent of *property*. Some begin this by considering the property of man in general in the inferior creatures.[14] Has he any right to use the lower irrational animals for labour, or food, or both?

It is needless to refine too much upon this subject. To use them for labor seems evidently lawful, as they are inferior, with strength fitted for it, and strength which they could not employ for the improvement and cultivation of the earth without the direction of man. They seem to be to man, some how as the body to mind. They help to produce food for themselves, and so increase their number and receive much more sensual pleasure, sharing in all respects with their masters the fruit of their toil.

To use them for food is thus argued to be lawful.—If suffered all to live, they would become too numerous, and could not be sustained, so that death to many of them in a much worse way must be the certain consequence. Further, nature seems to dictate the use of them for food in the plainest manner, for they are food for one another in a regular gradation, the insects to the birds and fishes, many of them to the beasts, and the smaller to the greater, or the tamer to the more rapacious of every order.

If we take tradition or Revelation for our guide, the matter is plain, that God made man lord of the works of his hands, and puts under him all the other creatures.[15] Only it appears that the grant of animal food was made no earlier than to Noah after the flood.[16]

Let us next consider the establishment of private property. Private property is every particular person's having a confessed and exclusive right to a certain portion of the goods which serve for the support and conveniency of life.[17]

In a very imperfect state of society community of goods may subsist in a great degree, and indeed its subsisting is one of the surest signs of an imperfect state of society. Some attempts have been made in civilized states to introduce it, but without any considerable effect, except in Sparta, the constitution of which was very singular.[18] In small voluntary societies, especially of the religious kind, it may be established, and will continue so long as the morals of the society are pure.[19] But in civil society full formed, especially if the state is at all extensive or intended to be so, private property is essentially necessary, and founded upon the reason of things and public utility. The reasons of it are (1) without private property no laws would be sufficient to compel universal industry. There never was such a purity of manners and

126

zeal for the public in the individuals of a great body, but that many would be idle and slothful and maintain themselves upon the labor of others.

2. There is no reason to expect in the present state of human nature, that there would be a just and equal distribution to every one according to his necessity, nor any room for distinction according to merit.

3. There would be no place for the exercise of some of the noblest affections of the human mind, as charity, compassion, beneficence, &c.

4. Little or no incitement to the active virtues, labor, ingenuity, bravery, patience, &c.

Some had laid down schemes for making property common, as Sir Thomas Moore in his Utopia; but in general they are chimerical and impracticable.[20] There is no instance in fact where any state that made a figure in the social life, had their goods wholly in common. Sparta had the most of it, but it was a very small state, and limited in its views; besides there was something so singular in the whole constitution of the Spartan government, that its subsisting so long, remains a phenomenon for politicians and reasoners yet to account for.

Supposing private property to be essential, or at least useful in the social state, the next question is, how does this property take its rise, or by what ways is it acquired?

The original ways of acquiring property may be reduced to these two (l) Prior occupation (2) Our own industry.

As to the first of these, it may be analysed thus. Of the things that lay in common for the use of man, I have a right to take what is convenient for me, and after I have taken it no body can have a better right, nor consequently any title to take it from me.

But many questions, difficult to be resolved, arise from the application of this principle. How far does this right extend? Must I take only what is sufficient for the present moment, or may I provide for future necessities and enjoyment. In vacant lands must I take only what I and my present followers can sufficiently occupy, or may I touch a continent and call it mine, though I shall not be able to fill it in many ages. I answer common utility must be the rule in all these cases, and any thing more particular, must be reserved till we come to the law of nations.[21]

Some say that the water in large bays and rivers ought to be common to all, because it is inexhaustible and one's using it cannot waste or spoil it for the use of others. But the security of societies will point out the measure of property that must be in all those things.

The extent or object of property contains three particulars (1) A

127

right to the fullest use. Whatever is a person's property he has a right to do with it as he pleases, with this single exception, if it may be called so, that he may not use it to the injury of others. Full property has no other exception, unless you call this an exception, that if any man would wantonly destroy the fruits of the earth, or his habitation; in that case though they were his own, people would hinder him, as supposing him to be mad, and deprive him not only of that liberty, but of all others.

(2) Property implies a right of exclusion. We may hinder others from any way intermedling with what is our property. This seems essential to the idea. Giving a full right to one, implies that others have none.

(3) It implies a power to alienate. That is to say, a right of alteration, commutation, donation, during life, and disposal at death. Thus property is said to be perpetual.

There are certain things called by Civilians *Res nullius*,[22] such as temples, public edifices, gates and walls of cities, &c. Temples used to be said to be given to God, and in the laws of civilized states, attention is paid to this circumstance. But as to the property or use, the case of them and of all the other things mentioned, is very clear. They are under the inspection of the magistrate, or such persons as represent the community, and are by them kept for common use.

NOTES

1. Witherspoon alludes to the eighteenth-century controversy on the historicity of the state of nature. The two great English theorists on this subject, Hobbes and Locke, were not concerned primarily with historical origins. Rather, both had postulated man in an original state of nature in order to erect their respective political theories. Yet Locke did argue that reason would lead one to conclude that man was originally free despite the historical evidence indicating that commonwealths were under the administration of one man in the beginning (John Locke, *An Essay Concerning the True Original Extent and End of Civil Government*, in *The Works of John Locke*, 9 vols., 12th ed. [London, 1824], 4: ch.2, sec. 104 & 105, pp. 399–400). Hutcheson asserted this premise even more strongly in an observation about the state of nature: "Tis no fictitious state; it always existed and must exist among men, unless the whole earth should become one empire" (*System of Moral Philosophy*, 1: 283).

On the other hand, David Hume essentially denied the historical reality of both the state of nature and the voluntary compact: "Almost all the governments, which exist at present, or of which there remains any record in story, have been founded originally, either on usurpation or conquest, or both, without any pretence of a fair consent, or voluntary subjection of the people" (David Hume, *Essays, Moral, Political, and Literary*, ed. by T. H. Green and T. H. Grose, 2 vols [London, 1875], Essay 7: "Of the Original Contract," 1: 447).

Witherspoon sides with Locke and Hutcheson, but his reasoning is specious. He argues that the state of nature and the voluntary compact are logical corollaries: if one can establish the historical existence of the voluntary compact, then it follows that the state of nature must have preceded it. However, Witherspoon fails to establish the fundamental premise: the historicity of the voluntary compact. He merely assumes it and then asserts the corollary that logically follows: the existence of a state of nature.

Later in this same lecture, Witherspoon asserts that there are historical traces of an original contract, but he fails to cite any evidence to substantiate this claim. Rather, like Locke, he believes that reason would force one to conclude that originally there existed some tacit consent between the governor and the governed (see n. 8).

2. The thesis of this paragraph may be found in Locke (*Of Civil Government*, ch. 2, sec. 14, p. 346). It was also restated by Hutcheson when he wrote, "[The state of nature] It still must subsist among the several independent states with respect to each other"(*System of Moral Philosophy*, 1: 283).

3. Concerning man's original state, Hobbes pessimistically affirmed, "Hereby it is manifest, that during the time men live without a common power to keep them all in awe, they are in that condition which is called war; and such a war as is of every man, against every man" (*Works*, Vol. 3: *Leviathan*, Pt. 1 cn. 13, pp. 112–13). Of the opposite opinion, Hutcheson took issue with Hobbes in these words: "This first state founded by nature is so far from being that of war and enmity, that it is a state where we are all obliged by the natural feeling of our hearts, and by many tender affections, to innocence and beneficence toward all; and that war is one of the accidental states arising solely from injury, when we or some of our fellows have counteracted the dictates of their nature" (*System of Moral Philosophy*, 1: 281).

Witherspoon's attempt to reconcile these opposing views is rather facile, although understandable. His Whiggish politics and orthodox Christianity would predispose him to disagree with the absolutist, heretical Hobbes. Yet his Calvinist theology with its emphasis on the depravity of man would lead him to a less optimistic view of man than that of Hutcheson and Shaftesbury. Thus he tries to syncretize these conflicting philosophical positions on the state of nature.

4. Witherspoon follows rather closely a similar list of Hutcheson's. In book 2, chapter 5 of his *System of Moral Philosophy*, Hutcheson labeled these "natural rights . . . of the perfect sort." Then, with more discussion than with Witherspoon, he presented the following list (1: 293-99):

     1. A right to life and safety
     2. A right to liberty of action
     3. A right of private judgment
     4. A right over one's own life
     5. A right to use what is common
     6. A right to society with others
     7. A right to the character of innocence
     8. A right to marriage

5. Here Witherspoon clearly and succinctly states the theory of the social compact. Although this political theory can be traced to ancient times, its classic formulation for the eighteenth-century mind was in the writings of John Locke. He affirmed that man had divested himself of natural liberty and put on the bonds of civil society by the means of a voluntary compact (*Of Civil Government*, ch. 8, sec. 95, p. 395). Scottish moral philosophy of the eighteenth century, the thought in which Witherspoon was steeped, generally expounded the same doctrine (e.g., Hutcheson, *System of Moral Philosophy*, 2: 227).

Another possible source of social contract theory for Witherspoon was Puritanism. After all, Puritans on the *Mayflower* had bound themselves together in covenant before disembarking upon American soil: "We do solemnly and mutually, in the presence of God and of one another, covenant and combine ourselves together into a civil body politic." The doctrine of the social contract constantly reappears in the constitutions of the Puritan colonies of New England. Perry Miller incisively discusses the church covenant in seventeenth-century New England in his essay "The Marrow of Puritan Divinity." His thesis is that these colonial Puritans were adherents of the federalist redaction of Calvinist theology (Perry Miller, *Errand into the Wilderness* [Cambridge, Mass.: Harvary University Press, 1956], pp. 48-98).

The evolution of the social contract theory was both lengthy and complex. A careful study of the development and formulation of this political doctrine may be found in *The Social Contract* by J. W. Gough (Oxford: Clarendon Press, 1936). Witherspoon's subscription to the social contract theory places him in the mainstream of American political thought during the Revolution era.

6. Witherspoon incorrectly charges Hobbes with treating the social compact theory contemptuously. As did Locke, Hobbes believed that men in the state of nature had voluntarily contracted among themselves to form a commonwealth. But unlike Locke, Hobbes believed that the original state of man was that of war. Therefore he concluded that an absolute monarchy resulted from this original social compact. Once this unlimited power had been granted to the sovereign, it should not be regained by the governed (*Works*, Vol. 3: *Leviathan*, ch. 18, pp. 159-70).

It seems clear that Witherspoon confuses Hobbes with Sir Robert Filmer (ca. 1588-1653). Both were royalists during the reign of Charles I. But Filmer differed sharply with Hobbes on the basis of absolute monarchy. He denied the social compact theory, choosing rather to justify monarchy by tracing it back to the original patriarchal dominion of Adam. Witherspoon obviously refers to this argument of Filmer in the subsequent paragraph.

The probable basis of Witherspoon's confusion was the belief that Locke was attacking Hobbes in his *Two Treatises on Government* (the fourth edition of this book, published in 1713, was in Witherspoon's library). Although in this work Locke had disputed such Hobbesean doctrines as the state of war being the original state, he made it clear that Filmer was his primary opponent. In fact, the first treatise of Locke's work was a careful refutation of Filmer's *Patriarcha*, a volume published posthumously in 1680. Still, Witherspoon haphazardly attributes Filmer's doctrines to Hobbes. He also makes the same mistake on page 136 of the *Lectures*.

7. Literally "a law of himself, his own law."

8. It is interesting to note Witherspoon's attempt to refute those who denied the historicity of the voluntary compact (cf. Hume, *Essays*, Essay 7: "Of the Original Contract," 1: 447). First, Witherspoon argues that the evolution of such a compact was so gradual as to be largely unrecorded. Secondly, he believes that since most subjects feel justified in rebelling against oppression this implies prior consent. Finally, he asserts that there are historical traces of a social contract; however, he fails to substantiate his claim with evidence. Actually, Witherspoon deals rather superficially with this hotly contested question of the historicity of the social contract.

9. The view of society presented by Witherspoon is essentially Lockean: "Men being, as has been said, by nature all free, equal and independent, no one can be put out of this estate and subjected to the political power of another, without his own consent, which is done by agreeing with other men, to join and unite into a community for their comfortable, safe and peaceable living" (Locke, *Of Civil Government*, ch. 8, sec. 95, p. 394).

10.This discussion of slavery is also considered later under the heading of "Relation of Master and Servant" in Lecture XI, p. 137. However, the latter discussion can hardly be considered a fuller exposition, as Witherspoon suggests.

Witherspoon generally follows the Whiggish premises of Locke and Hutcheson in his views on slavery (see Locke, *Of Civil Government*, ch. 4—"Of Slavery," pp. 351-52; Hutcheson, *System of Moral Philosophy*, bk. 3, ch. 3—"The Duties and Rights of Masters and Servants, " 2: 199-212). Both Locke and Hutcheson viewed slavery as illegitimate since the power exercised over the slave was not by his own consent. Locke did justify slavery by conquest, but only if the war against the defeated was just and the enslavement involved only those who fought for or aided the unjust cause.

Contrary to both Locke and Hutcheson, Witherspoon does justify slavery if the enslaved has given his consent. Yet he later makes it clear that even under these circumstances the master does not have the right "to take away life, or to make it unsupportable by excessive labor" 137).

11. Hutcheson had also justified life imprisonment for some criminals, although he had hedged it with certain qualifications—a prisoner had the right to defend himself by violence against savage tortures, prostitution or being forced to worship against his conscience (*System of Moral Philosophy*, 2: 201).

12. Although Witherspoon had moral questions about Negro slavery, he did not become an active participant in any abolition movement in America. He viewed slavery in America as an evil that would eradicate itself. For a fuller explanation of Witherspoon's views on slavery, see Introduction (p. 45).

13. The Old Testament ("the law of Moses") countenanced slavery, although it was not a widespread practice in Israel. Slavery in the ancient Near East generally arose from either capture in war, self-sale because of hunger or debt, insolvency, or being born of slave parents. Old Testament laws regulating slavery may be found in Exodus 21:1-11; Leviticus 25:39-46; and Deuteronomy 15:12-18.

Although slavery was not abolished in the Old Testament, its abuses were modified. Kidnapping for sale into slavery was a capital crime (Exodus 21:16). If a master killed a slave, he was subject to punishment; if he maimed a slave, the slave was to be granted his freedom (Exodus 21:20-27). Furthermore, all Hebrew debtor slaves were to be released after six years of service (Exodus 21:1-6).

Witherspoon followed the Old Testament on this subject, but Hutcheson believed that Christianity called for a higher standard. He particularly questioned the absolute power exercised by the Hebrews over foreign slaves. Thus he wrote, "Some of these rights granted over foreign slaves may justly be deemed only such indulgences as those of polygamy and divorces, granting only external impunity in such practices, and not sufficient vindication of them in conscience" (*System of Moral Philosophy*, 1: 211).

14. One who began his consideration of personal property with a discussion of man's right to use animals was Hutcheson. Witherspoon summarizes the arguments Hutcheson developed on this matter in chapter 6 of book 2—"The adventitious Rights, Real and Personal, Property or Dominion" (ibid., pp. 309-16).

15. "And God said, Let us make man in our image, after our likeness: and let them have dominion over the fish of the sea, and over the fowl of the air, and over the cattle, and over all the earth, and over every creeping thing that creepeth upon the earth" (Genesis 1:26).

16. In the creation account, it is only mentioned that every herb and every fruit of the tree is given man to eat (Genesis 1:29). But after the flood, God gave man animals for food: "Every moving thing that liveth shall be meant for you; even as the green herb have I given you all things" (Genesis 9:3).

17. Characteristically, Witherspoon follows eighteenth-century republican thought in his discussion of private property. Generally, he holds to the tenet of the inviolability of property (e.g., Locke, *Of Civil Government*, ch. 5—"Of property," pp. 352-67). The term *conveniency of life* is specifically Lockean: "The measure of Property, Nature has well set, by the Extent of Men's Labour, and the Conveniency of Life" (ibid., ch. 5, sec. 36, p. 358).

18. Ancient Sparta did not practice a pure community of goods. It is true that Spartan citizens were prohibited from (1) conventional alienation of land; (2) private ownership of precious metals; and (3) participation in trade and manufacture. On the other hand, some aristocrats owned their lands, and from the beginning of Sparta there were marked differences of wealth among the citizenry. Actually, most of the inhabitants of Sparta were not citizens, but slaves or helots.

19. Some form of communism appears to have occurred in the early Christian church at Jerusalem (Acts 2:44,45). This was a voluntary sharing of goods rather than a total abnegation of property. An occasional Christian sect, in emulation of this earlier example, has

practiced a community of goods (e.g., Oneida Community, Shakers, Hutterian Brethren, etc.). Most of these religious experiments in communism failed, but the Hutterites continue their sharing of goods and property today.

20. Thomas More (1478–1535) was Lord Chancellor of England under Henry VIII but was later executed because of his refusal to sanction the king's break with Rome. His famous work *Utopia* was published in 1516 under the Latin title, *De Optimo Reipublicae Statu, deque Nova Insula Utopia. Utopia* was an adaptation of Plato's *Republic*, and like that ancient work suggested that the people own and use all goods in common. More was not adamant in his advocacy of socialism, but did believe it to be the best possible economic form for society.

21. Witherspoon evades this thorny problem. On the other hand, Hutcheson clearly spoke out against unlimited occupation of land: "No person or society therefore can by mere occupation acquire such a right in a vast tract of land quite beyond their power to cultivate, as shall exclude others who may want to work, or sustenance for their numerous hands, from a share proportioned to the colonies they can send" (*System of Moral Philosophy*, 1: 326).

22. Civilians were those who were proficient in the civil law of Rome. *Res nullius* is a thing belonging to no one. This reference may be taken from Hutcheson's discussion of *res nullius* (ibid., pp. 331–36) or from the primary source, *The Institutes of Justinian*, bk. 2, title 1, sec. 7.

LECTURE XI

In the social life in general we may consider, (1) domestic, (2) civil society.

The first of these we must consider as implying and made up of several relations, the chief of which are (1) the relation of marriage, (2) that of parents and children, (3) that of master and servant.[1]

In marriage we ought to observe, that though all creatures may be said to be propagated in a way in a great degree similar, yet there is something peculiarly distinguished, dignified and solemn in marriage among men. This distinction is necessary and founded in reason and nature.

Human creatures at their birth are in a state weaker and more helpless than any other animals. They also arrive much more slowly at maturity, and need by far most assistance and cultivation. Therefore a particular union of the parents is absolutely necessary, and that upon such powerful principles as will secure their common care. Marriage is a relation expressly founded upon this necessity, and must be so conducted as to ascertain the property of the offspring, and to promise the most assiduous, prudent and extensive care.[2]

This is the foundation of marriage drawn from the public good. But we ought also to observe that man is manifestly superior in dignity to the other animals, and it was intended that all his enjoyments, and even his indulgence of instinctive propensities, should be of a more exalted and rational kind than theirs. Therefore the propensity of the sexes to one another, is not only reined in by modesty, but is so ordered as to require that reason and friendship, and some of the noblest affections, should have place. And it is certain that they have, if not a more violent, at least a more lasting and uniform influence in the married state than sensual desire.

It is further observed by moral writers, that though beauty and personal attraction may be considered as the first motives, yet these are always supposed to be indications of something excellent in the temper within. So that even love of beauty in man is an attachment to moral excellence. Let a person attend with seriousness, and he will find that the utmost perfection of form in an idiot, or one thoroughly known to be of a very bad temper, is really no object of desire. Though in those who are little known it is apt to prejudice the ignorant and unwary to judge favorably of the person.[3]

The particulars which reason and nature point out relating to the marriage contract are as follow:

1. That it be between one man and one woman. Polygamy is condemned by nature; for it is found that the males born, are to the females as 13 to 12, or as some say, as 20 to 19, the overplus being to supply the greater waste of the male part of the species by war and dangerous occupations, hard labor, and travelling by land and sea.

2. The fundamental and essential part of the contract is fidelity and chastity. This must immediately appear to be essential to the purpose of the union. Some writers say that this is especially binding upon the woman, in order to ascertain the offspring; but every body must see the absurdity of any distinction, because the contract would neither be equal, nor likely to be steadily observed if it were not mutual. Besides, as a late author has well observed, if chastity be a female virtue, how can men be unchaste without infringing upon it?

3. The contract should be for life—otherwise it would be short, uncertain, and mutual love and industry greatly weakened.

4. If superiority and authority be given to the man, it should be used with so much gentleness and love as to make it a state of as great equality as possible. Hutchinson and some other writers say there should be no superiority, and that their property being common, should not be alienated by the one without the other. Others think that perfect equality of power in two persons is not consistent with order, and the common interest, and therefore give authority to the man; and the laws of most nations give the man the disposal of property, with the reservation of particular rights to the woman.[4]

Some heathen writers gave the man power of life and death over the woman, a thing evidently barbarous and unjust.

5. Marriages are sometimes dissolved by divorces, which our law permits only on three accounts—adultery, wilful and obstinate desertion, and incapacity. The first two of these founded on the

New Testament, and the last on reason, being not so properly a dissolution of a marriage, as a declaration that it was void from the beginning, and never took place.[5]

Some writers of moral philosophy add as causes of divorce, contrariety of temper, incurable diseases, and such as would infect the offspring.[6] But none of them seem of sufficient moment. The first would be an evident temptation to causeless and wanton separations—and all the three may be guarded against by previous caution.

Hutchinson observes that in all nations, marrying in near degrees of consanguinity or affinity has been avoided and abhorred; and he adds, that the natural and general abhorrence of it has been greater than reason seems to dictate. Hence it has been conjectured to have been early tradition or revelation—and men have exercised their invention in finding out the true reason or ground of the prohibition.[7]

One reason assigned is, because if marriage were lawful to near relations, their frequent intercourse would be a strong temptation to uncleanness.[8]

Another; that if permitted, it would frequently confound or invert the duties of relations, by setting some above others whom they formerly used to obey.

A third reason, and perhaps the best is, that abstaining from blood relations in this voluntary contract extends the social ties, and produces a greater number of family relations.

Whatever be the moral reasons, it seems to have a strong sanction in nature; for it is observed that marriage between near relations, especially if repeated, greatly weakens the human race.

As to the extent of this prohibition, it has been various in different nations, but the most prevailing has been to forbid all within three degrees. The degrees are reckoned by the steps of descent between the parties and the common parent. Parent and child is the first—child and child the second—child and grand-child, the third—and two grand-children or first cousins the fourth—when it becomes lawful.[9]

Relation of Parents and Children

The first thing to be observed is, that this relation is distinguished by the strongest instinct of parental affection. This seems necessary, as the education of children is a duty requiring so much time, care and expense, which nothing but the most rooted affection would submit to.[10]

The rights of the parent may be summed up in these two:

1. Authority, which requires subjection in the children. 2. A right to a grateful return in due time from the children. The first is a perfect right, as far as it extends, but must be limited.[11]

Some nations have given parents the power of life and death over their children,[12] and Hobbs insists that children are the goods and absolute property of their parents, and that they may alienate them and sell them either for a time, or for life.[13] But both these seem ill founded, because they are contrary to the end of this right, viz. instruction and protection. Parental right seems in most cases to be limited by the advantage of the children.

Children are no doubt to judge for themselves in matters of religion when they come to years, though the parents are under the strongest obligation to instruct them carefully to the best of their judgment. Those who insist, that to leave them their judgment free they ought not to be taught any principles, ought to consider that their scheme is impracticable and absurd. If the parents do not instruct them, they will imbibe prejudices and contract habits, perhaps of the worst kind, from others.

Children in most nations are considered as having a right exclusive of their parents to property given them by others.

Many nations have given the parents a right to dispose of their children in marriage; but this seems to be carrying parental authority too far, if it be made absolute, because it puts in the power of the parent to dispose of what is most essential to their happiness through the whole of their future life. Yet it seems very contrary to reason and nature that children in early life should dispose of themselves in marriage without consulting their parents.

Since we have denied the power of life and death to parents, it will be asked, what is the sanction of their authority? I answer, moderate correction in early life, and as the very highest punishment, expulsion from their family, or a forfeiture of the privileges which they despise.[14]

As to the right to a grateful return, it is an imperfect right, but of the strongest kind—sometimes the civil authority interposes, and obliges children to maintain their aged parents.

To the disgrace of human nature it is often observed, that parental affection is much stronger than filial duty. We must indeed acknowledge the wisdom of Providence in making the instinctive impulse stronger in parents towards their children, than in children towards their parents; because the first is more necessary than the other to the public good; yet when we consider both as improved into a virtuous disposition by reason and a sense of duty, there seems to be every whit as much baseness in filial ingratitude, as in want of natural affection.

This relation is first generated by the difference which God hath permitted to take place between man and man. Some are superior to others in mental powers and intellectual improvement—some by the great increase of their property through their own, or their predecessors industry, and some make it their choice, finding they cannot live otherwise better, to let out their labor to others for hire.

Let us shortly consider (1.) How far this subjection extends. (2.) The duties on each side.

As to the first, it seems to be only that the master has a right to the labors and ingenuity of the servant, for a limited time, or at most for life. He can have no right either to take away life, or to make it insupportable by excessive labor. The servant therefore retains all his other natural rights.

The practice of ancient nations, of making their prisoners of war slaves, was altogether unjust and barbarous; for though we could suppose that those who were the causes of an unjust war deserved to be made slaves; yet this could not be the case of all who fought on their side; besides, the doing so in one instance, would authorise the doing it in any other; and those who fought in defense of their country, when unjustly invaded, might be taken as well as others. The practice was also impolitic, as slaves never are so good or faithful servants, as those who become so for a limited time by consent.

NOTES

1. Once again Witherspoon appears to be patterning his thought after Hutcheson. The first three chapters of book 3 in Hutcheson's *System of Moral Philosophy* (2:149-212) discuss the three items of domestic society about which Witherspoon writes in this lecture. Note the similarity of Hutcheson's wording to that of Witherspoon: "These states (adventitious) are either domestick or civil. The domestick are these three, of married persons, of parents and children, of masters and servants" (ibid., p. 149).
2. This was a familiar thesis of eighteenth-century moral philosophers. Thus, David Hume wrote, "Whoever considers the length and feebleness of human infancy, with the concern which both sexes naturally have for their offspring, will easily perceive, that there must be an union of male and female for the education of the young, and that this union must be of considerable duration" (*Treatise of Human Nature*, pt. 2, sec. 12, p. 331). In like manner Hutcheson wrote, "But the preservation of human offspring, and the giving it the education necessary for the higher purposes of a rational life, require a long, a constant, and troublesome attendance of many years, for which the mother without the aid of the father is not at all sufficient" (*System of Moral Philosophy*, 2:150).

3. Undoubtedly, one moral writer to whom Witherspoon refers in this paragraph is Lord Shaftesbury, who believed that "admirers of the fair sex" required a beauty of the mind to accompany physical beauty, even if unconsciously. For he asked, "Why else is the very Air of Foolishness enough to cloy a Lover at first sight? Why does an Idiot — Look and Manner destroy the effect of all those outward charms, and rob the Fair-One of her power; tho regularly armed in all the exactness of Features and Complexion?" (*Characteristics*, 1:137).

4. Hutcheson, in discussing this matter, wrote: "The powers vested in husbands by the civil laws of many nations are monstrous, such as that of life and death. To exercise any such power, or even that of any corporal punishment, must be tyrannical and unmanly. Committing to the husband the whole power over the whole stock of the family, including the wife's portion, is unjust and imprudent, as well as contrary to nature....Affairs of importance should rather be committed to both jointly, so that neither separately could transact validly about them; and a civil judge, or a prudent umpire be appointed to determine important matters of debate between them: or each should retain the power of managing their own shares" (*System of Moral Philosophy*, 2:165).

Although Locke denied that man possessed power over a woman's life, he did suggest that man should rule when conflict arose: "But the Husband and Wife, though they have but one common Concern, yet having different understandings, will unavoidably sometimes have different wills too; it therefore being necessary, that the last Determination, i.e. the Rule, should be placed somewhere, it naturally falls to the Man's share, as the abler and the stronger. But this reaching but to the things of their common Interest and Property, leaves the wife in the full and free possession of what by Contract is her peculiar Right, and gives the Husband no more power over her Life, than she has over his" (*Of Civil Government*, ch. 7, sec. 82, p. 385).

5. The New Testament passage that justifies adultery as sufficient reason for divorce is Matthew 19:9. Jesus had been questioned on the subject of divorce and in reply strongly affirmed the inviolability of marriage. However, he did indicate one exception: "Whosoever shall put away his wife, except it be for fornication, and shall marry another, committeth adultery: and whoso marrieth her which is put away doth commit adultery."

The passage that is cited to justify desertion as a cause for divorce is more ambiguous. In I Corinthians 7:12-15, Paul discussed the relationship of Christian and non-Christian mates. He encouraged the Christian husband or wife to remain with their pagan spouses if at all possible. However, he recognized this might not be possible in all circumstances: "But if the unbelieving depart, let him depart. A brother or a sister is not under bondage in such cases: but God hath called us to peace" (I Corinthians 7:15). In this context Paul was not writing of desertion in general, but desertion that occurred for religious reasons. Furthermore, Christian theologians disagree as to whether this scripture permits remarriage in such a case or simply sanctions a separation without the right of remarriage.

6. Hutcheson is one of those writers. In enumerating circumstances that make marriage "null and void from the beginning," Hutcheson not only lists "natural incapacity for marriage through an original bodily defect or other accidental causes," but also adds "perpetual madness or idiotism" and "some other incurable grievous diseases which are ordinarily transmitted to posterity" (*System of Moral Philosophy*, 2:167).

He later included "contrariety of temper" in his discussion of the causes of divorce. He suggested that a marriage might be dissolved when it proved "miserable to both parties, either by fault of both, or by some singular disagreement of their tempers, when upon a considerable trial 'tis found that there can be no hopes of any ease or peace while they cohabit; and both are willing to submit to any terms for a divorce" (ibid., p. 178).

7. Hutcheson discussed this subject in a section of chapter 1, book 3 of *System of Moral Philosophy* (2:170-75). His line of reasoning is similar to Witherspoon's, as indicated by Witherspoon, although Hutcheson's exposition is more thorough. Hutcheson suggested that this prohibition stemmed from an ancient divine command: "The abhorrence of such marriages was everywhere much higher than any reasons of expediency or prudence could have occasioned. Hence some ingenious men conclude that there has been some early divine

prohibition, the memory or tradition of which has been preserved among most nations, in some more distinctly, and in others less, as there was greater or less attention to the purity of manners" (ibid., p. 172).

8. This utilitarian reason for the prohibition of marriage of near relatives was stressed by Hume: "Those who live in the same family have such frequent opportunities of license of this kind, that nothing could preserve purity of manners, were marriage allowed, among the nearest relations, or any intercourse of love between them ratified by law and custom. Incest, therefore, being *pernicious* in a superior degree, had also a superior turpitude and moral deformity annexed to it" (*Enquiry Concerning the Principles of Morals*, sec. 4, p. 67).

9. Cf. Leviticus 18:6–18.

10. Witherspoon generally follows the ethical philosophy of Shaftesbury and Hutcheson in affirming that man possessed innate moral capabilities, among them the instinct of parental affection. Hutcheson had also asserted that nature implanted "the tendrest affections in the breasts of parents" in order to excite toward their children "long, laborious attention" (*System of Moral Philosophy*, 2:188).

Even John Locke, who denied the theory of innate ideas, wrote in a similar vein in his discussion of parental power: "The affections and tenderness which God hath planted in the breasts of parents toward their children makes it evident that this is not intended to be a severe arbitrary government, but only for the help, instruction and preservation of their offspring" (*Of Civil Government*, ch. 15, sec. 170, p. 440). However, Locke may have meant God planted this through the teaching of the Bible, not through intuitive moral sense.

11. The rights of parents are similarly developed in chapter 6 ("Of Parental Power") in *Of Civil Government* by John Locke (pp. 367–82).

12. Witherspoon may have gathered this information from an allusion in *The Spirit of Laws* (*De l' Esprit des lois*) by Montesquieu: "Fathers at Rome had the power of life or death over their children" (trans. Mr. Nugent [London, 1750], bk. 5, ch. 7, p. 71).

Charles Louis de Secondat Montesquieu (1689–1755) was a French man of letters and philosopher in the eighteenth century. His *Spirit of Laws*, a major contribution to political theory, was particularly influential in America on the subject of the separation of powers. James Madison wrote, "The oracle who is always consulted and cited on [separation of powers], is the celebrated Montesquieu. If he be not the author of this invaluable precept in the science of politics, he has the merit of at least displaying and recommending it most effectively to the attention of mankind" (*The Federalist: A Commentary on the Constitution of the United States*, ed. Paul Leicester Ford [New York, 1898], No. 47, p. 320).

Although *The Causes of the Grandeur and Declension of the Romans* (London, 1734) was the only Montesquieu volume listed in his library, Witherspoon's writings show that he had also read extensively from *The Spirit of the Laws*. In his manuscript biography of Witherspoon, Ashbel Green wrote that Montesquieu was Witherspoon's favorite political writer ("*The Life of Rev. John Witherspoon*," New Jersey Historical Society, Newark, N.J., n.p.)

13. Once again Witherspoon has confused the views of Thomas Hobbes with those of Sir Robert Filmer (see Lecture X, n. 6). It is true that Hobbes compared parental dominion to the rights of an absolute sovereign. Yet he disagreed with those who granted parental power on the basis of generation. Furthermore, he wrote, "A parent cannot be injurious to his son, as long as he is under his power" (*Works*, 2:119).

On the other hand, Filmer believed in absolute parental power over children, using it as one of his arguments to undergird monarchy. He specifically concurred with the view that children were the property of parents: "God also hath given to the father a right or liberty to alien his power over his children to any other; whence we find the sale and gift of children to have been much in use in the beginning of the world, when men had their servants for a possession and an inheritance, as well as other goods, whereupon we find the power of castrating and making eunuchs much in use in old times" (*Political Discourses. . . viz. Patriarca, or the Natural Power of Kings* [London, 1680], p. 155).

14. Cf. Hutcheson, *System of Moral Philosophy*, 2:190–91.

LECTURE XII[1]

OF CIVIL SOCIETY

Civil Society, as distinguished from domestic, is the union of a number of families in one state, for their mutual benefit.

We have before affirmed, that society always supposes an expressed or implied contract or agreement. Let us now see what this agreement necessarily implies.[2]

(1.) The consent of every individual to live in, and be a member of that society. (2.) A consent to some particular plan of government. (3.) A mutual agreement between the subjects and rulers; of subjection on the one hand, of protection on the other—These are all implied in the union of every society, and they complete the whole.[3]

Any objections that may be raised against this, are easily solved, e.g.—Though every individual has not given an actual consent, yet his determination to live with any society implies it. Again, if it be asked how children come to be members of a society; it is answered, they receive the benefits and partake of the rights of the society during the whole time of their education, and as they come to the use of reason, they both claim the privilege and acquiesce in the duty of citizens—And if they find any thing insupportable in their condition, they may alter it at their pleasure.[4]

Have then all subjects a right, when they see fit, to remove from the society in which they are? I answer, that in all ordinary cases they ought to have, at least in time of peace. Perhaps it may be affirmed with justice, that they who have enjoyed the privileges of any society in time of peace, if war or danger to the public should arise, they may be hindered from emigrating at that time, and compelled to contribute their share in what is necessary to the common defence.[5]

Whatever is the form of government in any society, the

members may be divided into two classes, the *rulers* and the *ruled*, the magistrates and subjects.

The rights of rulers may be divided into essential and accidental: the essential, such as in general must be vested in rulers in every society; the accidental, such as may be given to the rulers in some societies, but not in others.

The essential rights of rulers, are what require most to be enumerated, and these again by some good writers are divided into greater and lesser essentials.[6]

Of the first kind are, (1.) Legislation. (2.) Taxation for the public expense. (3.) Jurisdiction, or the administration of justice. (4.) Representation, or appearing and acting in name of the whole, in all transactions, with adjacent independent states, chiefly for the purpose of making war or peace.

The less essential rights of rulers are many, and they are called less essential, because they may be more varied than the others; such as, coining of money—possessing or managing public edifices—conferring honors on officers, &c.

The rights of subjects in a social state cannot be enumerated, but they may be all summed up in *protection*, that is to say, those who have surrendered part of their natural rights expect the strength of the public arm to defend and improve what remains.

It has been often said, that government is carried on by rewards and punishments; but it ought to be observed, that the only reward that a state can be supposed to bestow upon good subjects in general is protection and defence. Some few, who have distinguished themselves in the public service, may be distinguished by particular rewards; but to reward the whole is impossible, because the reward must be levied from those very persons to whom it is to be given.

After what has been said on the foundation of society, viz. consent, perhaps it may be necessary to mention two exceptions.[7]

1. It is said by some with apparent reason, that a few persons if accidentally armed with power, may constrain a large ignorant rabble to submit to laws which will be for their good. This I would admit in some cases, when there is an evident madness and disorder in the multitude, and when there is a moral certainty that they will afterwards be pleased with the violence done them. But in general it is but a bad maxim, that we may force people for their good. All lovers of power will be disposed to think that even a violent use of it is for the public good.

2. Though people have actually consented to any form of government, if they have been essentially deceived in the nature and operation of the laws, if they are found to be pernicious and

destructive of the ends of the union, they may certainly break up the society, recall their obligation, and resettle the whole upon a better footing.

Of the different forms of government

As soon as men began to consider and compare forms of government, they divided them into three general and simple kinds, (1) monarchy, (2) aristocracy, (3) democracy. These are called simple, because they are clearly distinguishable from each other in their nature and effects. The ancients generally divided the forms of government in this manner, because most of their governments were of one or other of these kinds, with very little mixture.[8]

Monarchy is when the supreme power is vested in a single person. Mr. Hutchinson says, monarchy may be either absolute or limited; but this is an inaccuracy, for limited monarchy is one of the mixed kinds of government.[9]

But monarchy may be either temporary or for life. The Roman dictators were absolute for a time, and so long as they continued, the government was purely monarchical, all other powers being dormant.

Monarchy may also be either hereditary or elective.

Aristocracy is that form of government in which the supreme power is lodged with a small number of nobles. This is capable of the same variations as monarchy, and it may be either temporary or perpetual, hereditary or elective, with this difference, that a temporary or elective aristocracy always puts some power in the hands of the people. The most complete aristocracy is when the ruling party have the power of cooptation[10] within themselves, and can fill up as they please, the vacancies made by deaths or resignation.

Democracy is when the supreme power is left in the multitude. But as in large governments the people in a collective body cannot well meet together, nor could they transact business with any convenience if they did, they may meet by representatives, chosen either by the whole, or by particular districts.

From those simple forms are generated many complex forms; two of them may be compounded together, either in equal or in different proportions, or all these may be united, as in the British government.

After pointing out the simple form of government, it will be proper to make some general observations upon government, and apply them to the various forms, to show whether any of them is

142

preferable to the other, and the advantages and defects of each in particular.

I. There are four things that seem to be requisite in a system of government and every form is good in proportion as it possesses or attains them. (1) Wisdom to plan proper measures for the public good. (2) Fidelity to have nothing but the public interest in view. (3) Secrecy, expedition, and dispatch in carrying measures into execution, and (4) Unity and concord, or that one branch of the government may not impede, or be a hindrance to another.[11]

Monarchy has plainly the advantage in unity, secrecy, and expedition. Many cannot so easily nor so speedily agree upon proper measures, nor can they expect to keep their designs secret; therefore, say some, if a man could be found wise enough, and just enough for the charge, monarchy would be the best form of government. Accordingly we find that in the command of a ship, fleet or army, one person is commonly intrusted with supreme power; but this does not apply to states, for many reasons. No man can be found who has either skill sufficient, or if he had, could give attention to the whole departments of a great empire. Besides, in hereditary monarchies there is no security at all for either wisdom or goodness; and an elective monarchy, though it may seem to promise ability, has been always found in experience worse than the other; because there is no reason to expect that an elected monarch will have the public good at heart; he will probably mind only private or family interest.

Aristocracy has the advantage of all the others for *wisdom* in deliberations; that is to say, a number of persons of the first rank must be supposed by their consultations to be able to discover the public interest. But it has very little, or no prospect of fidelity or union. The most ambitious projects, and the most violent and implacable factions, often prevail in such states.

Democracy has the advantage of both the others for fidelity; the multitude collectively always are true in intention to the interest of the public, because it is their own. They are the public. But at the same time it has very little advantage for wisdom, or union, and none at all for secrecy and expedition. Besides, the multitude are exceeding apt to be deceived by demagogues and ambitious persons. They are very apt to trust a man who serves them well, with such power as that he is able to make them serve him.[12]

If the true notion of liberty is the prevalence of law and order, and the security of individuals, none of the simple forms are favorable to it.

Monarchy, every one knows, is but another name for tyranny, where the arbitrary will of one capricious man disposes of the lives and properties of all ranks.

Aristocracy always makes vassals of the inferior ranks, who have no hand in government, and the great, commonly rule with greater severity than absolute monarchs. A monarch is at such a distance from most of his subjects, that he does them little injury; but the lord of a petty seignory is a rigorous task master to his unhappy dependents. The jealousy with which the members of an aristocratical state defend their own privileges is no security at all for humanity and easy treatment to their inferiors. Example—the Spartans; their treatment of the Helots—and the barons in all the feudal governments, in their treatment of their vassals.[13]

Pure democracy cannot subsist long, nor be carried far into the department of state—it is very subject to caprice and the madness of popular rage. They are also very apt to choose a favorite and vest him with such power as overthrows their own liberty,—examples, Athens and Rome.[14]

Hence it appears that every good form of government must be complex, so that the one principle may check the other. It is of consequence to have as much virtue among the particular members of a community as possible; but it is folly to expect that a state should be upheld by integrity in all who have a share in managing it. They must be so balanced, that when every one draws to his own interest or inclination, there may be an over poise upon the whole.[15]

II. The second observation upon the forms of government is, that where there is a balance of different bodies, as in all mixed forms, there must be always some *nexus imperii*,[16] something to make one of them necessary to the other. If this is not the case, they will not only draw different ways, but will often separate altogether from each other. In order to produce this *nexus*, some of the great essential rights of rulers must be divided and distributed among the different branches of the legislature. Example: in the British government, the king has the power of making war and peace,—but the parliament have the levying and distribution of money, which is a sufficient restraint.

III. The third observation is that the ruling part of any state must always have considerable property, chiefly of lands. The reason is, property has such an invariable influence, that whoever possesses property must have power. Property in a state is also some security for fidelity, because interest then is concerned in the public welfare.[17]

For this reason, did men in every state live entirely by agriculture, an agrarian law would be necessary to liberty; because if a vast proportion of property came into a few hands, they would soon take all power to themselves. But trade and commerce supercede the necessity of this, because the great and sudden fortunes accumulated by trade cause a rotation of property.

IV. In a well formed state the subjects should not be too numerous nor too few. If very numerous, the principles of government cannot exert their force over the whole. The Roman empire fell by its own weight. If the subjects are too few, they are not sufficient to suppress internal insurrections, or repel attacks from without.[18]

V. It is frequently observed, that in every government there is a supreme irresistible power lodged somewhere, in king, senate, or people. To this power is the final appeal in all questions. Beyond this we cannot go. How far does this authority extend? We answer, as far as authority in a social state can extend; it is not accountable to any other tribunal, and it is supposed in the social compact that we have agreed to submit to its decision. There is however an exception, if the supreme power wherever lodged, come to be exercised in a manifestly tyrannical manner, the subjects may certainly if in their power, resist and overthrow it. But this is only when it becomes manifestly more advantageous to unsettle the government altogether, than to submit to tyranny. This resistance to the supreme power, however, is subverting the society altogether, and is not to be attempted till the government is so corrupt as that anarchy and the uncertainty of a new settlement is preferable to the continuance as it is.[19]

This doctrine of resistance even to the supreme power is essentially connected with what has been said on the social contract, and the consent necessary to political union. If it be asked who must judge when the government may be resisted, I answer the subjects in general, every one for himself. This may seem to be making them both judge and party, but there is no remedy. It would be denying the privilege altogether, to make the oppressive ruler the judge.

It is easy to see that the meaning of this is not, that any little mistake of the rulers of any society will justify resistance. We must obey and submit to them always, till the corruption becomes intolerable; for to say that we might resist legal authority every time we judged it to be wrong, would be inconsistent with a state of society, and to the very first idea of subjection.[20]

The once famous controversy on passive obedience and nonresistance, seems now in our country to be pretty much over; what the advocate for submission used to say was, that to teach the lawfulness of resisting a government in any instance, and to make the rebel the judge, is subversive of all order, and must subject a state to perpetual sedition; to which I answer, to refuse this inherent right in every man, is to establish injustice and tyranny, and leave every good subject without help, as a tame prey to the ambition and rapacity of others. No doubt men may abuse the privilege, yet this does not make it void. Besides, it is not till a whole people rise, that resistance has any effect, and it is not easy to suppose that a whole people would rise against their governors, unless when they have really received very great provocation. Whereas on the other hand, nothing is more natural than for rulers to grasp at power, and their situation enables them to do it successfully by slow and insensible encroachments. In experience there are many instances of rulers becoming tyrants, but comparatively, very few of causeless and premature rebellions. There are occasional and partial insurrections in every government. These are easily raised by interested persons, but the great majority continues to support order.[21]

VI. Dominion, it is plain from all that has been said can be acquired justly only one way, viz. by consent. There are two other ways commonly mentioned, both of which are defective, inheritance and conquest. Hereditary power, which originally rose from consent and is supposed to be founded upon the continuance of consent, (as that of the hereditary power in a limited monarchy) is as lawful as any, but when they pretend such a right from nature, is independent of the people, it is absurd.[22]

That which is called the right of conquest ought to be exploded altogether. We shall see by and by what is the right of a conqueror in a just war. It was his right before, and he obtains possession of it by conquest. But to found any claim merely on conquest is not a right, but robbery.

Upon the whole, I will conclude with a few remarks upon the spirit and tendency of different forms of government.

1. Monarchical government has a tendency to politeness and elegance of manners, and generally to luxury. The submission and obsequiousness practised at the court of a monarch diffuses itself through the whole state.

2. Aristocracy narrows the mind exceedingly, and indeed cannot long submit in a large state. A small aristocracy however may submit as a form of government, as long as any other method, or longer.

3. Democracy tends to plainness and freedom of speech, and sometimes to a savage and indecent ferocity. Democracy is the nurse of eloquence, because when the multitude have the power, persuasion is the only way to govern them.

Let us now ask this short question, what is the value and advantage of civil liberty?

Is it necessary to virtue? This cannot be supposed. A virtuous mind and virtuous conduct is possible, and perhaps equally possible in every form of government.

Is it necessary to personal private happiness? It may seem so. We see the subjects of arbitrary governments, however not only happy, but very often they have a greater attachment to their form of government than those of free states have to theirs. And if contentment be necessary to happiness, there is commonly more impatience and discontent in a free state than in any other. The tyranny even of an absolute monarch does not affect with personal injury any of his subjects but a few, and chiefly those who make it their choice to be near him. Perhaps in free governments the law and the mob do more mischief to private property than is done in any absolute monarchy.

What then is the advantage of civil liberty? I suppose it chiefly consists in its tendency to put in motion all the human powers. Therefore it promotes industry, and in this respect happiness—produces every latent quality, and improves the human mind.—Liberty is the nurse of riches, literature and heroism.

NOTES

1. Witherspoon continues to draw upon Hutcheson's *System of Moral Philosophy* in this lecture, perhaps more heavily here than in the other lectures. The basic outline has been borrowed from chapters 5, 6, and 7 of book 3 of Hutcheson's work (2: 225-82). Witherspoon condenses and paraphrases Hutcheson; in some instances, he interposes his own thoughts or material drawn from other sources. But as subsequent footnotes in this lecture indicate—almost to the point of tedium—Witherspoon must have had Hutcheson's volume before him as he wrote this lecture.

2. On. pp. 123-24 of the *Lectures*, Witherspoon introduces the social contract theory. It is implicit in all his writings on politics.

3. Notice the agreement with Hutcheson: "Civil power is most naturally founded by these three different acts of a whole people. 1. An agreement or contract of each one with all the rest, that they will unite into one society or body, to be governed in all their common interests by one council. 2. A decree or designation, made by the whole people, of the form or plan of power, and of the persons to be intrusted with it. 3. A mutual agreement or contract between the governors thus constituted and the people, the former obliging themselves to a faithful administration of the powers vested in them for the common interest, and the later obliging themselves to obedience (*System of Moral Philosophy*, 2: 227).

4. Cf. Ibid., pp. 228-30.

5. In Hutcheson's volume, the consideration of the right to emigrate also followed immediately the discussion of children within a social contract. Witherspoon agrees essentially with Hutcheson's conclusion and paraphrases his argument (ibid., pp. 230-31).

6. In following Hutcheson, Witherspoon becomes slightly confused at this point. Hutcheson subdivided the essential rights of rulers into "internal" and "external"; not "greater" and "lesser" essentials, as Witherspoon does. In Hutcheson's system the lesser essentials are the same as Witherspoon's accidental powers. However, Witherspoon lists

the same four essential powers as Hutcheson did (ibid., pp. 234–38).

7. The same two exceptions that follow were given by Hutcheson (ibid., pp. 231–32). However, Witherspoon seems more hesitant than Hutcheson to allow power to be exercised contrary to the public's will, but ostensibly for the public's good. Witherspoon is keenly aware of how easily this procedure can become a pretext for increased power.

8. This stock division of government into these three basic forms can be traced back to Aristotle (*Politics* 3.7). However, Aristotle used the term *constitutional government* to describe a state administered by the citizens at large. He considered *democracy* to be a perversion of this constitutional government, having the interest of the poor only.

This three-fold division was common to eighteenth-century political philosophy (see Locke, *Of Civil Government*, pp. 415–16; Montesquieu, *Spirit of Laws*, bk. 2, pp. 11–18).

9. It seems rather disingenuous for Witherspoon to take issue with Hutcheson on this minor point after slavishly following him throughout this lecture and omitting any mention of it. Although disagreeing with Hutcheson's bifurcation of monarchy into absolute and limited, Witherspoon follows Hutcheson's two other divisions of monarchy: "hereditary—elective"; "during life—for a certain term" (*System of Moral Philosophy*, 2: 241–42).

10. This Latin term denoting elections to an office by colleagues in that office was used by Hutcheson in his exposition of aristocracy (ibid., p. 242).

11. The identical four advantages had been listed by Hutcheson in his consideration of the different forms of civil polity (ibid., p. 244). Witherspoon also generally follows Hutcheson in discussing the advantages and dangers of monarchy, aristocracy, and democracy, respectively.

12. This is one of the paragraphs that points conclusively to the fact that Witherspoon must have had Hutcheson's *System of Moral Philosophy* before him when he composed this lecture. He paraphrases Hutcheson, incorporating every one of his points. Notice the similarity to Hutcheson's paragraph:

> In all forms of Democracy one may be sure of fidelity. The popular assemblies always desire the good of the whole as it is their own. But where the whole power is lodged in such assemblies, without any check or controll by a prince or a senate, there is no security for wisdom, unity, or secrecy. This is obvious where all the free men meet in the assembly, there is no hope of wisdom, no avoiding seditions, no stability of councils. Suspicion and envy can be raised, by artful selfish demagogues, against all virtue and eminence, even where there is the greatest need for them. There resolutions are sometimes extravagantly bold; and again, when a pannick is raised, abjectly timerous. (*System of Moral Philosophy*, 2: 257).

13. Helots were the serfs of ancient Sparta. Although numerically superior to the citizens of Sparta, helots were denied citizenship and were forced to work the land.

14. The use of ancient Athens and Rome as lamentable illustrations of transition from democracy to despotism was common in eighteenth-century republican thought. A look at the books in Witherspoon's personal library indicates that his source of information may have been contemporary (e.g., *Causes of the Grandeur and Declension of the Romans* by Montesquieu) or ancient (e.g., *Bellrem piloponnesiacum* by Thucydides; *Opera lipsius greintum vecensuit* by Tacitus).

15. Witherspoon suggests a mixed form of government in order to insure a balance of power within government. This statement probably has several sources. First, it reflects Witherspoon's basic view of the nature of man. His Calvinist orientation naturally led him to conclude that men seek their own interests and thus need to be checked in their exercise of power (see Introduction, pp. 48–50.

Secondly, he probably draws upon Locke and Montesquieu in this advocacy of mixed government. Locke believed that the power of government should be balanced "by placing several parts of it in different hands" (Of Civil Government, ch. 8, sec. 107, p. 401). Montesquieu developed this Lockean thesis more fully in *The Spirit of Laws*: "But constant experience shows us that every man invested with power is apt to abuse it, and to carry his authority as far as it will go. Is it not strange, though true to say that virtue itself has need of limits? To prevent this abuse, it is necessary from the very nature of things that power should be a check to power" (bk. 11, ch. 4, p. 214).

16. *Nexus* is a tying or binding together, an interlacing; *imperii* is the power of authority or control. In this context, *nexus imperii* could be translated as "an interlacing of the power of control."

This Latin phrase was used by Hutcheson and the paragraph develops Hutcheson's argument, even to using the number that preceded it. Hutcheson had also used as one of his illustrations that the legislative should be empowered to raise the tribute for the wars into which the prince chooses to engage the nation (*System of Moral Philosophy*, 2: 244-45).

17. Again Witherspoon paraphrases and abbreviates Hutcheson (ibid., pp. 245-47). In Hutcheson's fuller exposition, he discussed the connection of property to all three forms of government: monarchy, aristocracy, and democracy. He suggested agrarian laws specifically for a democracy to insure the diffusion of property.

18. This is another summary of material from Hutcheson (ibid., pp. 249-51).

19. The topic of right of resistance engendered great controversy in seventeenth- and eighteenth-century England. Royalists such as Filmer and Hobbes denied that subjects of a king had the right to rebel. On the other hand, Locke affirmed that consent was the sole legitimate basis of government and that, consequently, rebellion was, under certain circumstances, a justifiable and desirable remedy for tyranny (*Of Civil Government*, ch. 19: "Of the Dissolution of Government," pp. 464-85).

Witherspoon wholeheartedly concurs with the latter view. The immediate sources for this section are Locke and Hutcheson (*System of Moral Philosophy*, 2: 270-82). Yet is clear that Witherspoon is not parroting someone else's thought in this instance. He clearly articulates the right of resistance and later enunciates this doctrine time and time again. For a thorough treatment of the influences that led Witherspoon to this conclusion and his own participation in rebellion, see Introduction (pp. 13-23, 46-48).

20. That Witherspoon was a conservative and not a radical revolutionist is clear from the caution he suggests in resisting legal authority.

21. The argument in this paragraph was familiar in eighteenth-century republican thought. Locke had similarly answered the objection that the right of resistance was a "ferment for frequent rebellion" (*Of Civil Government*, ch. 19, sec. 224, p. 479). Hutcheson had also argued that such a doctrine would not "cause continual seditions and rebellions." Rather, it was his conclusion that "mankind have generally been a great deal too tame and tractable" (*System of Moral Philosophy*, 2: 279-80).

22. Here Witherspoon may have used *The Principles of Natural and Politic Law* by Burlamaqui. In his discussion of the different ways of acquiring sovereignty, Burlamaqui wrote, "The only just foundation of all acquisition of sovereignty, is the consent, or will of the people." He, like Witherspoon denied that sovereignty could be acquired by "bare seizure." However, Witherspoon disagreed with Burlamaqui on the issue of hereditary power. Burlamaqui tied such power with consent in the following fashion: "The other manner of acquiring sovereignty, is the right of succession, by which princes, who have once acquired the crown, transmit it to their successors" (Burlamaqui, *Principles of Natural and Politic Law*, 2: 97, 99, 103). Witherspoon views this reasoning as "absurd."

LECTURE XIII[1]

OF THE LAW OF NATURE AND NATIONS

The next thing in order, is to treat of what is called the law of *nature* and *nations*. It has been before observed, that separate and independent states are, with regard to one another, in a state of natural liberty, or as man to man before the commencement of civil society.[2] On this several questions arise. (1) Is there any such law? (2) What is the law? (3) What is its sanction, or how is it to be enforced?

That there is such a law is plain from the reasons that show the obligation which one man lies under to another. If there are natural rights of men, there are natural rights of nations. Bodies politic, in this view, do not differ in the least from individuals. Therefore, as before, reason, conscience, and common utility, show that there is a law of nature and nations.[3]

The question what it is? must be considered in the same manner. I am not able to recollect any perfect or imperfect right that can belong to one man, as distinguished from another, but what belongs to nations, save that there is usually less occasion for the imperfect rights. If we read over the perfect rights, in a state of natural liberty, we shall see they all apply to nations.[4]

It will also appear that the imperfect rights apply; but the occasions of exerting them are much more rare. For example, it is more rare to see a nation in a state of general indigence, so as to require a supply. Yet this sometimes happens. It did so in the case of Portugal, at the time of the great earthquake at Lisbon. And the other nations of Europe lent them assistance. It is also from this principle that ships of different nations, meeting at sea, will do acts of humanity to one another. Some times also there are national favors that deserve national gratitude. But this is seldom merited and, I believe, still seldomer paid.[5]

As to the sanction of the law of nature and nations, it is no other than a general sense of duty, and such a sense of common utility, as makes men fear that if they notoriously break these laws, reproach and infamy along all nations will be the effect, and probably resentment and indignation by common consent.

The violation of the natural rights of mankind being a transgression of the law of nature, and between nations as in a state of natural liberty, there being no method of redress but force, the law of nature and nations has, as its chief or only object the manner of making *war* and *peace*.

In war it is proper to consider distinctly (1.) The causes for which a just war may be carried on. (2.) The times of commencing. (3.) The duration. (4.) The means by which it may be carried on.[6]

As to the first, the causes of commencing war are according to the principles above laid down, the violation of any perfect right—as taking away the property of the other state, or the lives of its subjects, or restraining them in their industry, or hindering them in the use of things common, &c. There is only one perfect right, the violation of which does not seem to be a cause of war; I mean that by which we have a right to character.[7] National calumny is scarcely a cause of war, because it cannot be frequent or of great effect. The violation of imperfect rights cannot usually be a cause of war between nations; yet a case may be supposed, in which even these would be a just cause of war. Suppose a ship of any nation should go into a port of another, in the greatest distress, and not only the people in general, but the governing part of the society should deny them all assistance—This would be an act of such notorious inhumanity, and of such evil sample, that is may justify national resentment; and yet even here, I think there should first be a demand of justice upon the offending persons, before vengeance should be taken upon the state.

These are the just and legitimate causes of making war. Some add to them, that when a nation is seen to put itself in such a situation as to defence, or as to the means of annoying others, that it seems to threaten hostilities, then we are not obliged to wait till it hath committed actual injury, but may put it in a state of incapacity: but there is no other truth in this, but what is founded upon the other; for the preservation of our property implies, that if others take such measures as are not to be accounted for but upon the supposition of an intention of wronging me, it is often easier and safer to prevent and disarm the robber, than to suffer him to commit the violence, and then to strip and rob him of his prey.[8]

One thing more is to be added, that every nation has a right to join which it pleases of two contending parties. This is easily resolved into the general principles; for the injured party may be supposed to go to war in defence of some perfect right; and the cause being just, the imperfect right of humanity, as well as general and common utility, calls for assistance to the oppressed. So that if we have a right to associate with any nation, we may be entitled to protect their property and rights.[9]

2. As to the time of commencing war, it seems to be no way contrary to natural law to say it is at any time the injured party pleases, after having received an injury; but accident or utility, or a desire in each party to manifest the equity of their cause, has introduced universally the custom of declaring war. This begun very early, and though not of absolute right, having been generally introduced, must be continued, though there is often more of form than of substance in it; for nations do often begin both attack and defence before declaration, as well as make all the necessary preparations for striking the most effectual blow. The meaning of a declaration of war seems to be, to call upon the injured party to prevent it by reparation—Likewise to manifest to all other states the justice of the cause.[10]

3. The duration of a war should be according to natural equity, till the injury be completely redressed, and reasonable security given against future attacks: therefore the practice, too common, of continuing a war for the acquisition of empire is to be condemned. Because one state has done some injury to another, it seems quite unreasonable that they should not only repair the injury, but subvert and ruin the offending state altogether—this would be unreasonable between man and man, if one had wronged another, not only to repair the wrong, but to take all the rest that he had, and reduce his family to beggary. It is even more unreasonable in states, because the offenders in states are not to be supposed to be the whole people, but only the rulers or perhaps only some individuals.[11]

Perhaps it may be asked, what is *reasonable* security against future injury? I answer, between equal independent nations, solemn treaties ought to be considered as security, but if faith has been often broken, perhaps something more may be required. The mutual complaints of nations against each other for breach of faith makes conquerors often demand such a degree of security, as puts the conquered altogether in their power.

4. As to the legitimate means of carrying on the war, in general, it may be said in one word, by force or open violence.[12] It is admitted on all hands, that this force may be used against the person and goods, not only of the rulers, but of every member of the hostile state. This may seem hard, that innocent subjects of the state

should suffer for the folly and indiscretion of the rulers, or of other members of the same state; but it is unavoidable. The whole individuals that compose a state are considered but as one body; it would be impossible for an enemy to distinguish the guilty from the innocent; and when men submit to a government, they risk their own possessions on the same bottom with the whole, in return for the benefits of society.

Open violence may be said to have no bounds, and therefore every method that can be invented and the most deadly weapons of annoyance may seem to be permitted—But from what has been said above, and upon the principles of general equity, all acts of cruelty and inhumanity are to be blamed,—and all severity that has not an immediate effect in weakening the national strength of the enemy is certainly inhumanity—Such as killing prisoners whom you can keep safely—killing women and children—burning and destroying everything that could be of use in life.[13]

The use of poisoned weapons has been also generally condemned—the poisoning of springs or provisions.

To the honor of modern times, and very probably I think the honor of Christianity, there is much more humanity in the way of carrying on war than formerly.

To aim particularly at the life of a leader or person of chief note, seems to have nothing in it unjust or improper, because the more important the life, it does more towards the finishing of the war; but what many seem to admit, the bribing of his own people to assassinate him privately, I cannot think honorable or fair.[14]

A question is often moved in morals, how far it is lawful to deceive an enemy, especially if we hold the general and universal obligation of truth. To this it may be answered, in the first place, that we may certainly with great justice conceal our own designs from an enemy—as indeed we may generally from friends by silence and guarding against every circumstances that may betray them. Neither do I think there is any thing at all blame-worthy in a general of an army using ambiguous signs, as feigned marches of a part or the whole, putting up lights or such things, because after a declaration of war he does not pretend to give information to his enemy of his motions, nay it is expected on both sides that they will do the best they can to over-reach one another in point of prudence. Yet I can scarce think it right to employ people to go to the enemy and professing to be sincere, tell direct falsehoods, and deceive them by that false intelligence.[15]

It is the custom of all to send spies to discover the enemy's designs, and also to bribe some of the enemies themselves to discover the designs of their leaders—The last of which is, I think, at least of a doubtful nature, or rather unjust—Though sending spies is by all approved, yet (what may seem a little unaccountable) such spies are always punished with instant death by the opposite side when detected. The reason probably is, that pretending friendship they have a right to consider them as traitors—Or as they are in an act of hostility they kill them as they would do an enemy in battle when in their power.

These circumstances apply to all war in general; but there is a distinction of wars by civilians into two kinds, *solemn* and *civil.* The first includes all wars between states formerly independent, the other internal insurrections of a part of one government against another.[16]

There has generally been a great difference in the behavior of the opposite parties in these different ways. In solemn wars there is a presumption of integrity in the plurality on both sides, each believes his own cause to be just. On this account they are to be treated with the more humanity. In civil wars the insurgents are considered as making unjust resistance to the ruling part of the society, and therefore guilty of the greatest crimes against society. Therefore they are often treated with great rigor, and when taken in battle, reserved to solemn trial and public execution. There is some reason for this in many cases, when it is indeed an unreasonable or unprovoked insurrection of disorderly citizens; but there are many cases in which the pretences on both sides are so plausible, that the war should be in all respects considered as solemn.

It·should be observed, notwithstanding the hostile disposition, there are occasions, both in a treaty for peace and during the continuance of the war, when enemies are under the strongest obligations to sincerity in their behavior to each other.—When proposals are made for accommodating the differences, for a suspension of arms, for an exchange of prisoners, or any thing similar.

It is worth while to inquire, whether the greatest honor and candor in war, with a strict adherence to all the laws above laid down, would give any party a great advantage who should take the liberty of transgressing them—as for example, who should use poisoned weapons—should send people to tell false stories—should bribe subjects to assassinate a hostile prince—I answer, that they would have no advantage at all, but probably the contrary. There is something powerful in magnanimity, which subdues the hearts of enemies; nay, sometimes terrifies them, and particularly inspires a general's army with invincible courage. Besides these, sinister arts are not so terrible as may be imagined—telling false news is as easily discovered as any trick whatsoever.[17]

Prudence and integrity have no need of any assistance from fraud—acts even of generosity from enemy to enemy are often as useful as any acts of hostility. There was something very handsome in the Roman general, who refused to avail himself of the treachery of a schoolmaster, as well as whimsical in the way in which he punished the traitor.[18]

Of Making Peace

As already hinted, all proposals tending to this purpose ought to be made with the utmost sincerity. Of all deceits in war the most infamous is that of making a treaty, or seeking a conference, only to take advantage of the security of one party to destroy him—by assassination, or by breaking a truce, to fight with advantage.[19]

The terms of peace ought to be agreeable to the end of making war. Damages should be repaired, and security given against future injury.

We have often said that nation to nation is as man to man in a state of natural liberty; therefore treaties of peace between nations should in general proceed upon the same principles as private contracts between man and man. There is however an exception, that contracts between individuals are (at least by war) always void when they are the effect of constraint upon one side. Now this must not hold in treaties between nations, because it would always furnish a pretext for breaking them. On the side of the conquered a treaty is always in a great degree the effect of necessity.[20]

It is generally, however, laid down in most authors as a principle, that the terms imposed and submitted to, may be sometimes so rigorous and oppressive, as to justify the injured party in revolting when they are able. This seems to me to be very lax in point of morals. It would be better I think to say, that the people who made the treaty should not recede from it. Their posterity, however, at some distance, cannot be supposed bound to unjust servitude by the deeds of their fathers.[21]

Let us conclude this subject by a few remarks on the situation of neutral states.[22]

1. Every state has a right, when others are contending, to remain neuter, and assist neither party.

2. They have a right to all their former privileges with both the contending parties—may carry on their traffic with both, and may show all the usual marks of friendship to both—only it has been generally agreed upon, that they are not to trade with any of them in certain articles supposed to be of consequence in carrying on war, particularly provisions and arms.

3. Neutral powers should keep their harbors alike open to both for common refreshment, and as an asylum to fly to. And it is held necessary that the contending powers must not carry on their quarrel, nor exercise any hostilities, within the territories of a neutral state.

4. Neutral states may purchase moveable goods from any of the contending parties which have been taken from the other. But not so with respect to lands or forts, because if the other party are able, they will re-take their possessions.

5. Deeds of a violent possessor are held to be valid, that is to say, if a conqueror prevails for a time, and levies tribute from any country, and afterwards the rightful possessor prevails, it would be unjust to demand the tribute again, because the true owner was not able to give protection to the subjects, and what was paid was lost through his weakness. The same thing may be said of a dependent state; if it owes any money and service to a supreme state, and an enemy exact it by force, the proper creditor cannot justly demand it again.

On the whole, those things that have been generally received as the law of nature and nations, are founded on the principles of equity, and when well observed, do greatly promote general utility.

NOTES

1. This lecture, like the preceding one, is largely based on Hutcheson's *System of Moral Philosophy*. In this lecture the chief source is chapter 10 of book 3: "The Laws of Peace and War" (2:347–71). Annotations throughout the lecture indicate how extensively Witherspoon borrowed from Hutcheson.

However, two other sources are influential upon both Hutcheson and Witherspoon in their exposition of this subject. The first of these is Hugo Grotius (1583–1645), Dutch jurist, theologian, and historian. His writings were of fundamental importance in the formulation of international law. His most celebrated work, *De jure belli ac pacis* (*On the Law of War and Peace*; 1625) was in Witherspoon's library. The third volume of this work explains the rules of warfare.

The other influential source is Grotius's disciple, Samuel von Pufendorf (1632–94). This learned German jurist and historian believed international law to be the link of all men. His most celebrated work was *De jure naturae et gentium* (*On the Law of Nature and Nations*, 1672). The abstract of this work, *De officio hominis et civis* (*On the Duty of Man and Citizen*, 1673) was in Witherspoon's library. Notice that the title for this lecture is taken from Pufendorf's earlier volume.

2. See Lecture X, n. 2.

3. Witherspoon makes no distinction between the law of nature and the law of nations. In this respect he sides with Pufendorf against Grotius, who viewed the law of nations, some of which had become obligatory because of the customary practice of great nations, as different from the inherent law of nature. Pufendorf disagreed, believing the two essentially synonymous. To him the law of nations was specifically the law of nature applied to national states, even as it could be applied to individual men.

4. On page 123 Witherspoon enumerates the following perfect rights of man in a state of natural liberty:

(1) A right to life.

(2) A right to employ his faculties and industry for his own use.

(3) A right to things that are common and necessary, as air, water, earth.

(4) A right to personal liberty.

(5) A power over his own life, not to throw it away unnecessarily, but for a good reason.

(6) A right of private judgment in matters of opinion.

(7) A right to associate, if he so incline, with any person or persons, whom he can persuade (not force)—under this is contained the right to marriage.

(8) A right to character, that is to say, innocence (not fame).

Since this list is specifically formulated to describe the perfect rights of individual man, it seems rather awkward and strained to use it to describe the perfect rights of nations.

5. Imperfect rights are defined by Witherspoon as those that one "cannot use force to obtain." Examples of such rights are gratitude, compassion, and so on (see page 123).

Witherspoon refers to the Lisbon earthquake of November 1, 1755, which largely destroyed the city and killed thousands. With aid from other nations, particularly England, Lisbon was reconstructed.

6. It is clear that Witherspoon merely paraphrases the following paragraph in Hutcheson: "In the war of states, as in those of individuals, we may consider the causes, the time of commencement, and the term to which they may be continued, and the lawful methods of carrying them on" (*System of Moral Philosophy*, 2:350).

7. Hutcheson similarly wrote about war, "The ordinary just causes are some violations of perfect rights" (ibid.). However, Witherspoon elaborates by naming some of these perfect rights and suggesting an exception, which Hutcheson failed to do.

8. The tangled syntax and length of this sentence makes it difficult to understand Witherspoon. He appears to be suggesting the possibility of preventive war if the enemy's intention is judged hostile. Hutcheson also suggested this possibility but recommended arbitration before such a precipitant step (ibid., pp. 350–51).

9. Witherspoon fails to make clear that a nation has only the right to assist another nation if that nation has a just cause. This confusion arises because of Witherspoon's artificial device of wedding the perfect rights of individuals with the perfect rights of nations. He thus attempts to compare the right of a nation to assist an oppressed nation with the right of an individual to associate with whomever he chooses.

10. Cf. ibid., p. 351. Hutcheson did not discuss the matter of the declaration of war.

11. See ibid., p. 352.

12. This statement draws upon a long line of just war theorists. Hugo Grotius wrote, "Modum agendi quod attinet, vis ac terror maxime propria bellorum": as to the mode of acting in war, force and terror are the proper means (*De jure belli ac pacis libri tres* [Leyden, Holland, 1939], lib. 3, cap. 2, sec. 6, 1, pp. 617–18). Hutcheson similarly asserted that "the most indisputable method of making war is by open force and violence against such as oppose us by violence" (*System of Moral lPhilosophy*, 2:352).

13. The chronicling of inhumane methods of warfare was common in ethical writings of this era. Grotius drew up an extensive list of acts he considered unlawful to use in war (such as poisoning and rape) in chapter 4 of *De jure belli ac pacis* (lib. 3, cap. 4, pp. 656–72). Pufendorf wrote that the more civilized nations consider "Poisoning or Bribing Subjects and Soldiers to assassinate their Masters" as "mean and base and cowardly" (Samuel Pufendorf, *Law of Nature and Nations*, trans. J. Spavan, 2 vols. [London, 1716], 2:342). Hutcheson in his *System of Moral Philosophy* had a similar list, having probably gathered his material from Grotius and Pufendorf and from the general teaching of eighteenth-century moral philosophy (2:352–54).

14. See Grotius, *De jure belli ac pacis* (lib. 3, cap. 4, sec. 18, pp. 668–71) and Hutcheson, *System of Moral Philosophy* (2:353).

15. Pufendorf justified deceit in general terms: "It is altogether as lawful to make use of Stratagem and Fraud, provided it be done without any Breach of Faith. Accordingly an Enemy may very justly be imposed on by false Reports and false News" (*Law of Nature and Nations*, 2:335-36). Hutcheson believed that the use of misleading signs to an enemy was permissible, but demurred on the use of false narratives: "But it must ever be a disagreeable method to a candid mind, especially if joined to any profession of friendship" (*System of Moral Philosophy*, 2:354). Witherspoon concurs with Hutcheson in his dislike of the latter method of deceit.

16. Pufendorf used the terminology of "solemn" and "less solemn" in his bifurcation of wars. However, he not only included civil wars among the "less solemn" but also wars waged between nations that were not "proclaimed at all" (*Law of Nature and Nations*, 2:335). Burlamaqui followed Pufendorf's definition of wars in his *Principles of Natural and Politic Law* (2:250).

17. Here there is an interesting divergence between Witherspoon and Hutcheson. Hutcheson admitted that certain barbarities might bring the enemy to terms more quickly, although such would be unjust to innocents and would establish "horrid precedents, which may be turned against ourselves" (*System of Moral Philosophy*, 2:352). Conversely, Witherspoon argues that magnanimity actually strengthens an army and is the best practical policy.

18. This celebrated incident was recorded by Titus Livius (ca. 59 B.C.-A.D. 17) in his *History of Rome* (5. 27). Marcus Furius Camillus, the Roman general, was laying siege to the city of Falerii in 394 B.C. A schoolmaster from the city treacherously led his youths into the Roman camp. Camillus refused his treachery, pointing out that there were rights of war to be honored. The teacher was stripped, his hands bound behind his back, and the boys were given rods with which to beat him. Thus the entourage returned to Falerii. According to Livius, the people of the city were so moved by Camillus's magnanimity that they sued for peace and Falerii fell into Roman hands.

19. See Hutcheson, *System of Moral Philosophy*, 2:354-55.

20. The same principle is in Hutcheson, ibid., p. 364.

21. Witherspoon raises a thorny ethical question: to what degree are the conquered committed to a treaty imposed by oppression? Locke left no doubt about his answer to the question: "It remains only to be considered, whether Promises, extorted by Force, without Right, can be thought Consent, and how far they bind. To which I shall say they bind not at all; because whatsoever another gets from me by force, I still retain the Right of, and he is obliged presently to restore" (*Of Civil Government*, ch. 16, sec. 186, p. 45).

With some qualification, Hutcheson agreed with Locke since he believed that treaties, extorted by violence and inconsistent with emity, produce no obligation (*System of Moral Philosophy*, 2:365).

Witherspoon disagrees with both Locke and Hutcheson. Probably his orthodox Christian background made him squeamish about any falsity, regardless of the circumstances.

22. Witherspoon takes his list of the rights of neutral states in time of war from Hutcheson (ibid., pp. 357-63). It is essentially the same as Hutcheson's, although with some variation and condensation. For instance, Witherspoon chooses to take two topics that Hutcheson discusses under the first item and make them "4" and "5" in his list.

Grotius also had a discussion of neutrals in war in his famous work, *De jure belli ac pacis* (lib. 3, cap. 17, pp. 803-8). However, his exposition was more limited than Hutcheson's.

LECTURE XIV

JURISPRUDENCE

Jurisprudence is the method of enacting and administering civil laws in any constitution.

We cannot propose to go through a system of civil laws, and therefore what I have in view is to make some preliminary remarks, and then to point out the *object* of civil laws, and the manner of their operation.

1. The first preliminary remark is, that a constitution is excellent, when the spirit of the civil laws is such as to have a tendency to prevent offences and make men good, as much as to punish them when they do evil.[2]

This is necessary in some measure; for when the general disposition of a people is against the laws, they cannot long subsist, even by a strict and rigorous execution on the part of the rulers. There is, however, more of this in some constitutions than in others. Solon and Xenophon, as well as Lycurgus, seem to have formed their plan very much with this view, to direct the manners of the people in the first place, which will always make the observation of particular laws easy.[3]

But how shall the magistrate manage this matter, or what can be done by law to make the people of any state virtuous? If, as we have seen above, virtue and piety are inseparably connected, then to promote true religion is the best and most effectual way of making a virtuous and regular people. Love to God, and love to man, is the substance of religion; when these prevail, civil laws will have little to do.

But this leads to a very important disquisition, how far the magistrate ought to interfere in matters of religion. Religious sentiments are very various—and we have given it as one of the perfect rights in natural liberty, and which ought not to be

159

alienated even in society, that every one should judge for himself in matters of religion.[4]

What the magistrate may do on this subject seems to be confined to the three following particulars:

(1.) The magistrate (or ruling part of any society) ought to encourage piety by his own example, and by endeavoring to make it an object of public esteem. Whenever the general opinion is in favor of any thing, it will have many followers. Magistrates may promote and encourage men of piety and virtue, and they may discountenance those whom it would be improper to punish.[5]

(2.) The magistrate ought to defend the rights of conscience, and tolerate all in their religious sentiments that are not injurious to their neighbors. In the ancient heathen states there was less occasion for this, because in the system of polytheism the different gods and rites were not supposed to be opposite, but co-ordinate and consistent; but when there is believed to be but one God, the sentiments about his nature and worship will often be considered as essentially repugnant one to another.

The pretence of infidels, that persecution only belongs to the Christian religion, is absurd; for the Christian was the first religion that was persecuted, and it was the necessary consequence of saying, that the gods of the heathens were no gods.

At present, as things are situated, one of the most important duties of the magistracy is to protect the rights of conscience.

It is commonly said, however, that in case any sect holds tenets subversive of society and inconsistent with the rights of others, that they ought not to be tolerated. On this footing Popery is not tolerated in Great Britain; because they profess entire subjection to a foreign power, the see of Rome, and therefore must be in opposition to the proper interest of their own state; and because violence or persecution for religion is a part of their religion, which makes their prosperity threaten ruin to others—as well as the principle imputed to them, which they deny, that faith is not to be kept with heretics. But however just this may be in a way of reasoning, we ought in general to guard against persecution on a religious account as much as possible; because such as hold absurd tenets are seldom dangerous. Perhaps they are never dangerous, but when they are oppressed. Papists are tolerated in Holland without danger to liberty. And though not properly tolerated, they are now connived at in Britain.[6]

In ancient times, in great states the censorial power was found necessary to their continuance, which inspected the manners of men.[7] It seems probable, that supporting the religious sects in modern times answers this end, for the particular discipline of each sect, is intended for the correction of manners.

(3.) The magistrate may enact laws for the punishment of acts of profanity and impiety. The different sentiments of men in religion, ought not by any means to encourage or give a sanction to such acts as any of them count profane.

Many are of opinion, that besides all this, the magistrate ought to make public provision for the worship of God, in such manner as is agreeable to the great body of the society; though at the same time all who dissent from it are fully tolerated. And indeed there seems to be a good deal of reason for it, that so instruction may be provided for the bulk of common people, who would, many of them, neither support nor employ teachers, unless they were obliged. The magistrates right in this case seems to be something like that of a parent, they have a right to instruct, but not to constrain.[8]

(2) The second preliminary remark is, that laws should be so framed as to promote such principles in general, as are favorable to good government, and particularly that principle, if there be one, that gave rise to the constitution, and is congenial to it.

Such a principle as I have in view, is generally the point of honor in a country, and this lawgivers and administrators of law should endeavor to preserve in its full vigor, for whenever it is undermined, the constitution goes to ruin.[9]

Of these principles, sobriety, industry, and public spirit are the chief. Some states are formed to subsist by sobriety and parsimony, as the Lacedemonians.[10]

Industry is the prevailing principle, in others, as in Holland. Public spirit in others, as in Greece, ancient Rome, and Britain. Only public spirit may be diversified; sometimes it is a passion for acquiring glory and dominion, as in Rome, and sometimes for preserving liberty, as in Greece and Britain.

When I say, that in the management of a state, the utmost attention should be given to the principle of the constitution to preserve it in its vigor, I mean that though all other crimes are bad, and in part tend to the ruin of a state, yet this is much more the case with crimes against that principle than any other. Any act of immorality was bad at Sparta, but to make poverty and parsimony reproachful, and to introduce fine houses and furniture and delicate entertainments, would have been instant ruin.

Any act of immorality would be hurtful in Holland, but to make fraudulent bankruptcy less infamous than it is, would immediately destroy them.

Sobriety, industry, and public spirit are nearly allied, and have a reciprocal influence upon one another. Yet there may be a great degree of some of them in the absence of the others. In Sparta there was much sobriety and public spirit, but little industry. In Athens, industry and public spirit, with very little parsimony.

In opposition to the whole of this, Mandeville wrote a book called *The Fable of the Bees*,[11] which seems to be levelled against sobriety, industry and public spirit, all at once; his position is, *that private vices are public benefits*, and that the waste and luxury of one man supplies the wants of another; but it is easy to overthrow his reasoning, for though sober and industrious persons spend each less than a profuse person, yet sobriety and industry tend much more to population, and by that means they are mutually serviceable to each other. Luxury and vice only waste and destroy, they add nothing to the common stock of property or of happiness. Experience fully justifies this, for though from the luxury of one man another may reap some gain, the luxury of a nation always tends to the ruin of that nation.

(3) A third preliminary remark is, that laws may be of two kinds, either written or in the breasts of magistrates. In every constitution of note, there is something of each of these kinds. It is uncertain whether it is better to have many or few special laws. On the one hand, it seems to be the very spirit of a free constitution to have every thing as strictly defined as possible, and to leave little in the power of the judge. But on the other hand, a multiplicity of laws is so apt to lead to litigation and to end in ambiguity, that perhaps judges of equity, chosen by the district in which they live and are to act, and chosen but for a time, would be a more just and equitable method of ending differences. But the difficulty of settling a constitution so as always to secure the election of impartial judges, has made modern states, where there is liberty, prefer a multiplicity of written laws.[12]

(4) The last preliminary remark is, that no human constitution can be so formed, but that there must be exceptions to every law. So that there may be in every nation oppression under form of law, according to the old maxim, *summum jus, summa injuria*.[13] This further shows the necessity of forming the manners of a people.

After having laid down these preliminaries, we may observe that the objects of civil laws may be divided into the three following particulars.[14]

1. To ratify the moral laws by the sanction of the society. The transgression of such laws are called *crimes* as profanity, adultery, murder, calumny, &c. And they are prosecuted and punished by order of the public according to the spirit of every constitution.

2. To lay down a plan for all contracts in the commerce or inter-

course between man and man. To show when a contract is valid, and how to be proved. The transgressions of such laws are called *frauds*. They chiefly regard the acquisition, transmission, or alienation of property.

3. To limit and direct persons in the exercise of their own rights, and oblige them to show respect to the interfering rights of others. This contains the whole of what is called the police of a country.—And the transgression of such laws are called trespasses. A number of things in this view may become illegal, which before were not immoral.

Of the Sanction of the Moral Laws

In all polished nations, there are punishments annexed to the transgression of the moral laws, whether against God, our neighbor, or ourselves; in the doing of which, the three following things are chiefly necessary.

(1.) To determine what crimes, and what degree of the same crime, are to be inquired into by the civil magistrate. It is of necessity that in a free state crimes should be precisely defined, that men may not be ignorantly or rashly drawn into them. There are degrees of every crime—profanity, impurity, violence, slander, that are blameable in point of morals, nay, even such as may fall under the discipline of a religious society—that if they were made cognizable by the civil magistrate, would multiply laws and trials beyond measure.

(2.) To appoint the methods of ascertaining the commission of crimes. This is usually by testimony, in which we are to consider the number and character of the witnesses. Generally through Christendom, and indeed most other parts of the world, two witnesses have been esteemed necessary to fix crimes upon an accused person; not but that the positive evidence of one person of judgment and untainted character is, in many cases, sufficient to gain belief, and often stronger than two of unknown or doubtful credit, but it was necessary to lay down some rule, and two are required to guard against the danger of hired evidence, and to give an opportunity of trying how they agree together. To have required more would have made a proof difficult or impossible in many cases.

It seems to be a maxim in law, and founded on reason, that in the case of what are called occult crimes, such as murder, adultery, forgery, and some others, where the nature of the thing shows that there must be a penury of evidence, they sometimes content themselves with fewer witnesses, if there are corroborating cir-

163

cumstances to strengthen their testimony.

It seems to be a matter not easily decided, whether it be agreeable to reason and justice, in the case of very atrocious crimes, that on account of the *atrocity*, *less* evidence should be sufficient for conviction, or that *more* should be required. On the one hand, the more atrocious the crime, the greater the hurt to society, and the more need of public vengeance. On the other hand, the more atrocious the crime, and the heavier the punishment, it seems agreeable to justice that the conviction should be upon the more unquestioned evidence. Lawyers are seen to take their common places, sometimes the one way, sometimes the other. It is often thought that in practice, less evidence is sufficient to convict a man of murder, forgery, rape, and other crimes of a deep dye. But I am persuaded that the appearance is owing to the greater and more general eagerness to discover the perpetrators of such crimes. Others are suffered to escape more easily, not that more evidence is necessary, but that it is more difficult to get at the evidence.

Evidence may be distinguished into two kinds, *direct* and *circumstantial*. Direct evidence is when the witnesses swear to their sight or knowledge of the accused committing the crime. Circumstantial, when they only swear to certain facts, which cannot be supposed to have existed unless the crime had been committed. As a man found dead—another found near the place—with a weapon bloody—or clothes bloody, &c. Some have affirmed that circumstantial evidence is stronger than direct, but it must be taken with very great caution and judgment.

(3.) The law is to proportion and appoint the punishment due to every crime when proven.

Punishment in all regular states is taken wholly out of the hands of the injured persons, and committed to the magistrate, though in many or most cases the injured party is suffered to join the magistrate in the prosecution, and to have a certain claim, by way of reparation, as far as that is practicable.[15]

Therefore the punishment in general must consist of two parts, (1) reparation to the sufferer, (2) the vindicta publica,[16] which has sometimes two ends in view, to be an example to others, and to reclaim and reform the offenders, as in corporal punishment less than death. Sometimes but one, the good of others in the example, as in capital punishments and banishment.

The kind of punishment and the degree, is left wholly to different lawgivers, and the spirit of different constitutions. Public utility is the rule. Punishment is not always proportioned to the atrociousness of the crime in point of morals, but to the frequency of it, and the danger of its prevailing.

Some nations require, and some will bear, greater severity in punishments than others.[17]

The same or similar conduct often produces opposite effects. Severe laws and severe punishments sometimes banish crimes, but very often the contrary. When laws are very sanguinary, it often makes the subjects hate the law more than they fear it, and the transition is very easy from hating the law to hating those who are entrusted with the execution of it. Such a state of things threatens insurrections and convulsions, if not the dissolution of a government.

Another usual effect of excessive severity in laws is, that they are not put in execution. The public is not willing to lend its aid to the discovery and conviction of offenders; so that in time the law itself becomes a mere brutum fulmen[18] and loses its authority.

I may make one particular remark, that though many things are copied from the law of Moses into the laws of the modern nations, yet, so far as I know, none of them have introduced the *lex talionis* in the case of injuries, an eye for an eye, and a tooth for a tooth, &c. and yet perhaps there are many instances in which it would be very proper. The equity of the punishment would be quite manifest, and probably it would be as effectual a restraint from the commission of injury as any that could be chosen.[19]

The concluding remark shall be, that it is but seldom that very severe and sanguinary laws are of service to the good order to a state; but after laws have been fixed with as much equity and moderation as possible, the execution of them should be strict and rigorous. Let the laws be *just* and the magistrate *inflexible*.

NOTES

1. In this lecture Witherspoon borrows from book 3, chapter 9 ("Of the Nature of Civil Laws and their Execution") in Hutcheson's *System of Moral Philosophy* (2: 310-47). However, this borrowing is selective, for he frequently injects his own views or follows another source (e.g., Montesquieu or Locke).

2. This thesis was common in liberal political thought of the eighteenth century. Note the similar comment of Hutcheson on this matter: "It is poor policy merely to punish crimes when they are committed. The noble art is to contrive such previous education, instruction, and discipline, as shall prevent vice, restrain these passions, and correct these confused notions of great happiness in vicious courses, which enslave men to them" (ibid., p. 310). Montesquieu also wrote, "In those states [moderate governments] a good legislator is less bent upon punishing then preventing crimes; he is more attentive to inspire good morals than to inflict penalties" (*Spirit of Laws*, bk. 6, ch. 9, p. 81).

3. In commending governments whose primary aim was to prevent vice rather than punish crimes, Hutcheson gave several examples in a footnote: "the institutions of Lycurgus, Solon, Plato, Numa, and the old Persians, according to Xenophon, and of the Chinese" (*System of Moral Philosophy*, 2: 310). If Witherspoon selected his three names from Hutch-

eson's list, he mistakenly grouped Xenophon with Solon and Lycurgus as a lawmaker. In Hutcheson's footnotes, Xenophon was rightly identified as a historian who tells of the polity of the old Persians.

Solon (ca. 638-559 B.C.), an Athenian statesman and poet, instituted thoroughgoing economic and constitutional reform. He constructed a milder civil code, widened suffrage, created popular courts, and realigned tax rates to aid the poor.

Xenophon (ca. 430-354 B.C.) was a Greek historian and military leader. Although Athenian by birth, he became disgusted with the deterioration of democracy in Athens and later wrote an essay lauding Spartan institutions.

Lycurgus (396-324 B.C.) was an Athenian statesman who was chief guardian of the public revenue. He also served as superintendent of the city and as censor. He worked diligently to raise both public and private morals in ancient Athens.

4. In Witherspoon's list of perfect rights (p. 123), he includes the freedom of religious opinion under the heading "A right of private judgment in matter of opinion."

In his advocacy of religious toleration, Witherspoon again demonstrates that he stands in the stream of eighteenth-century liberal political thought. John Locke eloquently argued for freedom of religious opinion in *A Letter Concerning Toleration* (London, 1689). Toleration had continued to grow in intellectual prestige during the Age of Reason, and by this time advocates of religious persecution were clearly on the defensive.

5. Hutcheson also suggested that virtue is promoted by "the example of those in supreme power, and the preferring of virtuous men to all station and offices of dignity, while the vicious are made contemptible" (*System of Moral Philosophy*, 2: 317).

6. Witherspoon suggests his approval of increased toleration for Roman Catholics. Those who justified this restriction of religious liberty generally did so upon the grounds of political subversion, not religious heterodoxy. For instance, Locke believed that Catholicism should not be tolerated because its adherents owed their allegiance to a foreign jurisdiction (John Locke, *A Letter Concerning Toleration*, in *The Works of John Locke*, 9 vols., 12th ed. [London, 1824], 5: 46-47).

At this time Roman Catholics were still technically subject to the penalties and disabilities prescribed by the Toleration Act of 1689. Although granting toleration to Protestant dissenters, this act denied similar freedom to Catholics. The Oath of Allegiance required by the act effectively denied civil or military office to Catholics. Priests were subject to imprisonment, the right to inherit land was denied to Catholics, and a host of other restrictions specifically applied to them. However, as Witherspoon indicates above, the harsher aspects of these penal laws were seldom enforced in the late eighteenth century.

In 1778 and 1791 the British Parliament passed measures of Catholic relief, lessening these penalties and broadening toleration of Catholics. Yet it was not until the Act of Emancipation of 1829 that Roman Catholicism achieved full religious toleration in Great Britain.

7. Censor was the title of two magistrates in ancient Rome, whose task it was to draw up the register or census of the citizens and to supervise the public morals. One function of this office, which was instituted in 443 B.C., was to exclude from public life those citizens guilty of disgraceful immorality.

8. Although an advocate of religious toleration, Witherspoon does not suggest the total separation of church and state. Rather, he believes that the state should support the majority religion within a context of toleration. After all, Witherspoon had been a clergyman in the Church of Scotland, the established religion of his native land. At this time ten of the thirteen American colonies had an established religion, although New Jersey, Witherspoon's new home, was not one of them. The American Revolution greatly accelerated the separation of church and state, yet establishment of religion was not completely abolished in America until 1833, the date of its occurrence in Massachusetts.

9. Here Witherspoon evidently draws upon the thought of Montesquieu. In *The Spirit of Laws*, Montesquieu ably developed the thesis that a nation's polity and laws should corres-

166

pond to the spirit that animates that nation. He suggested that the spirit of a nation is shaped by various causes: "by the climate, by the religion, by the laws, by the maxims of government; by precedents, morals, and customs" (bk. 19, ch. 4, 1:418). Thus he concluded that it should be "the business of the legislature to follow the spirit of the nation when it is not contrary to the principles of the government" (ibid., bk. 19, ch. 5, 1: 419).

Witherspoon obviously concurs with Montesquieu's hypothesis. Witherspoon's illustrations are a mixture of his own and those of Montesquieu. For instance, Montesquieu specifically mentioned the gaiety of the Athenians in contrast to the sobriety of the Spartans (ibid., bk. 19, ch. 7, 1: 420).

10. Lacedemonia was an ancient name for Sparta.

11. See p. 89, n. 15 for a brief biographical sketch of Mandeville and a discussion of *The Fable of the Bees*.

12. Unlike Witherspoon, Hutcheson clearly opted for few laws with wise judges: "It is plain that right and property are better preserved by a very few simple laws leaving much to the judges, provided there be a good plan for obtaining wise and disinterested judges" (*System of Moral Philosophy*, 2: 322).

13. This legal phrase is defined as "a strict and oppressive insistence on a legal right" (Max Radin, *Radin Law Dictionary* [New York: 1955], p. 335).

14. Witherspoon appears to borrow partially from Hutcheson here, since his list is quite similar to Hutcheson's (*System of Moral Philosophy*, 2: 327). However, Witherspoon explains these three objects of civil laws more fully and with greater clarity than did Hutcheson.

15. Notice that Witherspoon takes punishment out of the hands of the individual only "in all regular states." Witherspoon believed, as did Locke and other advocates of natural rights, that man in the natural state had the right to punish violations of the law of nature. However, this right is surrendered when man joins a political society (see Locke, *Of Civil Government*, ch. 9, sec. 128, p. 413).

16. The punishment belonging to the public; the vengeance of the community.

17. Witherspoon's subsequent discussion suggests a lessening of the severity of punishment. A similar thesis was developed by Montesquieu in his *Spirit of the Laws* (bk. 6, chs. 9–21, 1: 118–36).

18. "Brutum fulmen" means a harmless thunderbolt, an empty threat. An illustration of its original usage may be found in Pliny's *Natural History* (2.43). Its common usage in England dates back to the seventeenth century (A. J. Bliss, *A Dictionary of Foreign Words and Phrases in Current English* [London: Routledge & Kegan Paul, Ltd., 1966], p. 103).

19. *Lex talionis* translates as "the law of retaliation." It refers to the Old Testament concept of retribution recorded in Exodus 21:23–25: "Thou shalt give life for life, eye for eye, tooth for tooth, hand for hand, foot for foot, burn for burning, wound for wound, stripe for stripe."

LECTURE XV[1]

The second object of civil laws being to regulate the making of contracts,[2] and the whole intercourse between man and man relating to the acquisition, possession and alienation of property, we must consider carefully the nature of

Contracts

A contract is a stipulation between two parties before at liberty, to make some alteration of property, or to bind one or both parties to the performance of some service.

Contracts are absolutely necessary in social life. Every transaction almost may be considered as a contract, either more or less explicit.

The principal thing which constitutes a contract is, *consent*. But in some kinds of contracts, viz. the gratuitous, the consent of the receiver is presumed. In the transmission of estates by donation or testament this is presumed—and those who are incapable of giving their consent through infancy may notwithstanding acquire property and rights. When a man comes into a settled country and purchases property, he is supposed, besides every other part of the bargain, to purchase it under such conditions, and subject himself to such laws as are in force in that country.[3]

Contracts are said to be of three degrees in point of fulness and precision—(1.) A simple affirmation of a design as to futurity—as when I say to any one that I shall go to such a place to-morrow; this is not properly binding, and it is supposed that many things may occur to make me alter my resolution—yet a frequent alteration of professed purposes gives the character of levity; therefore a prudent man will be cautious of declaring his purposes till he is well determined. (2.) A gratuitous promise of doing some favor to me. This is not made binding in law, nor does it usually convey a perfect right, because it supposes that the person who was the object of good will, may, by altering his behaviour, forfeit his title to it, or that the person promising may find it much more inconvenient, costly or hurtful to himself, than he supposed; or, lastly, that what was intended as a service, if performed, appears plainly to be an injury. In the last case every one must see, that it cannot be binding; but in the two former, I apprehend that in all ordinary cases a distinct promise is binding in conscience, though it may not be necessary to make it binding in law. I say all ordinary cases, because it is easy to figure a case in which I may make a promise to another, and such circumstances may afterwards occur as I am quite confident, if the person knew, he would not hold me to my promise.

3. The third degree is a complete contract, with consent on both sides, and obligation upon one or both.

The essentials of a contract which render it valid, and any of which being wanting, it is void, are as follow:

That it be, (1.) Free. (2.) Mutual. (3.) Possible. (4.) Lawful. (5.) With a capable person. (6.) Formal.[5]

First. It must be free. Contracts made by unjust force are void always in law, and sometimes in conscience. It must however be unjust force, because in treaties of peace between nations, as we have seen before, force does not void the contract;[6] and even in private life sometimes men are forced to enter into contracts by the order of a magistrate, sometimes by the threatening of legal prosecution, which does not make them void.[7]

2. They must be mutual, that is, the consent of the one as well as that of the other must be had. Contracts in this view become void, either by fraud on one side, or by essential error.[8] If any man contrives a contract so as to bind the other party, and keep himself free, this fraud certainly nullifies the agreement—or if there is an essential error in the person or the thing, as if a person should oblige himself to one man supposing him to be another.

3. Contracts should be of things evidently possible, and probably in our power. Contracts, by which men oblige themselves to do things impossible, are no doubt void from the beginning; but if the impossibility was known to the contracting party, it must have been either absurd or fraudulent. When things engaged for become impossible by the operation of Providence without a man's own fault, the contract is void, and he is guiltless—as if a man should covenant to deliver at a certain place and time a number of cattle, and when he is almost at the place of destination they should be killed by thunder, or any other accident, out of his power.[9]

169

4. Contracts must be of things lawful. All engagements to do things unlawful are from the beginning void; but by unlawful must be understood the violation of perfect rights. If a man oblige himself for a reward to commit murder, or any kind of fraud, the engagement is void; but it was criminal in the transacting, and the reward ought to be returned, or given to public uses. There are many contracts, however, which are very blameable in making, that must, notwithstanding, be kept, and must not be made void in law—as rash and foolish bargains, where there was no fraud on the other side. If such were to be voided, great confusion would be introduced. The cases of this kind are numerous, and may be greatly diversified.[10]

5. Contracts must be made with a capable person, that is to say, of age, understanding, at liberty, &c. It is part of the civil law, or rather municipal law, of every country, to fix the time of life when persons are supposed capable of transacting their own affairs. Some time must be fixed, otherwise it would occasion numberless disputes, difficult to be decided. A man at the age of fourteen, and a woman at twelve, may choose guardians, who can alienate their property, and at the age of twenty-one they have their estate wholly in their own hand.[11]

6. Contracts must be formal.

The laws of every country limit a great many circumstances of the nature, obligation, extent and duration of contracts.

Having pointed out something of the essential characters of all lawful contacts; I observe they may be divided two different ways, (1) contracts are either absolute or conditional. The absolute are such as are suspended upon no condition, but such as are essential to every contract, which have been mentioned above. Such as when a person makes a settlement upon another, without reserve, then, whether he behave well or ill, whether it be convenient or inconvenient, it must fulfilled. Conditional contracts are those that are suspended on any uncertain future contingency, or some performance by the opposite party. Of this last sort are almost all transactions in the way of commerce,—which leads to the (2) way of dividing contracts into beneficent and onerous.[12] The first is when one freely brings himself under an obligation to bestow any favor or do any service, as donations or legacies, and undertaking the office of guardian of another person's estate.

The onerous contract is when an equal value is supposed to be given on both sides, as is the case for the most part in the alienation of property—and the transactions between man and man, and between society and society.

To this place belongs the question about the lawfulness of lend-ing money upon interest. If we consider money as an instrument of commerce and giving an opportunity of making profit, there seems plainly to be nothing unjust, that the lender should share in the advantage arising from his own property.[13]

The chief thing necessary is, that the state or government part of the society should settle the rate of interest and not suffer it to depend upon the necessity of the poor or the covetousness of the rich. If it is not settled by law, usury will be certain consequence.

The law of Moses does not seem to have admitted the taking of interest at all from an Israelite. It is thought, however, that the main reason of this must have been drawn from something in their constitution as a state, that rendered it improper; for if it had been in itself immoral they would not have been permitted to take it of strangers.[14]

Of the Marks or Signs of Contracts

All known and intelligent marks of consent, are the signs and means of completing contracts. The chief of these, however, are words and writing, as being found the most easy and useful. Words are of all others the most natural and proper for giving immediate consent, and writing to perpetuate the memory of the transaction. There are, however, many other signs that may be made use of, and wherever there is a real purpose of signifying our intention, by which others are brought to depend upon it, the engagement is real, and we are bound in conscience, though the law in every country must of necessity be more limited. The whole rests ultimately on the obligation to sincerity in the social life.

This obligation arises from the testimony of conscience, and from the manifest utility and even necessity of sincerity to social intercourse.[15]

Signs are divided into *natural, instituted* and *customary*.[16] Natural signs are those which have either a real likeness to the thing signified, or such a known and universal relation to it, that all men must naturally be led from the one to the other—As a picture is a natural sign, because a representation of the thing painted. An inflamed sullen countenance and fiery eyes are natural signs of anger, because they are the universal effects of that passion.

Instituted signs are those that have no other connection with the thing signified, than what has been made by agreement; as if two persons shall agree between themselves, that if the one wants to signify to the other at a distance, that he wishes him to come to his assistance, he will kindle a fire upon a certain hill, or hang out a flag upon a certain pinnacle of his house, or some part of his ship. Words and writing are properly instituted signs, for they have no relation to the thing signified but what original agreement and long custom has given them.

Customary signs are no other than instituted signs which have long prevailed, and whose institution has either been accidental or has been forgotten. It is also usual to apply the word customary to such signs as depend upon the mode and fashion of particular countries. There are some signs and postures, which though they may seem perfectly arbitrary, have obtained very generally, perhaps universally, as bending down the body, or prostration, as a sign of respect and reverence; kneeling and lifting up the hands as a sign of submission and supplication.—Perhaps both these are natural, as they put the person into the situation least capable of resistance.

Sometimes there is a mixture of natural and instituted signs, as if a man sends a pair of wings, or the figure of them, to a friend, to intimate his danger, and the necessity of flying.[17]

In the use of signs, the great rule of sincerity is, that wherever we are bound, and whatever we profess to communicate our intention, we ought to use the signs in the least ambiguous manner possible. When we have no intention, and are under no obligation to communicate any thing to others, it is of small moment what appearances are; it is their business not to make any unnecessary or uncertain interferences. A light in a house, in the middle of the night, will perhaps suggest most probably, to a traveller accidently passing, that there is somebody sick in that house; yet perhaps it is extraordinary study or business that keeps some person awake.[18]

Nay, when there is no obligation to give, nor any reason for the party to expect true information, it is held generally no crime at all, to use such signs as we have reason to suppose will be mistaken; as when one who does not desire to be disturbed, keeps his chamber close shut, that people may conclude he is not there. When a general of an army puts a fire in the camp, to conceal his march or retreat. And probably none would think it faulty when there was an apprehension of thieves, to keep a light burning in a chamber to lead them to suppose the whole family is not at rest.

There are some who place in the same rank, evasive phrases, when there is an apparent intention to speak our mind, but no right in the other to obtain it.[19] Such expressions may be strictly true, and yet there is all probability that the hearer will misunderstand them. As if one should ask if a person was in any house, and should receive for answer, he went away yesterday morning; when perhaps he returned the same evening. I look upon these evasions, however, as very doubtful, and indeed rather not to be chosen, because they seem to contain a profession of telling our real mind.

Some mention ironical speech as an exception to the obligation to sincerity. But it is properly no objection at all, because there is no deception. Truth lies not in the words themselves, but in the use of them as signs. Therefore, if a man speaks his words in such a tone and manner as the hearer immediately conceives they are to be taken in an opposite sense, and does really take them in the sense the speaker means them, there is no falsehood at all.[20]

Mr. Hutchinson and some others allow a voluntary intended departure from truth, on occasion of some great necessity for a good end. This I apprehend is wrong, for we cannot but consider deception as it itself base and unworthy, and therefore a good end cannot justify it. Besides to suppose it were in men's power on a sufficient occasion to violate truth, would greatly destroy its force in general, and its use in the social life.[21]

There are two sorts of falsehood, which because no doubt they are less aggravated than malicious interested lies, many admit of, but I think without sufficient reason.

(1) Jocular lies, when there is a real deception intended, but not in any thing material, nor intended to continue long. However harmless these may seem, I reckon they are to be blamed, because it is using too much freedom with so sacred a thing as truth. And very often such persons, as righteous punishment in Providence, are left to proceed further, and either to carry their folly to such excess, as to become contemptible, or to go beyond folly into malice.

(2) Officious lies, telling falsehoods to children or sick persons for their good.[22] These very seldom answer the end that is proposed. They lessen the reverence for truth; and particularly with regard to children, are exceedingly pernicious, for as they must soon be discovered, they lose their force, and teach them to deceive. Truth and authority are methods infinitely preferable in dealing with children, as well as with persons of riper years.

NOTES

1. In this lecture Hutcheson's *System of Moral Philosophy* is again Witherspoon's primary source. Book 2, chapter 9 of Hutcheson's work—"Concerning Contracts or Covenants" (2: 1-27)—is the source for the section entitled "Contracts" and book 2, chapter 10—"The Obligations in the Use of Speech" (2: 28-43)—is the source for the last half of the lecture, beginning with the title "Of the Marks or Signs of Contracts."

Witherspoon also seems to borrow from Pufendorf's *Law of Nature and Nations* in this lecture, although not as extensively as from Hutcheson. Pufendorf's influence upon Witherspoon may have been mediated directly, since *De officio hominis et civis* was in

Witherspoon's library, or Pufendorf's impact may have been of a secondary nature through Hutcheson's work.

2. The three objects of civil laws are listed by Witherspoon on pp. 162, 163.

3. Hutcheson used a similar, although slightly different, example to illustrate tacit consent: "When lands are offered only to such as are willing to settle in a colony upon certain conditions of civil subjection; one who takes possession of such lands, is deemed to consent to the conditions" (*System of Moral Philosophy*, 2: 7, 8).

4. This classification of the three degrees of contracts is obviously borrowed from Hutcheson (ibid., pp. 5, 6). Although Witherspoon injects some of his own thoughts into this discussion, much of the wording is similar to Hutcheson's. However, Hutcheson chose to label them as "three forms of speaking about our future actions or prestations" rather than three degrees of contracts. Similarly, Grotius in *De jure belli ac pacis* had indicated there were three ways of speaking of the future, which he illustrated by the following phrases: I intend to give you, I will give you, and I promise you (lib. 2, 11, secs. 2–4, pp. 328–30).

5. This list appears to be a condensation of material found in Hutcheson's *System of Moral Philosophy* under the heading of "Valid exceptions against contracts" (2: 8–27). Hutcheson's discussion was more thorough (for example, he also listed drunkenness as a cause to invalidate a contract—ibid., pp. 11–12).

Both Grotius and Pufendorf stipulated conditions that were necessary to validate a contract. Grotius spoke of these conditions as "Sed quae ad perfectae promissionis vim requirantur videamus" ("conditions required to produce the force of a perfect promise"—*De jure belli ac pacis*, lib. 2, cap. 11, sec. 5–22, pp. 330–39). Pufendorf entitled an entire chapter in his *Law of Nature and Nations* "Of the Consent requir'd in Promises and Contracts" (1: 298–313).

6. See p. 155 of the *Lectures*; also Hutcheson, *System of Moral Philosophy*, 2: 19–20).

7. Hutcheson wrote, "Contracts to which one is compelled by fear upon the just sentence of a judge, are plainly valid, since the sentence is just" (ibid., p. 18). Earlier, Pufendorf similarly had written, "All such Covenants, as are made, out of Dread or Respect of Lawful Authority, or thro' Deference to a Person we are extremely oblig'd to, stand firm and good" (*Law of Nature and Nations*, 1:311–12).

8. In Hutcheson's categories of conditions essential to a contract, he chose to discuss "mutual consent" and "error and fraud" separately (*System of Moral Philosophy*, 2: 12–16). Witherspoon subordinates "error and fraud" under the category of "mutual consent," although the grouping is somewhat strained.

9. Cf. ibid., p. 23 and Pufendorf, *Law of Nature and Nations*, 1: 314–19.

10. See Hutcheson, *System of Moral Philosophy*, 2: 24–26 and Pufendorf, *Law of Nature and Nations*, 1: 319–22.

11. Hutcheson's discussion of this point was considerably fuller than Witherspoon's (*System of Moral Philosophy*, 2:8–11). Hutcheson specified the age at which minors can legally act through their guardians and the age at which they are no longer minors.

In commenting on the issue of capability, Pufendorf simply wrote, "But to give a real and binding Consent, a Man must, be so far Master of his Reason as to understand what he is doing" (*Law of Nature and Nations*, 1: 299).

12. In like manner, Hutcheson classified contracts as "either beneficient, where a gratuitous favour is professedly done on one side; or onerous, where men profess to give mutually equal values" (*System of Moral Philosophy*, 2:64).

13. See ibid., pp. 71–74.

14. "Thou shalt not lend upon usury to they brother; usury of money, usury of victuals, usury of any thing that is lent upon usury: Unto a stranger thou mayest lend upon usury; but unto thy brother thou shalt not lend upon usury: that the lord thy God may bless thee in all that thou settest thine hand to in the land whither thou goest to possess it" (Deuteronomy 23:19,20).

15. Hutcheson also cited conscience and utility as obligations to sincerity. Hutcheson, who

believed in an innate conscience, affirmed that nature had "implanted a moral feeling in our heart" to regulate the power of speech. He went one to state, "We are naturally prone to communicate our sentiments. Truth is the natural production of the mind when it gets the capacity of communicating it, dissimulation and disguise are plainly artificial effects of design and reflection, and an immediate approbation naturally attends both this communicativeness, and the steadfast purpose of speaking according to our sentiments" (*System of Moral Philosophy*, 2:28). Furthermore, Hutcheson asserted that veracity was essential to social relationships. He argued that deceit "tends to deprive human life of all these advantages from mutual confidence in conversation" (ibid., p. 31).

16. Hutcheson used the same categorization although he considered "instituted" and "customary" as synonymous (ibid., p. 30). Witherspoon's elucidation of each of these signs is more thorough than Hutcheson's.

17. This illustration is borrowed from Hutcheson (ibid.). Some of the other examples in this section (such as the man who keeps his chamber shut) are taken from the same source.

18. Hutcheson similarly indicated that a sign might deceive someone for whom it was not intended. For instance, no one is culpable merely because an observer falsely assumed there was a fire after seeing smoke (ibid., p. 29).

19. It seems certain that Witherspoon has in mind a passage from Hutcheson's *System of Moral Philosophy*. Hutcheson considered it lawful to give an evasive answer "in cases where we are not obliged to declare our sentiments, on account of the bad conduct or intentions of some hearers, or where our refusing to answer some captious questions might discover as much as direct speech, what the inquirers have no right to know, and would abuse to the worst purposes, if they knew it" (ibid., p. 35).

20. Samuel Pufendorf likewise discounted ironical speech: "Nor do we attribute a Power of Obliging to any Promises, but to such as are made seriously and upon a mature Deliberation. One must be monstrously silly to insist upon the Letter of a Jest" (*Law of Nature and Nations*, 1: 296).

21. Throughout this section there is a philosophical disagreement between Witherspoon and Hutcheson on the issue of whether a falsehood is ever justified. Hutcheson argued that an untruth would be lawful under certain circumstances. For instance, he supposed a situation in which a just prince was hiding in a house from an inhuman usurper. Would it not be better to lie if this was the only possible way to prevent the usurper from discovering the prince? (*System of Moral Philosophy*, 2: 127).

To Hutcheson a supreme good (such as the saving of a human life) superseded a lesser good (such as the telling of truth). He developed this thesis rather fully in chapter 17 of book 2 of *A System of Moral Philosophy*: "The extraordinary Rights arising from singular Necessity" (ibid., pp. 117-40). In this respect he was a precursor of contemporary situation ethicists such as Joseph Fletcher, James Pike, and John A. T. Robinson.

Witherspoon, on the other hand, hates to justify a falsehood under any circumstances. He legalistically adheres to telling the truth, viewing it primarily as an end in itself rather than as a means to an end. He repeatedly takes issue with Hutcheson on this point.

22. Hutcheson justified falsehoods by a physician to a patient if used sparingly and told to benefit the patient (ibid., p. 33).

LECTURE XVI[1]

OF OATHS AND VOWS

Among the signs and appendages of contracts, are oaths and vows.

An oath is an appeal to God, the searcher of hearts, for the truth of what we say, and always expresses or supposes an imprecation of his judgment upon us, if we prevaricate.[2]

An oath therefore implies a belief in God, and his Providence, and indeed is an act of worship, and so accounted in Scripture, as in that expression, *Thou shalt fear the Lord thy God, and shalt swear by his name.*[3] Its use in human affairs is very great, when managed with judgment. It may be applied and indeed has been commonly used (1) in the contracts of independent states, who have no common earthly superior. In ancient times it was usual always to close national treaties by mutual oaths. This form is not so common in modern times, yet the substance remains; for an appeal is always supposed to be made to God, against the breach of public faith.[4]

(2.) It has been adopted by all nations in their administration of justice, in order to discover truth. The most common and universal application of it has been to add greater solemnity to the testimony of witnesses. It is also sometimes made use of with the parties themselves, for conviction or purgation. The laws of every country point out the cases in which oaths are required or admitted in public judgment. It is, however, lawful and in common practice, for private persons, voluntarily, on solemn occasions, to confirm what they say, by oath. Persons entering on public offices are also often obliged to make oath, that they will faithfully execute their trust.

Oaths are commonly divided into two kinds, *assertory* and *promissory*[5]—Those called purgatory fall under the first of these divisions.[6] There is perhaps little necessity for a division of oaths, for they do not properly stand by themselves; they are confirmations and appendages of contracts, and intended as an additional security for sincerity in the commerce between man and man.

Therefore oaths are subject to all the same regulations as contracts; or rather oaths are only lawful, when they are in aid or confirmation of a lawful contract. What therefore voids the one will void the other, and nothing else. A contract otherwise unlawful, cannot be made binding by an oath: but there must be a very great caution used not to make any unlawful contract, much less to confirm it by an oath.

It is easy to see the extreme absurdity of our being obliged to fulfill a criminal engagement by oath, for it would imply that out of reverence to God we ought to break his commands; but nothing can be more abominable, than the principle of those who think they may safely take an unlawful oath, because it is not binding: this is aggravating gross injustice by deliberate profanity.[7]

I have said that oaths are appendages to all lawful contracts; but in assertory oaths which are only confirmations of our general obligation to sincerity, it is necessary not only that what we say be true, but that the occasion be of sufficient moment to require or justify a solemn appeal to God. Swearing on common occasions is unnecessary, rash, profane and destructive of the solemnity of an oath and its real use.[8]

From the general rule laid down, that oaths are lawful when applied to lawful contracts, it will follow that they become unlawful only when the fulfilling of them would be violating a perfect right;[9] but perhaps an additional observation is necessary here. Contracts must be fulfilled, when they violate an imperfect right; whereas some oaths may be found criminal and void, though they are only contrary to imperfect rights: as for example, some persons bind themselves rashly by oath, that they will never speak to or forgive their children who have offended them.[10] This is so evidently criminal, that nobody will plead for its being obligatory, and yet it is but the violation of an imperfect right. The same persons, however, might in many ways alienate their property to the prejudice of their children, by contracts which the law would oblige them to fulfil.

In vows there is no party but God and the person himself who makes the vow: for this reason, Mr. Hutchinson relaxes their obligation very much—Supposing, any person had solemnly vowed to give a certain part of his substance to public or pious uses, he says if he finds it a great inconvenience to himself or family, he is not bound; this I apprehend is too lax. Men ought to be cautious in making such engagements; but I apprehend that when made, if not directly criminal, they ought to be kept.[11]

Of the use of Symbols in Contracts[12]

Besides promises and oaths, there is sometimes in contracts a use of other visible signs called symbols; the most common among us are signing and sealing a written deed. There is also, in some places, the delivery of earth and stone in making over land—and sundry others. In ancient times it was usual to have solemn symbols in all treaties—mutual gifts—sacrifices—feasts—setting up pillars.[13]—The intention of all such things, whenever and wherever they have been practised, is the same. It is to ascertain and keep up the memory of the transaction. They were more frequent and solemn in ancient times than now, because before the invention of writing they were more necessary.

Of the Value of Property

Before we finish the subject of contracts, it may be proper to say a little of the nature and value of property, which is the subject of them. Nothing has any real value unless it be of some use in human life, or perhaps we may say, unless it is supposed to be of use, and so becomes the object of human desire—because at particular times, and in particular places, things of very little real importance acquire a value, which is commonly temporary and changeable. Shells and baubles are of great value in some places; perhaps there are some more baubles highly valued in every place.

But though it is their use in life that gives things their value in general, it does not follow that those things that are of most use and necessity, are therefore of greatest value as property, or in commerce. Air and water, perhaps we may add fire, are of the greatest use and necessity; but they are also in greatest plenty, and therefore are of little value as a possession or property. Value is in proportion to the plenty of any commodity, and the demand for it. The one taken in the inverse, and the other in the direct proportion.[14]

Hence it follows that money is of no real value. It is not wealth properly, but the sign of it, and in a fixed state of society the certain means of procuring it. In early times traffic was carried on by exchange of goods—but being large, not easily divided or transported, they became very troublesome. Therefore it soon became necessary to fix upon some sign of wealth, to be a standard by which to rate different commodities.

Anything that is fit to answer the purpose of a common sign of wealth, must have the following properties: It must be (1.) valuable, that is, have an intrinsic commercial value, and rare, otherwise it could have no comparative value at all. (2.) Durable, otherwise it could not pass from hand to hand. (3.) Divisible, so that it might be in larger or smaller quantities as are required. (4.) Portable, it must not be of great size, otherwise it would be extremely inconvenient.[15]

Gold and silver were soon found to have all these properties, and therefore are fixed upon as the sign of wealth. But besides being the sign of the value of other commodities, they themselves are also matters of commerce, and therefore increase or decrease in their value by their plenty or scarceness.

It may seem to belong to the ruling part of any society to fix the value of gold and silver as signs of the value of commodities—and no doubt they do fix it nominally in their dominions. But in this they are obliged to be strictly attentive to the value of these metals as a commodity from their plenty or scarceness, otherwise their regulations will be of little force—other nations will pay no regard to the nominal value of any particular country, and even in internal commerce the subject would fix a value upon the signs according to their plenty.[16]

It is as prejudicial to commerce to make the nominal value of the coin of any country too small as too great.

We shall close this part of the subject by speaking a little of the

Rights of Necessity, and common Rights[17]

These are certain powers assumed both by private persons and communities, which are supposed to be authorised by the necessity of the case, and supported by the great law of reason.[18]

There will remain a great number of cases in which these rights of necessity are to be used, even in the best regulated civil society, and after the most mature deliberation and foresight of probable events, and provision for them by specific laws.

Were a man perishing with hunger, and denied food by a person who could easily afford it him, here the rights of necessity would justify him in taking it by violence. Were a city on fire, and the blowing up of an house would save the far greater part, though the owner was unwilling, men would think themselves justified in doing it, whether he would or not. Much more would men in cases of urgent necessity make free with the property of others, without asking their consent, but presuming upon it.

In our own government, where, by the love of liberty general among the people, and the nature of the constitutions, as many particulars have been determined by special laws as in any government in the world—yet instances of the rights of necessity occur every day. If I see one man rob another upon the highway, or am informed of it, if I have courage and ability I pursue the robber, and apprehend him without any warrant, and carry him before a magistrate to get a warrant for what I have already done. Nothing is more common in Britain than to force people to sell their inheritance, or a part of it, to make a road or street straight or commodious. In this instance it is not so much necessity as great utility.[19]

The question of the greatest moment here is, whether the establishing these rights of necessity does not derogate from the perfection and immutability of the moral laws. If it be true, that we may break in upon the laws of justice for the sake of utility, is not this admitting the exploded maxim, that we may do evil that good may come?[20] I answer, that these rights of necessity have in general property as their object, or at most the life of particular persons—and it seems to be inseparable from the establishment of property in the social state, that our property is to be held only in such manner, and to such a degree, as to be both consistent with, and subservient to, the good of others. And therefore these extraordinary cases are agreeable to the tacit or implied conditions of the social contract.

In rights of necessity we are to consider not only the present good or evil, but for all time to come, and particularly the safety or danger of the example. Where the repetition of the thing in similar circumstances would have a fatal effect, it ought not to be done. If a city were under all the miseries of famine, and a ship or two should arrive with grain, the owner of which would not sell it but at a most exorbitant price, perhaps equity might admit that they should be compelled; but if any such thing were done it would prevent others from going near that place again.[21]

It would be of no consequence to determine these rights of necessity by law. If the law described circumstantially what might be done, it would be no longer a right of necessity, but a legal right. To forbid them by law would be either ineffectual, or it would abolish them altogether, and deprive the society of the benefit of them when the cases should occur. Things done by the rights of necessity are by supposition illegal, and if the necessity does not excuse, the person who pretends them may be punished. If I am aiding in pulling down a man's house on pretence of stopping a fire, if he afterwards makes it appear that there was not the least occasion for it, or that I, being his enemy, took the opportunity of this pretence to injure him, he will obtain reparation.

As property, or at most life is concerned in the rights of necessity—still the moral laws continue in force. Whatever expresses an evil disposition of mind does not fall under the rule, because it can never be necessary to the doing of any good. The pretence of its being necessary in some cases is generally chimerical, and even were it real, the necessity could not justify the crime—as suppose a robber very profane should threaten a man with death unless he would blaspheme God or curse his parents, &c.[22]

There are certain things called common rights,[23] which the public is supposed to have over every member: the chief of them are (1.) diligence. As a man must eat the community have a right to compel him to be useful—and have a right to make laws against suicide. (2.) They have a right to the discovery of useful inventions, provided an adequate price be paid to the discoverer. (3.) They have a right to insist upon such things as belong to the dignity of human nature. Thus all nations pay respect to dead bodies, though there is no other reason for it but that we cannot help associating with the body, even dead, the ideas which arise from it, and belonged to the whole person when alive.

3. The third and last object of civil laws is, limiting citizens in the exercise of their rights, so as they may not be injurious to one another, but the public good may be promoted.[24]

This includes the giving directions in what way arts and commerce may be carried on, and in some states extends as far as the possessions of private persons.

It includes the whole of what is called the police of a community—the manner of travelling, building, marketing, time and manner of holding all sorts of assemblies—In arts and commerce particularly the police shows its power.

It will only be necessary here to make a few remarks on the nature and spirit of those laws.

1. Those things in themselves are arbitrary and mutable, for there is no morality in them but what arises from common utility. We may sometimes do things in a way better than that appointed by law, and yet it is not allowed.

2. Men in general have but a very light sense of the malignity of transgressing these laws, such as running of goods, breaking over a fence, &c.

3. In the best constitutions some sanctions are appointed for the breach of these laws. Wherever a state is founded upon the principles of liberty, such laws are made with severity and executed with strictness.

Finally, a man of real probity and virtue adopts these laws as a part of his duty to God and the society, and is subject not only for wrath, but also for conscience sake.[25]

NOTES

1. Witherspoon discusses many topics in this lecture, some of which are unrelated to one another and to the lecture title, "Of Oaths and Vows." Apparently Witherspoon wanted to cover a host of subjects before concluding the *Lectures*. Hence the transition from one theme to another is often strained and awkward.

In this lecture Witherspoon borrows material from four chapters of Hutcheson's *System of Moral Philosophy* in the following order:
1) book 2, chapter 11—"Concerning Oaths and Vows" (2: 44-53)
2) book 2, chapter 12—"The Value of Goods in Commerce and the Nature of Coin" (2: 53-64)
3) book 2, chapter 17—"The extraordinary Rights arising from singular Necessity" (2: 117-40)
4) book 2, chapter 16—"Concerning the general Rights of Human Society, or Mankind as a System" (2: 104-16)

2. Hutcheson defines an oath as "a promise made to God, binding us to some performance, and an invocation of divine punishment if we omit it" (ibid., p. 50). Pufendorf had earlier defined an oath as "a religious Asseveration by which we either renounce the Mercy, or imprecate the Vengeance of God, if we speak not the Truth" (*Law of Nature and Nations*, 2: 11).

3. Witherspoon omits one phrase in this Biblical injunction—"Thou shalt fear the Lord thy God and serve him, and shalt swear by his name" (Deuteronomy 6:13).

4. Witherspoon obviously does not share the conviction held by some Protestant dissenters of that era (such as Quakers) that oaths of any kind are wrong. Quakers based their refusal to swear on the following words of Jesus: "Swear not at all: neither by heaven; for it is God's throne: nor by the earth; for it is his footstool: neither by Jerusalem; for it is the city of the great King. Neither shalt thou swear by thy head, because thou canst not make one hair white or black. But let your communication be, Yea, yea; Nay, nay: for whatsoever is more than these, cometh of evil" (Matthew 5:33-37).

5. The division of oaths into assertory and promissory was common among seventeenth-century jurists such as Pufendorf. Pufendorf defined an assertory oath as one in which "a Man Swears to clear a Matter of Fact not yet sufficiently prov'd, and which cannot be conveniently made out any other Way." Whereas he viewed a promissory oath as that which is "annex'd to Promises and Contracts, to render 'em more Sacred and Inviolable" (*Law of Nature and Nations*, 2: 19).

6. Hutcheson listed five different sub-divisions under assertory oaths: necessary, judicial, voluntary, purgatory, and expletory. It is not easy to understand why Witherspoon chooses to list one of these (purgatory) with no accompanying illustration. Hutcheson defined a purgatory oath as one "enjoined upon the party accused in a criminal action, in which he is to be absolved upon swearing to his innocence" (*System of Moral Philosophy*, 2: 49).

7. Hutcheson had similarly decried oaths connected with disobedience to God or the state: "An oath cannot bind us to what is directly impious toward God, or contrary to the perfect right of another; or to what is specifically prohibited by a law excluding our moral power of transacting in those matters. Could oaths bind us in such cases, they would be the most pernicious engines of evading every obligation to God, or man; and of destroying all the rights of others" (*System of Moral Philosophy*, 2: 47-48).

In like manner, Pufendorf wrote: "Farthermore, an Oath is likewise Void, when what we have sworn to do, is unlawful; or what we have sworn not to do is expressly enjoyn'd by the laws of God or Man" (*Law of Nature and Nations*, 2: 15).

8. This is in agreement with the spirit of the third commandment of the Decalogue: "Thou shalt not take the name of the Lord thy God in vain; for the Lord will not hold him guiltless that taketh his name in vain" (Exodus 20:7).

9. Witherspoon's list of perfect rights is on page 123 of the *Lectures*.

10. Hutcheson had previously employed the same example to illustrate wicked vows that should be observed (*System of Moral Philosophy*, 2: 52).

11. In the preceding lecture Witherspoon took issue with Hutcheson on the matter of veracity (see p. 173). He was much more reluctant to justify a falsehood, even if it served a good purpose.

Once again there is disagreement on this point. The particular passage from Hutcheson to which Witherspoon refers is as follows: "Thus should the parent of a numerous family, in any danger, vow to give the half of his goods to the poor, or to certain orders called religious, or for building or adorning certain edifices; or should he undertake useless penances; while all the indigent are sufficiently provided otherways, or might be so by a far smaller proportion of the goods of the wealthy; while all useful orders of men have sufficient support, and there are sufficient buildings and utensils for all religious uses; and while the penances vowed are no way useful for his improvement in virtue; he is under no obligation as God cannot be supposed to accept of such promises; and there's no conveyance made of any rights to men" (*System of Moral Philosophy*, 2: 51).

12. The reason for the inclusion of this brief section here is not clear. Logically it should have been included under the discussion entitled "Of the Marks or Signs of Contracts" in the preceding lecture.

13. These are allusions to symbols used to ratify covenants in Biblical times. Illustrations of the use of each symbol are as follows:

(1) Mutual gifts—The Gibeonites' gift of goods and wine to the Israelites (Joshua 9:3-15) and the exchange of gifts between Hiram and Solomon (I Kings 5:7-12).

(2) Sacrifices—The offering of livestock by Israel after receiving the covenant at Sinai (Exodus 24:4-8).

(3) Feasts—The eating of a feast together to seal a league between Isaac and Abimelech, Ahuzzath, and Phichol (Genesis 26:26-33).

(4) Setting up pillars—The heap of stones left to memorialize the pact between Jacob and Laban (Genesis 31:43-55).

14. The thesis that the value of goods is determined by their usefulness and scarcity was common in the writings of the moral philosophers of the Enlightenment (e.g., Pufendorf, *Law of Nature and Nations*, 2: 85-86).

15. This paragraph is a condensation and restatement of material found in Hutcheson. By paraphrasing, Witherspoon seems to improve the clarity of Hutcheson's statement: "The qualities requisite to the most perfect standard are these; it must be something generally desired so that men are generally willing to take it in exchange. The very making any goods the standard will of itself give them this quality. It must be portable; which will often be the case if it is rare, so that small quantities are of great value. It must be divisible without loss into small parts, so as to be suited to the values of all sorts of goods; and it must be durable, not easily wearing by use, or perishing in its nature" (*System of Moral Philosophy*, 2: 55-56).

16. This is a hurried and inadequate summary of a lengthy section in Hutcheson's volume (ibid., pp. 58-64). Hutcheson indicated the futility of governors of states arbitrarily changing the value of coinage and the ensuing harm that would result from such an action.

17. The transition here is quite abrupt. Witherspoon wants to discuss this subject, but its connection with the preceding material is unclear.

In explaining the rights of necessity, Witherspoon reacts to and borrows from material found in book 2, chapter 17 ("The extraordinary Rights arising from some singular

Necessity'') in Hutcheson's volume (ibid., pp. 117-40).

18. Hutcheson excused acts of necessity: "Such conduct as in ordinary cases would be vicious, and contrary to law, does in some rarer cases of necessity become good and lawful" (ibid., p. 120).

19. The illustrations used by Witherspoon to justify certain rights of necessity are original and not borrowed from Hutcheson. In justifying acts of necessity, Hutcheson's examples presented the moral dilemma in a more graphic way: lying to prevent a murder, theft of property to save lives, murder to prevent the spread of disease, and so on (ibid., pp. 123-27).

Perhaps Witherspoon shies away from these illustrations because he desires to avoid Hutcheson's utilitarian ethic (or means that promote the general good are by definition, good). Thus, in the subsequent paragraph, Witherspoon attempts to restrict the rights of necessity to property matters or at the most, to "the life of particular persons." Nevertheless, he concedes ground on this issue by admitting that general laws may be broken in certain extreme cases.

20. Witherspoon may be referring to a passage in the New Testament. Paul disagreed with those who justified sin on the basis that it was an occasion for God's mercy: "What shall we say then? Shall we continue in sin, that grace may abound? God forbid" (Romans 6:1-2).

Hutcheson did not believe that this statement was applicable as a moral tenet, for he affirmed that an action was either good or evil in reference to its end (ibid., pp. 132-33). Witherspoon does not concur with this conclusion, but fails to resolve logical problems raised by his position.

21. Hutcheson used this same illustration, although with some variation. In Hutcheson's writing, the ship is loaded with both food and ammunition, the city is impoverished because of a siege, and the ship may sell his provisions to the besiegers rather than the inhabitants of the city. Under these circumstances, Hutcheson strongly believed that seizing the goods by force would be justified (ibid., p. 125). Yet Witherspoon argues against such an action since the long-range effects will be detrimental.

22. Hutcheson also refused to justify any impious act toward God: "No necessity can justify such actions as evidence impiety, or contempt of the Deity; such as blasphemy, perjuring, or abjuring the true God, or that worship we believe acceptable to him" (ibid., p. 139).

23. In moving from a discussion of the rights of necessity to common rights, Witherspoon once again lacks adequate transition. This particular section borrows from book 2, chapter 16 ("Concerning the general Rights of Human Society, or Mankind as a System") of Hutcheson's work (ibid., pp. 104-16).

Hutcheson's explanation of common rights lists seven. Witherspoon chooses to enumerate three of these and combine another ("to prevent suicide") under the general heading of "diligence." He omits the other three general rights given by Hutcheson, which are "to preserve the human race, to prevent the destruction of any thing useful, and the right of repelling all injuries and punishing them."

24. On pages 162, 163 Witherspoon outlines the three objects of civil laws: "1. To ratify the moral laws by the sanction of the society. 2. To lay down a plan for all contracts in the commerce or intercourse between man and man. 3. To limit and direct persons in the exercise of their own rights, and oblige them to show respect to the interfering rights of others." Although he fails to make this clear, Witherspoon evidently intends that the remaining material in the *Lectures* will be organized under these three headings. Therefore, at this point, he introduces the third object of civil laws.

Not only is this organizational pattern hazy but the emphasis given to the three topics is quite disproportionate. The first object of civil laws (to sanction moral laws) is discussed on pages 163-65. The second object, which dealt with contracts, covers fourteen pages of the *Lectures* (pp. 168-81) and involves such diverse topics as signs of contracts, oaths and vows, symbols in contracts, rights of necessity, and common rights. Yet the third object of civil laws is dispensed within eight brief paragraphs of inadequate treatment.

25. This phrase is taken from Romans 13:1-7, where Paul encouraged Christians to be obedient to the civil authorities. After warning that rulers "execute wrath upon him that doeth evil," he wrote, "Wherefore ye must needs be subject, not only for wrath, but also for conscience sake" (Romans 13:4,5).

RECAPITULATION

Having gone through the three general divisions of this subject, Ethics, Politics, and Jurisprudence, I shall conclude with a few remarks upon the whole, and mention to you the chief writers who have distinguished themselves in this branch of science.

1. You may plainly perceive both how extensive and how important moral philosophy is. As to extent, each of the divisions we have gone through might have been treated at far greater length. Nor would it be unprofitable to enter into a fuller disquisition of many points; but this must be left to every scholar's inclination and opportunities in future life. Its importance is manifest from this circumstance, that it not only points out personal duty, but is related to the whole business of active life. The languages, and even mathematical and natural knowledge, are but hand-maids to this superior science.

2. The evidence which attends moral disquisitions is of a different kind from that which attends mathematics and natural philosophy; but it remains as a point to be discussed, whether it is more uncertain or not. At first sight it appears that authors differ much more, and more essentially on the principles of moral than natural philosophy. Yet perhaps a time may come when men, treating moral philosophy as Newton and his successors have done natural, may arrive at greater precision. It is always safer in our reasonings to trace facts upwards, than to reason downwards, upon metaphysical principles. An attempt has been lately made by Beatty, in his Essay on Truth, to establish certain impressions of common sense as axioms and first principles of all our reasonings on moral subjects.[1]

3. The differences about the nature of virtue are not in fact so great as they appear: they amount to nearly the same thing in the issue, when the particulars of a virtuous life come to be enumerated.[2]

4. The different foundations of virtue are many of them, not opposite or repugnant to each other, but parts of one great plan—as benevolence and self-love, &c. They all conspire to found real virtue: the authority of God—the dictates of conscience—public happiness and private interest all coincide.[3]

5. There is nothing certain or valuable in moral philosophy, but what is perfectly coincident with the scripture, where the glory of God is the first principle of action, arising from the subjection of the creature—where the good of others is the great object of duty, and our own interest the necessary consequence.[4]

In the first dawn of philosophy, men began to write and dispute about virtue. The great inquiry among the ancients was, what was the *summum bonum*? by which it seems they took it for granted, that virtue and happiness were the same thing. The chief combatants here, were the Stoics and Epicureans. The first insisted that virtue was the *summum bonum*, that pleasure was no good, and pain no evil: the other said that the *summum bonum* consisted in pleasure, or rather that pleasure was virtue: the Academics and Platonists went a middle way between these.[5]

I am not sensible that there is any thing among the ancients, that wholly corresponds with the modern dispute upon the foundation of virtue.

Since the disputes arose in the sixteenth and seventeenth centuries, some of the most considerable authors,[6] chiefly British, are Leibnitz, his Theodicee and his Letters; Clark's Demonstration and his Letters. Hutcheson's Inquiries into the ideas of beauty and virtue, and his System. Wollaston's Religion of Nature Delineated. Collins on Human Liberty. Nettleton on Virtue and Happiness. David Hume's Essays. Lord Kaim's Essays. Smith's Theory of Moral Sentiments. Reed's Inquiry. Balfour's Delineation of Morality. Butler's Analogy and Sermons. Balguy's Tracts. Theory of Agreeable Sensations, from the French. Beatty on Truth. Essay on Virtue and Harmony.

To these may be added the whole Deistical writers, and the answers written to each of them in particular, a brief account of which may be seen in Leland's View of the Deistical Writers.

Some of the chief writers upon government and politics are Grotius, Puffendorf, Barbyrac, Cumberland, Selden, Burlamaqui, Hobbs, Machiavel, Harrington, Locke, Sydney, and some late books, Montesquieu's Spirit of Laws; Ferguson's History of Civil Society; Lord Kaime's Political Essays, Grandeur and Decay of the Roman Empire; Montague's Rise and Fall of Ancient Republics; Goguet's Rise and Progress of Laws, Arts and Sciences.

NOTES

1. Witherspoon's preference for inductive reasoning, rather than deductive reasoning, is quite clear. He is hopeful that the inductive method employed by Newton in the natural sciences will be used to construct a science of morals. James Beattie and his *Essays on the Nature and Immutability of Truth* is discussed in Lecture VI, n. 4.

2. See pp. 83-85 for Witherspoon's discussion of the nature of virtue and his attempted synthesis of opposing views.

3. See pp. 85-87.

4. This appears to be a summary sentence of a lengthy section in the *Lectures* dealing with man's three duties: to God (pp. 95-108); to man (all of Lecture VIII); and to ourselves (all of Lecture IX). At the very beginning of Lecture I, Witherspoon averred that reason would validate the Bible.

5. These references to ancient Greek philosophies by Witherspoon are cursory, although not inaccurate. A comprehensive and readable treatment of this subject may be found in *Outlines of the History of Greek Philosophy* by Eduard Zeller (trans. L. R. Palmer, rev. Wilhelm Nestle, 13th ed. [New York: Harcourt, Brace & Co., 1931].

Stoicism was founded by Zeno (334/33-262/61 B.C.) in Athens about 300 B.C.. The name of the philosophy was derived from its adherents' meeting place, the Stoa Poikile. Zeno taught that man should govern his life totally according to the laws of nature. He believed that virtue is the only good; passions and emotions are to be overcome (ibid., pp. 227-46).

The founder of Epicureanism was Epicurus (344-270 B.C.). The philosophy originated in Athens and was contemporary with the beginning of Stoicism. Epicurus asserted that the feeling of pleasure and pain that accompany sense experiences are the ultimate good and evil. Thus pleasure is the sole good; pain is the sole evil (ibid., pp. 248-60).

It is difficult to identify exactly Witherspoon's reference to the "Academics and Platonists." The Platonic heritage, as transmitted by the Academy, has a very long history. Its beginning was about 387 B.C. with the establishment of the Academy by Plato and its actual conclusion did not occur until 529 A.D., when Justinian closed the Athenian school. One can, however, reasonably restrict the term "Academics" to the first four centuries following Plato (or the eras of the Old Academy and New Academy).

"Platonists and Academics" possibly may refer to Antiochus of Ascalon (d. 68 B.C.). Head of the Academy and eclectic in his ethical philosophy, Antiochus taught that although virtue suffices for happiness, for the highest grade of happiness bodily and external goods are also necessary. This may be the "middle way" to which Witherspoon alludes. Cicero (106-43 B.C.), some of whose works were in Witherspoon's personal library, studied under Antiochus and subscribed to his ethical views (ibid., pp. 272-77).

6. The following bibliography by Witherspoon is significant in indicating the works that its authors considered important in moral and political thought. It is also helpful in ascertaining the sources for *Lectures on Moral Philosophy*. See Appendix 1 for details of this bibliography.

Appendix 1

Bibliography of Chief Writers on Ethical and Political Thought

At the conclusion of *Lectures on Moral Philosophy*, Witherspoon suggested a bibliography of the chief writers on ethical and political thought. Information about that bibliography is given in this appendix.

When only the name of an author was given by Witherspoon (for example, Grotius), the most probable work or works is enclosed in brackets. A work preceded by an asterisk indicates that the book was in Witherspoon's personal library (Appendix 2). A citation accompanying a bibliographical entry (e.g., "See p. 7") indicates that a reference or allusion to that particular author appears in the body of the *Lectures*. The page number cited is the first reference to the author by Witherspoon, and at that point brief biographical information may be found.

Leibniz, Gottfried Wilhelm (1646-1716). *Essais de Theodicée. . .* ("Theodicy. Essays on the Goodness of God, the Freedom of Man and the Origin of Evil"; 1710). *A Collection of Papers* ("which passed between the late learned Mr. Leibnitz, and Dr. Clarke, in the years 1715 and 1716, relating to the Principles of Natural Philosophy and Religion"; 1717).

Clarke, Samuel (1675-1729). **A Discourse Concerning the Being and Attributes of God, the Obligations of Natural Religion and the Truth and Certainty of the Christian Revelation* (1705-6). The fourth edition of this book (1716), which was in Witherspoon's library, contained the parts described in the Recapitulation: the first section entitled "A demonstration of the being and attributes of God," and the appendix containing the letter exchange of Samuel Clarke and Joseph Butler. See p. 68.

Hutcheson, Francis (1694-1747). *Inquiry into the Original of Our Ideas of Beauty and Virtue* (1725). *A System of Moral Philosophy* (1755). See p. 75.

Wollaston, William (1659-1724). *The Religion of Nature Delineated* (1722). See p. 88.

Collins, Anthony (1676-1729). *Inquiry Concerning Human Liberty and Necessity* (1715).

Nettleton, Thomas (1683-1742). *Some Thoughts Concerning Virtue and Happiness* (1729).

Hume, David (1711-76). *Essays, Moral and Political* (1741-42). See p. 74.

Kames, Henry Home, Lord (1696-1782). **Essays on the Principles of Morality and Natural Religion* (1751). See p. 89.

Smith, Adam (1723-90). *The Theory of Moral Sentiments* (1759). See pp. 75, 88.

Reid, Thomas (1710-96). *An Inquiry into the Human Mind on the Principles of Common Sense* (1763). See pp. 75, 100.

Balfour, James (1705-95). *A Delineation of the Nature and Obligations of Morality, with Reflections upon "An Enquiry Concerning Morals"* (1753).

Butler, Joseph (1692-1752). **Fifteen Sermons Preached at the Chapel of Rolls Court* (1726). *The Analogy of Religion, Natural and Revealed, to the Constitution and Course of Nature* (1736). See p. 82.

Balguy, John (1686-1748). *A Collection of Tracts, Moral and Theological* (1734).

Pouilly, Louis-Jean Levesque de (1692-1750). *Theorie des Sentimens agreables* ("The Theory of Agreeable Sensations"; 1747).

Beattie, James (1735–1803). *Essay on the Nature and Immutability of Truth, in Opposition to Sophistry and Scepticism* (1770). See p. 100.

On page 143 of his edition of Witherspoon's *Lectures on Moral Philosophy*, Varnum Lansing Collins added this note: "The 'Essay on virtue and harmony' has eluded identification." Perhaps Witherspoon referred to an essay in *Characteristics of Men, Manners, Opinions, Times* (1711) by Lord Shaftesbury, Anthony Ashley Cooper (1677-1713). The essay was entitled "An Inquiry Concerning Virtue, or Merit" (*Characteristics*, 2: 3-176). See p. 69.

Leland, John (1691-1766). *A View of the Principal Deistical Writers* (1754-1756). In these three volumes Leland chose to attack such Deists as Matthew Tindal (1657-1733), Hume, and Lord Bolingbroke, Henry St. John (1678–1751). See p. 100.

Grotius, Hugo (1583–1645). [*De jure belli ac pacis* ("On the Law of War and Peace"; 1625)] See p. 156.

Pufendorf, Samuel von (1632-94). [*De jure natural et gentium* ("On the Law of Nature and Nations"; 1672). **De officio homini et civis* ("On the Duty of Man and Citizen"; 1673).] See p. 156.

Barbeyrac, Jean (1674-1744). [Barbeyrac's chief contribution to political thought was not original work but rather his commentaries on Grotius and Pufendorf. English editions of Grotius's *On the Law of War and Peace* and Pufendorf's *On the Duty of Man and Citizen* with "the notes of Mr. J. Barbeyrace" were available in the time of Witherspoon.]

Cumberland, Richard (1631-1718). [*De legibus naturae disquisitio philosophica* ("A Philosophical Inquiry into the Laws of Nature"; 1672)]

Selden, John (1584-1654). [His many legal and philosophical works may be found in *Opera omnia* (D. Wilkins, ed., 3 vols., 1726.]

Burlamaqui, Jean Jacques (1694-1748). [Principles du droit naturel ("The Principles of Natural Law"; 1747). *Principes du droit politique*

("The Principles of Political Law"; 1751).] See p. 99.

Hobbes, Thomas (1588-1679). [*Leviathan, or the Matter, Forme, and Power of a Commonwealth, Ecclesiasticall and Civil* (1651). Other political writings by Hobbes are included in *The Moral and Political Works of Thomas Hobbes of Malmesbury* (1750).] See p. 75.

Machiavelli, Niccolo (1469-1527). [*Il Principe* ("The Prince"; 1532.] Harrington, James (1611-77). [*Oceana (1656)].*

Locke, John (1632-1704). [*Two Treatises of Government* (1690)]. See pp. 74-75.

Sydney, Algernon (1622-83). [*Discourses Concerning Government* (1698)].

Montesquieu, Charles Louis de Secondat, Baron (1689-1755). *De l'esprit des lois* ("The Spirit of Laws"; 1748). See p. 39.

Ferguson, Adam (1723-1816). *An Essay on the History of Civil Society* (1766).

Kames (see previous note).

Montesquieu (see note above). *Considerations sur les causes de la grandeur des Romains et de leur decadence* ("Considerations on the Cause of the Grandeur and Declension of the Romans"; 1734).

Montague, Edward Wortley (1713-76). *Reflections on the Rise and Fall of the Ancient Republicks, Adapted to the Present State of Great Britain* (1759).

Goguet, Antoine Yves (1716-58). *De l'origine des lois, des arts, et des sciences* ("The Origin of Laws, Arts, and Sciences"; 1758).

Appendix 2

John Witherspoon's Personal Library in 1794

The following list of books represents John Witherspoon's personal library at his death in 1794. These volumes had been willed to Witherspoon's son-in-law, Samuel Stanhope Smith. Smith, president of the college from 1795 to 1812, sold the collection to the college shortly after a fire on May 6, 1812 had devastated the school's library. Smith's relinquishing of the collection was fortunate, for this allowed Witherspoon's library to remain intact.

It should not be assumed that this list of books is the complete library of John Witherspoon. These books are simply the ones that Witherspoon possessed when he died and that were still in Smith's possession in 1812. There is no way to establish definitely which books or how many books are missing from Witherspoon's original library. It is worth noting that *A System of Moral Philosophy* by Francis Hutcheson (2 vols. [London, 1753]) is not on this list, and yet, as noted in this edition of *Lectures on Moral Philosophy*, the volume was used extensively by Witherspoon. Furthermore, Witherspoon had a large collection of bound pamphlets that is not included on this list (see Stewart MacMaster Robinson, "Notes on the Witherspoon Pamphlets," *Princeton University Library Chronicle* 27 [Autumn 1965]: 53–59).

This inventory was collected at the Princeton University Library from a large volume entitled *Donations in Books and Apparatus Received for the use of the College of New Jersey Since it was consumed by fire March 6th MDCCCII*. Because the bibliographical entries were made by hand, it is difficult to process the list. However, the following appendix represents the book list exactly as it appears in the above volume.

"Titles of volumes once belonging to president Witherspoon, and bought by the college from president Smith."

Helwig (Christopher) Historical and chronological theatre. 1687. f°.
Usher (James) Annales Veteris Testamenti. Londini, 1650. f°.
Dufresnoy's Chronological tables of universal history. 2v. London, 1762. 8°.
Strauchius (Giles) Breviarium chronologicum. London, 1704. 8°.
Gordon (James) Chronologia. annorum serium, etc. complutins. Bordigalae, 1611. 8°.

Bossuet (J.B.) Discours surl' histoire universalle. 7' ed. 2v. La Haye, 1702, 12°.
Universal history. 18v. London, 1747-48. 8°.
Blair (J.) Chronological tables of the world to 1753. f°.
Goguet (A.Y.) Origin of laws arts and sciences, 3v. Edinburgh, 1761. 9°.
Arbuthnot (J.) Tables of ancient coins, weights and measures explained. London, 1727. 4°.
Carver (J.) Three years travels through North America, [1766-68]. Philadelphia, 1784. 8°.
Edwards (J. sen.) Life of Brainerd, with his journal. Edinburgh, 1765. 8°.
Gordon. History of the U.S. 3v. New York, 1789. 8°.
Zimmerman (E.A.W.) Political survey of Europe. Dublin, 1788. 8°.
Present state of Great Britain and Ireland. etc. London, 1738. 8°.
Burnet (G.) History of his own time, v. 1. 1724. f°.
Buchanan (G.) Rerum Scoticarum historia. Edinburgh, 1583, f°.
Boswell (J.B.) Account of Corsica. etc. 2nd ed. London, 1768. 8°.
Brantome (J. de B. d.) Anecdotes tochant les duels. Seyde, 1722. 12°.
Temple (Sir M.) Observations on the United Provinces. Edinburgh, 1747. 12°.
Journey through the Christian Netherlands. 2nd ed. London, 1732. 8°.
Vertot (J.R. de) History of the revolutions of Portugal. 4th ed. London, 1735. 8°.
Volney. Travels in Syria and Egypt [1783-5]. 2v. in 1. Dublin, 1788. 8°.
Montesquieu. Causes of the grandeur and declension of the Romans. London, 1734. 16°.
Flouis cumnotis Min - ellij. et Ampelius. Rotorodami, 1680. 24° or 8m. 12°.
Suetonius. XII Caesares, with a translation by J. Clarke. 1732. 8°.
Tacitus. Opera, Lipsius quintum recensuit. Lugd. Bat., 1598. 8° 8m.
——— do. Excudebat. J. Stoer. 1598. 24°.
Cicero. do omnia, Lambini ed. cum Gostrossedi notes. Lugdani, 1587. 4°.
——— do. Epistolarum ad familiares v.8 xvi. Must. J. Ross. Cantabngrai, 1749. Qr.
Horace. OEuvres, en latin eten francois par M. Dacier. 10v. 5th ed. Hambourg, 1733. 16°.
Mavrocordato (er.) περι ΧαΘηχουΤων βιβλος. De officiis liber. Londini, 1724. 8m. 8°.
Lucanus. Pharsalia, cum supplemento. Maj. Amsteladami, 1714. 16°.
Horatius. Excecensione Heinsius. Edinburgh, 1704. 12°.
——— do. Frajecti Batavonum, 1713. 12°.
C. Nepotis Vitae imperatorum. Lugd. Bat., 1675. 8°.
C. Phynii naturae historiarum libri xxxvii. Romae, 1513. f°.
Terentius. Comocdiae sex. Glasguae. Foulei, 1742. 1.p. 8°.
Beaumont (Joseph). Psyche, orlore's mystery. 2nd ed. London, 1702. f°.
Potter (J) Archaeologiae Graecae. Antiquities of Greece. 2v. 8th ed. London, 1704. 8°.
Pindarus. Olympia, Pythia, Nemea, Isthmia. Lugd. Bat., 1590. 8m. 8°.

Thucydides. Bellum peloponnesiacum. T. I. ex ed. Napii et Dukers Glasguae Foulis, 1759. 8m. 8°.

Restaut (P.) Principes ret a grammaire francaise. 9th ed. Paris, 1765. 12°.

Bathe (W.) Janua Linguarum. 1400 sentences. 8th ed. by T. Horne. London, 1634. 8°.

Mair (J.) Tyro's dictionary Latin and English. Edinburgh, 1763. 12°.

Ruddiman (J.) Grammaticaelatinae institutiones. 2v. Edinburgh, 1725-31. 8m. 8°.

Willymott (W.) English examples to Lily's grammar rules. London, 1727. 8°.

Adam (A.) Principles of Latin and English grammar. Edinburgh, 1772. 8°.

Lang (J.) Loci communes, sive florilegium - sententiarum Argentorati, 1622. 8°.

Reland (A.) Brevis introductio inlinguam hebraicam. Glaguae, 1721. 18°,

Maunovy (G.) Grammaire et dictionnaire francois et espagnol. Paris, 1707. 8m. 12°.

Voyages et avantures de Jacques Massi [par Tvssot de Patot.] Bourdeaux, 1710. 12°.

Holmes (J.) Art of rhetoric made easy. 3rd ed. London, 1766. 8°.

Lexiphanes, a dialogue imitated from Lucian . . . 2nd ed. London, 1767. 12°.

Lamy (B.) Rhetorique. 5th ed. Amsterdam, 1712. 12°.

Boileau. Oluvus diserses. 2v. in 1. Amsterdam, 1701. 12°.

Choise collection (Watson's) of scots poems. 3v. in 1. Glasgow, 1709-13. 16°.

Roscommon. Masks. Glasgow, Foulis. 1753. 16°.

West (G.) Observations on the resurrection of Christ. 3rd ed. London, 1747. 8°.

Saurin (J.) Sermons. 10v. La Haye, 1749. 8°.

Pascal (B.) Pensies ed. [de Filleau de Les Chaise]. Amsterdam, 1700. 12°.

Ruddiman (T.) Vindication of Buchanan's Psalms. Edinburgh, 1745. 8°.

Baxter (A.) Enquiry into the nature of the soul (1st ed.). London, 1730. 4°.

Discourse concerning the certainty of a future state. London, 1706. 8°.

Cudworth. Intellectual system of the universe. 2nd ed. by Birch. 2v. London, 1743. 4°.

Chillingworth. Religion of protestants. etc. 2nd ed. London, 1638. f°.

Watts (I.) Logick. 4th ed. London, 1731. 8°.

Nicoly (P.) Essais de morale. 6th ed. 6v. La Haye, 1688. 8m. 12°.

Puffendorf (S.) De officio hominis et civis . . . ed. 2da. Edinburgi, 1724. 24°.

Rollin (Charles) De la manière d'Enseigner et d'etudier les belles lettres. 2nd. ed. 4v. Paris, 1728. 12°.

—— True (the) conduct of persons of quality. [from] the French. [*anon.*] London, 1694. 12°.

Home (H.) Lord Kames. Essays on the principles of morality. 3rd ed. [*anon.*] Edinburgh, 1751. 8°.

Epictetus. Morals, with Simplicius his comment. Made English by G. Stanhope. 5th ed. London, 1741. 8°.

Jackson (J.) A defense of human liberty. 2nd ed. London, 1730. 16°.

Locke (J.) Two trestises of government . . . 4th ed. London, 1713. 12°.

Gordon (J.) The character of a generous prince . . . London, 1703. 12°.

Dickinson (J.) Essay on the . . . power of Great-Britain over the colonies . . . Philadelphia, 1774. 8°.

Goguet (A.Y.) The origin of laws, arts and sciences . . . fr. the French. 3v. Edinburgh, 1761. 8°.

Grotius (H.) De jure belli et pacis . . . ed nova . . . Amsterdami, 1646. 8°.

Wallace (R.) A dissertation on the numbers of mankind [*anon.*] Edinburgh, 1753. 8°.

Home (H.) Lord Kaimes. Six sketches on the history of man . . . Philadelphia, 1776. 12⁰.

Political Essays concerning the present state of the British Empire . . . [*anon.*] London, 1772. 4ᵍ.

Maclaurin (C.) An account of . . . Newton's philosophical discoveries. London, 1748. 4°.

Martin (B.) The philosophical grammar . . . London, 1769. 8°.

Strauch (A.) Tabulae Sincuum, tangentium logarithmorum . . .Amstelodami, 1700. 16⁰.

Frewin (R.) The book of rates . . . [*anon.*] Dundee, 1787. 16°.

Kearsley (g.) Tax tables . . . 96th ed. London, 1788. 16°. [Bound together with above.]

Maraldi (J.D.) Connoissance des temps pour . . . 1756 . . . Paris, 1755. 12°.

Leclerc (J.) Physica sive de rebus corporeis . . . Amstelodami, 1696. 18°.

Crookshank (W.) The history of the church of Scotland . . . 2nd ed. 2v. Edinburgh, 1751. 16°.

Dundas (J.) An abridgement of the acts of the general assemblies . . . Edinburgh, 1721. 16⁰.

Apology (an) for . . . the . . . ministers . . . of . . . the church of Scotland . . . [*anon.*] n.p., 1677. 16°.

Authentic memoirs concerning the Portuguese inquisition . . . [*anon.*] London, 1769. 8°.

Heidegger (J.H.) Historia papatus . . . [recen.] H. Wetsten. Amstelaedami, 1698. 4°.

Pascal (B.) Les provinciales . . . avec notes de G. Wendrock. n.p., 1700. 16°.

Stewart (W.) Collections and observations concerning . . . the church of Scotland. Edinburgh, 1770. 12°.

Wodrow (R.) The history of the sufferings of the church of Scotland. 2v. Edinburgh, 1821-22. f°.

Burnet (G.) Historia reformationis ecclesiae Anglicanae . . . 2v. in 1. Genevae, 1689. f°.

Hooke (J.) Catholicism without popery . . . [*anon.*] 2 pts. in 1v. London, 1699-1704. 8°.
Knox (J.) The historie of the reformation . . . within . . . Scotland. Edinburgh, 1732. f°.
Aristotelis. Rhetorica, edente Th. Goulston. Londini, 1696. 8m, 4°. unbound.
Abbadie (J.) Traité de la vérité de la religion Chrétienne. 2v. Rotterdam, 1715. 16°.
—— Traité de la divinité de . . . Christ. Rotterdam, 1709. 16°.
—— Le triomphe de la providence . . . 4v. Amsterdam, 1723. 16°.
Ames (W.) De conscientia et ejus jure . . . Amstelodami, 1631. 24 .
Amyraut (M.) Discours de l'estat des fideles aprés la mort. Sausuur, 1646. 8°.
Béze (T. de) Annotationes majores in Novum Testamentum. 2v. in 1. 8°. [no t.p.]
Bourignon (A.) The renovation of the gospel-spirit (From the) French. London, 1707. 8°.
Bartoli (D.) L'huomo al punto cioé l'huomo in punto di morte. Bologna, 1671. 24°.
Bates (W.) The harmony of the divine attributes . . . 4th ed. London, 1697. 8°.
Baxter (R.) The cure of church divisions . . .3rd ed. London, 1670. 16⁰.
—— Of the imputation of Christ's righteousness to believers . . . London, 1675. 16°.
Bellamy (J.) True religion delineated . . . Boston, 1750. 8°.
Patience (La) de Job selon l'historie de la Bible . . . Lyon, 1512. 16°.
Boistuau (P.) Le théatre du monde . . . Lyon, 1612. 16°.
Robert (A.) L'anti balladin . . .Lyon, 1611. 16⁹.
Benson (G.) The history of the first planting the Christian religion. 2v. London, 1735. 4°.
Paraphrase (a) . . . on the first epistle of St. Peter . . . [*anon.*] London, 1742. 4°.
Diodati (J.) Pious . . . annotations upon the holy Bible . . . London, 1643. 8°.
Cyprianus (T.C.) Opera . . . Adnotationes Pamelii . . . Ed. ultima. Coloniae, 1617. f°.
Justinus *martyr*. Opera . . . Ed. nova. Coloniae, 1686. f°.
Novum Testamentum Graecum . . .Recensuit L. Kusterus. Roterodami, 1710. f⁹.
Pearson (J.) An exposition of the creed. 11th ed. London, 1723. f°.
Burnet (G.) An exposition of the thirty-nine articles . . . 3rd ed. London, 1705. f°.
Erasmus (D.) In Novum Testamentum annotationes . . . Basileae, 1542. f°.
Calvin (J.) Praelectiones in duodecim prophetas . . .minores . . . Genevae, 1567. f⁹.
—— In librum Psalmorum . . . commentarius. [Parisiis], 1557. f°.
Ainsworth (H.) Annotations upon the five bookes of Moses . . . London, 1639. f°.

Baxter (R.) Practical works . . . 4v. London, 1707. f°.

Attempt (an) to explain the words reason, substance [tc.] . . . [*anon.*] London, 1766. 12°.

Binning (H.) Several sermons . . . Glasgow, 1760. 16°.

Blackburne (T.) Considerations on the controversy [of] protestants and papists. London, 1768. 8°.

Confessional (the) . . . in protestant churches . . . 2nd ed. [*anon.*] London, 1767. 8°.

Blackwell (A.) The sacred classics defended and illustrated. London, 1725. 4°.

Calamy (E.) Thirteen sermons concerning the Trinity . . . London, 1722. 8°.

Calderwood (D.) Altare Damascenum. Sou ecclesiae Anglicanae politia. Lugdum, 1708. 4°.

Castalion (S.) Dialogorum sacrorum libri IV . . . ed. 18no. Londini, 1750. 16°.

Chauncy (C.) A compleat view of episcopacy . . . Boston, 1771. fa. 8°.

Clarkson (D.) A discourse concerning liturgies. London, 1689. 16°.

Clarke (S.) A paraphrase on the four evangelists . . . 3rd ed. 2v. London, 1717. 8°.

Calvin (J.) In omnes . . .epistolas . . .commentarii . . .Parisiis, 1556. f°.

Bull (G.) Defensio fidei nicaenae, ex scriptis . . . Catholicorum . . . Oxonii, 1688. 8°.

Bullock (T.) The reasoning of Christ . . . in defence of Christianity . . . 3rd ed. London, 1730. 8°.

Burnet (T.) De statu mortuorum et resurgentium . . . Londini, 1726. 8°.

Burnet (G.) A discourse of the pastoral care. 3rd ed. London, 1713. 16°.

Butler (J.) Fifteen sermons preached at the rolls chapel . . . 2nd ed. London, 1729. 8°.

Claude (J.) L'examen de soi-même pour . . .la communion . . . Amsterdam, 1730. 24⁰.

Cave (W.) Primitive Christianity . . . 7th ed. London, 1714. 8°.

Cawdrey (D.) and Palmer (H.) Sabbatum redivivum . . . London, 1652. sm. 4°.

Chandler (T.B.) The appeal defended . . .in answer to . . .Chauncy . . . New York, 1769. 8⁰.

Collection (a) of discourses . . .against the . . .church of Rome . . . Edinburgh, 1687. p. 8⁰.

Rome . . . Edinburgh, 1687. p. 8°.

Scotland, Church of. A collection of confessions of faith, catechisms, (etc.) . . . 2v. Edinburgh, 1719-22. 16°.

Coles (E.) A practical discourse on God's sovereignty . . .7th ed. London, 1718. p. 8⁰.

Cooper (A.) An essay upon the chronology of the world . . . Edinburgh, 1722. 16°.

Daille (J.) Mélange de sermons. 2v. in 1. Amsteldam, 1658. 16°.

Daneaus (L.) Examen libri de duabus in Christo naturis . . . Genevae, 1581. 16°.

——— De tribus . . .quaestionibus . . .responsio triplex . . .Genevae, 1581. 16°. [Bound together with above.]

Ditton (H.) A discourse concerning the resurrection of Christ . . .2nd ed. London, 1714. 8°.

Dickson (D.) Therapeutica sacra: . . . concerning regeneration. 2nd ed. Edinburgh, 1697. 16°.

Doddridge (P.) The family expositor: . . . 3v. London, 1739-48. 4°.

——— Sermons on the religious education of children. 3rd ed. London, 1743. 12°.

Drelincourt (C.) Les visites charitables . . . 3v. in 2. Charenton, 1665-67. p. 8°.

Du Bosc (P.T.) Sermons sur divers textes . . . 2v. Rotterdam, 1692. p. 8°.

Legendre (P.) La vie de Pierre Du Bosc . . . eurichie de lettres . . . Rotterdam, 1694. 8°.

Du Moulin (P.) Traitté de la paix de l'ame . . . Charenton, 1663. p. 8°.

——— Defense de la foy catholique . . . 2v. in 1. Geneve, 1610-12. 24°.

Vray (le) iuge des differens entre . . . l'église . . . Rotterdam, 1614. 24°. [Bound together with above.]

Durham (J.) The dying man's testament to the church . . . (Ed.) by J. Carstares. Edinburgh, 1680. 16°.

——— The blessednesse of the death of these that die in the Lord . . . [London], 1682. 16°.

Essen (A.) Compendium theologiae dogmaticum . . . Ultrajecti, 1669. 8°.

Erskine (J.) Theological dissertations . . . London, 1765. 12°.

Estimate (an) of the profit and loss of religion . . . [anon.] Edinburgh, 1753. 8°.

Fisher (E.) The marrow of modern divinity. 14th ed. by T. Boston. Glasgow, 1752. 16°.

Alsop (V.) Melius inquirendum . . . 3rd ed. London, 1681. 8°.

Clarke (S.) A discourse concerning . . . God . . . and . . . revelation . . . 4th ed. London, 1716. 8°.

Blount (C.) Miscellaneous works. London, 1695. 8°.

Daillé (J.) XI, IX sermons upon . . . Colossians. 3 pts. in lv. London, 1672. f°.

Firmin (G.) The real Christian . . . London, 1670. sm. 4°.

Findlay (R.) A vindication of the sacred books . . . from . . . Voltaire. Glasgow, 1770. 8°.

Flavel (J.) Whole works. 7th ed. 2v. Edinburgh, 1762. f°.

Forbes (J.) Instructiones historico-theologicae . . . Amstelodami, 1645. f°.

Geier (M.) Proverbia . . . Salomonis, cum cura enucleata . . . Lipsiae, 1653. sm. 4°.

Grotius (H.) De veritate religionis Christianae. Ed. Novissima. Amstelodami, 1680. 24°.

Zinzendorf (N.F.) Maximus . . . out of . . . his . . . discourses. Extracted by J. Gambold. [anon.] London, 1751. 8°.

Gentleman (the) instructed, in the conduct of a . . . happy life . . . 6th ed. [*anon.*] London, 1716. 8°.

Marlorah (A.) *editor*. Genesis cum catholica expositione . . . [*anon.*] 2v. in 1. Morgiis, 1585. 8°.

Gilpin (R.) Daemonologia sacra . . . 3 pts. in lv. London, 1677, sm. 4°.

Government (the) of the tongue. [*anon.*] Oxford, 1674. 8°.

Grotius (H.) De veritate religionis Christianae. Ed. novissima. Amstelodami, 1662. 24°.

Hall (A.) An humble attempt to exhibit . . . the . . . gospel church. Edinburgh, 1769. 12°.

Henry (M.) A method for prayer . . . 3rd ed. London, 1712. 8°.

────── A discourse on meekness . . . [with] a sermon . . . 2nd ed. London, 1717. 16°.

Hervey (J.) Aspasio vindicated, and . . .imputed righteousness defended . . .Edinburgh, 1765. 12°.

Sandeman (R.) Letters on Theron and Aspasio . . . [*anon.*] 2v. Edinburgh, 1757. 12°.

Hildrop (J.) Miscellaneous works . . . 2v. London, 1754. 8°.

Hopkins (E.) The doctrine of the two covenants . . . London, 1712. 8°.

Howe (J.) The blessedness of the righteous opened . . . New ed. Glasgow, 1742. 8°.

────── A treatise of delighting in God . . . London, 1674. 8°.

────── The prosperous state of the Christian interest . . . [Ed.] by J. Evans. London, 1726. 8°.

Hunter (H.) Sacred biography: or, the history of the patriarchs . . . 2v. London, 1783-84. 8°.

Grotius (H.) The truth of the Christian religion . . . Done into English by J. Clarke. London, 1711. 12°.

La Placette (J.) La mort des justes . . . Amsterdam, 1695. 12°. The same 2 de. ed. 2v. Amsterdam, 1714. 16°.

Le Clerc (J.) De l'incrédulité . . . Amsterdam, 1714. 8°.

La Placette (J.) Eclaircissemens sur quelques difficultez . . . de la liberté [morale] . . . Amsterdam, 1709. 12°.

────── Traité de la foi divine . . . 2 de. éd. augmentée. 4v. Rotterdam, 1716. 16°.

────── Réponse à deux objections . . . sur l'ongine du mal et sure . . . la trinité . . . Amsterdam, 1707. 12°.

────── Traité de l'aumone . . . Amsterdam, 1699. 12°.

────── Divers traitées sur des matières de conscience . . . Amsterdam, 1697. 12°.

────── Réponse à une objection . . . Amsterdam, 1709. 12°.

────── Nouvelles réflexions sur la prémotion physique . . . La Haye, 1714. 12°. [Bound together with above.]

────── Nouveaux essais de morale . . . 2v. La Haye, 1715. 12°.

────── La communion devote . . . 7 me. éd. 2v. in 1 Amsterdam, 1716-17. 12°.

────── Traité de la restitution . . . Amsterdam, 1696. 12°.

────── Traité de l'orgueil. 2 de. éd. Amsterdam, 1700. 12°.

Larroque (M. de) Histoire de l'eucharistic . . . 2 de éd. Amsterdam, 1671. 16°.

Riccaltoun (R.) An inquiry into . . . letters on Theron and Aspasio . . . [anon.] Glasgow, 1762. 12°.

Jurieu (P.) Histoire critique des dogmes et des cultes . . . dans l'église . . . Amsterdam, 1704. 4°.

King (P.) The history of the apostles' creed . . . 3rd ed. [anon.] London, 1711. 8°.

Knight (J.) Eight sermons . . . in defence of the divinity of . . . Christ . . . London, 1721. 8°.

Knox (H.) Select sermons on interesting subjects. 2v. Glasgow, 1776. 12°.

Lardner (N.) The credibility of the gospel history . . . Part II. 4v. London, 1734-40. 8°.

Laurentius (J.) S. apostoli Petri epistola . . . posterior . . . commentario explicata . . . Amsteldami, 1641. sm. 4°.

Leighton (R.) Select works . . . Edinburgh, 1746. 8°.

Leland (J.) The advantage and necessity of the Christian revelation . . . 2v. London, 1768. 8°.

Locke (J.) A paraphrase and notes on the epistles . . . [anon.] 4th ed. London, 1742. 8°.

Lubbert (S.) De Jesu Christo servatore . . . Academia Franekerana Franecker, 611. 4°.

Hopkins (E.) Works . . . 3rd ed. London, 1710. f°.

Malebranche (N.) Traité de la nature et de la grace. Deruière éd. [anon.] Rotterdam, 1684. 12°.

———— Défense de l'auteur de la Recherche de la verité . . . [anon.] Rotterdam, 1684. 12°.

Marshall (W.) The gospel-mystery of sanctification opened . . . 10th ed. Glasgow, 1771. 16°.

M'Laurin (J.) Sermons and essays. [Ed.] by J. Gillies. Glasgow, 1755. 12°.

Pasor (G.) Lexicon Graeco-Latinum in . . .N. Testamentum . . . Postrema ed. Genevae. 1662. 8⁰.

Moses *ben Maimon*. De idolatria liber, cum interpretatione Latina . . . D. Vossii. Amsterdami, 1642. sm. 4°.

Minucius Felix (M.) Octavius, et C. Cypriani de idolar. vanitate. Nova ed. N. Rigaltii. Lutetiae, 1643. 8°.

Mistakes about religion, amongst the causes of our defection . . . [anon.] Edinburgh, 1737. 8⁰.

Muir (G.) An essay on Christ's cross and crown. [With] six sermons. 2nd ed. Paisley, 1769. 12°.

Nichols (W.) Defensio ecclesiae Anglicanae . . . ed. 2 da. Londini, 1712. 12°.

Le Blanc (L.) Theses theologicae . . . Londini, 1675. f°.

Limborch (P. van) Theologia Christiana . . . Ed. 4ta. Amstelaedami, 1715. f°.

Lowth (W.) A commentary upon the large and lesser prophets . . . London, 1727. f°.

Peirce (J.) Vindiciae fratrum dissentientium in Anglia . . . Londini, 1710. 8°.

Millar (R.) The history of the propagation of Christianity . . . 2v. Edinburgh, 1723. 8°.

Hildesley (M.) Plain instructions for young persons in . . . the Christian religion . . . [anon.] London, 1762. 8°.

Poiret (P.) L'occonomie divine . . . 7v. Amsterdam, 1687. 12°.

Earle (J.) and others. Practical discourses of singing in the worship of God . . . London, 1708. 12°.

Liverpool. Unitarian Church. A form of prayer, and a new collection of psalms . . . London, 1763. 8°.

Reynolds (T.) and others. Practical discourses upon reading the scriptures. London, 1717. 12°.

Pictet (B.) La théologie Chrétienne . . . 2v. Nlle. éd. Genève, 1708. 4°.

Peirce (J.) A paraphrase . . . on Colossians, Philippians and Hebrews . . . 2nd ed. London, 1733. 4°.

Baker (T.) Reflections upon learning . . . 5th ed. [anon.] London, 1714. 8°.

Renoult (J.B.) Histoire des variations de l'église Gallicane . . . Amsterdam, 1703. 8°.

Ross (A.) παντε βεια: or, a view of all religions in the world . . . 6th ed. London, 1696. 8°.

Fontaine (N.) L'histoire du Vieux et du Nouveau Testament . . . [anon.] Paris, 1697. 12°.

Richelet (P.) editor. Les plus belles lettres Francoises . . . avec des notes. 4 me. ed. 3v. La Haye, 1708. 12°.

Petitdidier (M.) Apologie desoletires provinciales . . . (anon) 2v. Rouen, 1698. 12°.

Fontenelle (B.L. de) Nouveaux dialogues des morts. Nlle. ed. Amsterdam, n.d. 12°.

Balzac (J.L.G. de) Oeuvres. Dernière éd. 2v. in 1. Rouen, 1657. 12°.

France (N.) Dialoghi piacevolissimi. Venezia, 1590. 8°.

Belligarde (J.B.M. de). Reflexions sur le ridicule . . . 7me. éd. Amsterdam, 1707. 12°.

Whole (the) duty of man . . . [anon.] London, 1741. 18°.

Quick (J.) Synodicon in Gallia reformata . . . London, 1692. 2v. f°. (v. II wanting.)

Sainte (la) Bible traduite en Francois . . . Nlle. éd. 2v. Anvers, 1717. f°.

Spurstowe (W.) The wells of salvation opened . . . London, 1655. 8°.

Sarpi (P.) Traité des bénéfices. 3md. éd. Amsterdam, 1692. 12°.

Alsop (V.) Anti-sozzo, sive Sherlocismus enervatus . . . [anon.] London, 1675. 8°.

Seed (J.) Discourses on several important subjects . . . 2nd ed. 2v. London, 1745. 8°.

Sherlock (W.) A discourse concerning the divine providence. 5th ed. London, 1715. 8°.

Sherlock (T.) The use and intent of prophecy . . . 3rd ed. London, 1732. 8°.

Sherlock (W.) A discourse concerning the happiness of good men . . . in the next world . . . 3rd ed. London, 1719. 8°.

Shuckford (S.) The sacred and prophane history of the world connected . . . 2nd ed. 3v. London, 1731-40. 8°.

Scripture's (the) sufficiency demonstrated . . . [with] Clarke's Promises of scripture . . . [anon.] 2nd ed. London, 1769. 12°.

Scriptural life . . . [anon.] Edinburgh, 1727. 12°.

Werenfels (S.) Sermons sur des vérités importantes . . . 4me éd. Amsterdam, 1723. 8°.

Stillingfleet (E.) Irenicum . . . The divine right of particular forms of church-government . . . 2nd ed. London, 1662. sm. 4°.

Stillingfleet (J.) Shecinah: or, a demonstration of the divine presence in . . . religious worship . . . London, 1663. 8°.

Schmidt (E.) Novi Testamenti . . . Graeci . . . ταμειον . . . ed. E.S. Cyprianus. Gothae, 1717. f°.

Scott (J.) Works . . . 2v. London, 1718. f°.

Tracts concerning patronage . . . [anon.] Edinbugh, 1770. 12°.

Sherlock (W.) A practical discourse concerning a future judgment. 8th ed. London, 1717. 8°.

Simson (J.) The case of J. Simson . . . Glasgow, 1715. 8°. The same 2nd ed. Edinburgh, 1727. 8°.

Dundas (J.) editor. State of the processes . . . against J. Simson . . . Edinburgh, 1728. 8°.

Ursinus (Z.) Corpus doctrinae Christianae . . . Studio D. Parei. Genevae, 1623. 8°.

Spanheim (T.) Opera. Lugdimi Batavorum, 1701-03. 3v. in 2. f°. [v. II. and III. wanting.]

Weile (T.R.V.) Theatrum lucidum, exhibens verum Messiam . . . Amstelodami, 1671. 12°.

Walker (T.) Essays and sermons on doctrinal and practical subjects. Edinburgh, 1782. 8°.

Walker (T.) A vindication of the discipline and constitutions of the church of Scotland . . . Edinburgh, 1774. 8°.

Warburton (W.) The principles of . . . religion . . . explained; in a course of sermons . . . 2v. London, 1753-54. 8°. [v. II. wanting.]

Waterland (D.) Eight sermons . . . in defense of the divinity of . . . Christ . . . London, 1720. 8°.

——— A vindication of Christ's divinity . . . 3rd ed. Cambridge [Eng.], 1720. 8°.

Wilkins (J.) A discourse concerning the gift of prayer . . . London, 1674. 8°. The same. 9th ed. London, 1718. 8°.

Wishart (W.) Discourses on several subjects. London, 1753. 12°.

Wyttenbach (D.A.) Tentamen theologiae dogmaticae . . . 3v. Francofurti, 1747-49. 8°.

N . . . (S.) A concordance to the holy scriptures . . . 3rd ed. Cambridge [Eng.], 1682. f°.

Hosius (S.) Confutatio prolegomenon Brentii . . . Ultima aed. Antverpiae, 1571. f°.

Trustees of the widow's fund of the Church of Scotland. An account of

the . . . fund . . . Edinburgh, 1759. f°.
Calvin (J.) Institutionum Christianae religionis libri quatuor. Ed. postrema . . . Lugduni, 1654. f°.
Toussain (R.) Inde in sacra Biblia . . . Hanoviae, 1624. f°.
Biblia Hebraica, cum Novo . . . Testamento, eorundem Latina interpretatio X. Pagnini . . . Genevae, 1619. f°.
Walther (R.) In Acta apostolorum . . . homiliae CLXXV. Tiguri, 1580. f°.
――――In Pauli . . . epistolam ad Romanos homiliae. Tiguri, 1580. f°. [Bound together with above.]
Hemming (N.) Commentarii inomnes epistolas . . . Lipsiae, 1572. f°.
Calvin (J.) Opera omnia theologica . . .7v. Genevae, 1617. f⁰. [v. I. only.]
Saint Amour (L.G. de) Journal . . . concerning . . . Jansenists and Molinists. Rendered only of French. London, 1664. f°.
History of the republick of Holland. London, 1703. 8°.

Works Cited and Selected Bibliography

PRIMARY SOURCES

1. Manuscript Collections

Newark, N.J. New Jersey Historical Society. Witherspoon Papers.
New York. New York City Public Library. Letters, Emmet Collection.
Philadelphia. Presbyterian Historical Society. Witherspoon Papers.
Princeton, N.J. Princeton University Library. Witherspoon Papers.
Washington, D.C. Library of Congress. Papers of John Witherspoon.

2. Intellectual Writings of the Seventeenth and Eighteenth Centuries

Baxter, Andrew. *Enquiry into the Nature of the Human Soul*. London, 1730.

Beattie, James. *An Essay on the Nature and Immutability of Truth in Opposition to Sophistry and Scepticism*. 5th ed. London, 1774.

Bolingbroke, Henry St. John, Viscount. *The Works of Lord Bolingbroke*. Edited by David Mallet. 5 vols. London, 1754.

Brown, John. *Essays on the Characteristics*. London, 1752.

Burlamaqui, Jean Jacques. *The Principles of Natural and Politic Law*. Translated by Mr. Nugent. 2 vols. 2d ed. London, 1763.

Butler, Joseph. *Fifteen Sermons Preached at the Rolls Chapel—to which are added Six Sermons Preached on Publick Occasions*. 4th ed. London, 1749.

———. *The Works of Joseph Butler, D.C.L.* Edited by W. E. Gladstone. 2 vols. Oxford, 1896.

Calvin, John. *Institutionum Christianae Religionis*. London, 1654.

Campbell, Archibald. *An Enquiry into the Original of Moral Virtue . . . Against the Author of The Fable of the Bees*. Edinburgh, 1733.

Clarke, Samuel. *A Discourse Concerning the Being and Attributes of God, The Obligations of Natural Religion, and the Truth and Certainty of the Christian Revelation*. 4th ed. London, 1716. 8th ed. London, 1732.

Cudworth, Ralph. *The True Intellectual System of the Universe.* London, 1743.

Edwards, Jonathan. *The Works of President Edwards.* Edited by Sereno E. Dwight. 10 vols. New York, 1830.

Endemann, Samuel. *Institutiones Theologicae Dogmaticae.* Hanover, 1777-78.

Ferguson, Adam. *An Essay on the History of Civil Society.* Edinburgh, 1767.

Filmer, Robert. *Political Discourses . . .viz. Patriarcha, or the Natural Power of Kings.* London, 1680.

Grotius, Hugo. *De jure belli ac pacis libri tres (On the Law of War and Peace).* Amsterdam, 1646.

Hamilton, Alexander; Jay, John; and Madison, James. *The Federalist: A Commentary on the Constitution of the United States.* Edited by Paul Leicester Ford. New York, 1898.

————. *The Federalist.* 2 vols. New York, 1788.

Hobbes, Thomas. *The English Works of Thomas Hobbes.* Edited by William Molesworth. 11 vols. London, 1839-45.

Home, Henry (Lord Kames). *Essays on the Principles of Morality and Natural Religion.* Edinburgh, 1751.

Hume, David. *Dialogues Concerning Natural Religion.* Edited by N. Kemp Smith. Oxford: The Clarendon Press, 1935.

————. *An Enquiry Concerning Human Understanding.* London, 1748.

————. *Enquiry Concerning the Principles of Morals.* London, 1751.

————. *Essays, Moral, Political, and Literary.* Edited by T. H. Green and T. H. Grosse. 2 vols. London, 1875.

————. *Philosophical Works.* Edited by T. H. Green and T. H. Grosse. 4 vols. London, 1874-75.

Hutcheson, Francis. *An Inquiry into the Original of Our Ideas of Beauty and Virtue.* London, 1725.

————. *A Short Introduction to Moral Philosophy, in Three Books; Containing the Elements of Ethicks and the Law of Nature.* Translated from the Latin. Glasgow, 1747.

————. *A System of Moral Philosophy.* 2 vols. London, 1755.

Leechman, William. *The Nature, Reasonableness and Advantages of Prayer.* Glasgow, 1743.

Leland, John. *The Advantage and Necessity of the Christian Revelation in the Ancient Heathen World . . .* 2 vols. London, 1764.

————. *A View of the Principal Deistical Writers That Have Appeared in England in the Last and Present Century.* 3 vols. London, 1754-56.

Locke, John. *An Essay Concerning Human Understanding.* 4th ed. London, 1700.

————. *A Letter Concerning Toleration.* London, 1689.

————. *Two Tracts on Government.* Edited by Philip Abrams. Cambridge: At the University Press, 1967.

————. *Two Treatises of Government*. A critical edition with an introduction and apparatus criticus by Peter Laslett. Cambridge: At the Unversity Press, 1967.

————. *The Works of John Locke*. 9 vols. 12th ed. London, 1824.

Mandeville, Bernard de. *The Fable of the Bees; or, Private Vices, Publick Benefits*. London, 1714.

Mather, Cotton. *Manuductio ad Ministerium: Directions for a Candidate of the Ministry*. Boston, 1726.

————. *Reasonable Religion: Or, the Truths of the Christian Religion Demonstrated with Incontestable Proofs, that those who would Act Reasonably must Live Religiously*. London, 1713.

Montesquieu, Charles Louis de Secendat. *The Causes of the Grandeur and Declension of the Romans*. London, 1734.

————. *De l'Esprit des lois (The Spirit of Laws)*. Translated by Mr. Nugent. London, 1750.

Polansdorf, Amandus Polanus a. *Syntagma Theologiae Christianiae*. 2 vols. Hanover, 1624.

Pufendorf, Samuel. *The Law of Nature and Nations*. Translated by J. Spavan. 2 vols. London, 1716.

Reid, Thomas. *An Inquiry into the Human Mind, on the Principles of Common Sense*. Edinburgh, 1764.

Riccaltoun, Robert. *An Inquiry into Letters on Theron and Aspasio*. Glasgow, 1762.

Shaftesbury, Anthony A. Cooper, Third Earl of. *Characteristics of Men, Manners, Opinions, and Times*. 3 vols. London, 1711.

Smith, Adam. *The Theory of Moral Sentiments*. London, 1759.

Wollaston, William. *The Religion of Nature Delineated*. London, 1722.

3. Other Published Material

Adams, John. *Diary and Autobiography*. Edited by L. H. Butterfield. 4 vols. Cambridge, Mass. Harvard University Press, Belknap Press, 1961.

————. *The Works of John Adams, Second President of the United States: With a Life of the Author, Notes and Illustrations*. Edited by Charles Francis Adams. 10 vols. Boston: Little, Brown & Co., 1856.

Boudinot, Elias. *Journal of Historical Recollections of American Events During the Revolutionary War*. Philadelphia: F. Bourquin, 1894.

Butterfield, L. H., ed. *John Witherspoon Comes to America*. Princeton, N.J. Princeton University Library, 1953.

Carlyle, Alexander. *The Autobiography of Dr. Alexander Carlyle of Inveresk, 1722-1805*. Edited by John Hill Burton. London: T. N. Foulis, 1910.

Dexter, Franklin Bowditch, ed. *The Literary Diary of Ezra Stiles*. 3 vols. New York: C. Scribner's Sons, 1901.

Force, Peter, ed. *American Archives*. 4th ser., vol. 5. Washington,

D.C.: Prepared and Published under Authority of an Act of Congress, 1844.

Ford, Worthington Chauncey, ed. *Warren-Adams Letters; Being Chiefly a Correspondence Among John Adams, Samuel Adams, and James Warren . . . 1743-1814.* 2 vols. Vols. 72 and 73 of the Collections of the Massachusetts Historical Society. Boston: Massachusetts Historical Society, 1917-25.

General Catalogue of Princeton University, 1746-1906. Preface written by Varnum Lansing Collins. Princeton, N.J.: Princeton University, 1908.

Horn, David Bayne and Ransome, Mary, eds. *English Historical Documents, 1714-1783.* Vol. 10 of *English Historical Documents.* Edited by David C. Douglas. London: Eyre and Spottiswoode, 1957.

Mills, W. Jay. ed. *Glimpses of Colonial Society and the Life at Princeton College, 1766-1773,* by one of the class of 1763. Philadelphia: J. B. Lippincott Co., 1903.

Morison, Samuel Eliot, ed. *Sources and Documents Illustrating the American Revolution, 1764-1788, and the Formation of the Federal Constitution.* Oxford: Clarendon Press, 1929.

Morren, Nathaniel, ed. *Annals of the General Assembly of the Church of Scotland From. . .1739 to. . .1766, with An Appendix of Biographical Sketches, Illustrative Documents and Notes.* 2 vols. Edinburgh: Johnstone, 1838-40.

Records of the Presbyterian Church in the United States of America. Philadelphia: Presbyterian Board of Publication, 1841.

Smith, Samuel Stanhope. *The Lectures correct and improved, which have been delivered for a series of years in the College of New Jersey, on the subjects of moral and political Philosophy.* Trenton, N.J.: D. Fenton, 1812.

Whitehead, William A., et al. *Archives of the State of New Jersey.* Newark, N.J.: Printed at the Daily Journal Establishment, 1880-present.

Witherspoon, John. *Lectures on Moral Philosophy.* 2d ed. Philadelphia: William W. Woodward, 1822.

——. *Lectures on Moral Philosophy.* Edited by Varnum Lansing Collins. Princeton, N.J.: Princeton University Press, 1912.

——. *The Works of The Rev. John Witherspoon.* 4 vols. 1st ed. Philadelphia: William W. Woodward, 1800-1801.

——. *The Works of John Witherspoon.* 9 vols. 3d ed. Edinburgh: Printed for Ogle and Aikman, 1804-5.

SECONDARY SOURCES

1. *Works on Witherspoon and Princeton*

Blair, Samuel. *An Account of the College*. Woodbridge, N.J.: Printed by James Parker, 1764.

Collins, Varnum Lansing. *The Continental Congress at Princeton*. Princeton, N.J.: The University Library, 1908.

———. *Early Princeton Printing*. Princeton, N.J.: Princeton University Press, 1911.

———. *President Witherspoon: A Biography*. 2 vols. Princeton, N.J.: Princeton University Press, 1925.

———. *Princeton*. New York: Oxford University Press, 1914.

———. *Princeton, Past and Present*. Princeton, N.J.: Princeton University Press, 1931.

Dodds, Harold W. *John Witherspoon 1723-1794*. Address delivered on April 26, 1944, to the Newcomen Society. Princeton, N.J.: Princeton University Press, 1944.

Green, Ashbel. "The Life of the Reverend John Witherspoon, D.D. LL.D., With a Brief Review of His Writing; and a Summary Estimate of His Character and Talents." MS. Newark, N.J.: New Jersey Historical Society, n.d.

McCosh, James. *John Witherspoon and His Times*. Philadelphia: Presbyterian Board of Publication, 1890.

Maclean, John. *History of the College of New Jersey*. 2 vols. Philadelphia: J. B. Lippincott, 1877.

Pomfret, John Edwin. "Witherspoon, John (1723-1794)." *Dictionary of American Biography*. Edited by Dumas Malone. Vol. 20. New York: Charles Scribner's Sons, 1936.

Rice, Howard Crosby. *The Rittenhouse Orrery: Princeton's Eighteenth-Century Planetarium, 1767-1954*. Princeton, N.J.: Princeton University Library, 1954.

Schmidt, George P. *Princeton and Rutgers: The Two Colonial Colleges of New Jersey*. New Jersey Historical Series, vol. 5. Princeton, N.J.: Van Nostrand, 1964.

Thorp, Willard, ed. *The Lives of Eighteen From Princeton*. Princeton, N.J.: Princeton University Press, 1946.

Wertenbaker, Thomas Jefferson. *Princeton, 1746-1896*. Princeton, N.J.: Princeton University Press, 1946.

Woods, David Walker, Jr. *John Witherspoon*. New York: F. H. Revell Co., 1906.

2. *Works on Intellectual History*

Becker, Carl Lotus. *The Heavenly City of the Eighteenth-Century Philosophers.* New Haven, Conn.: Yale University Press, 1932.

Blackstone, William T. *Francis Hutcheson and Contemporary Ethical Theory.* Athens, Ga.: University of Georgia Press, 1965.

Blau, Joseph L. *Men and Movements in American Philosophy.* Englewood Cliffs, N.J.: Prentice-Hall, Inc., 1952.

Brett, R. L. *The Third Earl of Shaftesbury: A Study in Eighteenth-Century Literary Theory.* London: Hutchinson's University Library, 1951.

Cassirer, Ernst. *The Philosophy of the Enlightenment.* Translated by Fritz C. A. Koelin and James P. Pettigrove. Boston: Beacon Press, 1951.

Clough, Wilson Ober. *Intellectual Origins of American National Thought.* New York: Corinth Books, 1961.

Cohen, Morris R. *American Thought: A Critical Sketch.* Glencoe, Ill.: Free Press, 1954.

Cragg, Gerald Robertson. *Reason and Authority in the Eighteenth Century.* Cambridge: At the University Press, 1964.

Davies, Hugh Sykes and Watson, George, eds. *The English Mind: Studies in the English Moralists Presented to Basil Willey.* Cambridge: At the University Press, 1964.

Ferguson, John. *Moral Values in the Ancient World.* London: Barnes & Noble, 1958.

Fowler, Thomas. *Shaftesbury and Hutcheson.* London: Sampson Low, Marston, Searle and Revington, 1882.

Gough, J. W. *The Social Contract: A Critical Study of its Development.* Oxford: Clarendon Press, 1936.

Grave, S. A. *The Scottish Philosophy of Common Sense.* Oxford: Clarendon Press, 1960.

Grean, Stanley. *Shaftesbury's Philosophy of Religion and Ethics: A Study in Enthusiasm.* Athens, Ohio: Ohio University Press, 1967.

Hanham, H. J. *The Scottish Political Tradition. An Inaugural Lecture Delivered Before the University of Edinburgh on February 26, 1964.* Edinburgh: University of Edinburgh, 1964.

Harvey, Ray Forrest. *Jean Jacques Burlamaqui: A Liberal Tradition in American Constitutionalism.* Chapel Hill, N.C.: University of North Carolina Press, 1937.

Hearnshaw, F. J. C., ed. *The Social and Political Ideas of Some English Thinkers of the Augustan Age, A.D. 1650–1750.* New York: G. G. Harrap & Co., Ltd., 1928.

Hunt, George L., ed. *Calvinism and the Political Order.* Philadelphia: Westminster Press, 1965.

Lamprecht, Sterling Power. *The Moral and Political Philosophy of John Locke.* New York: Russell & Russell, 1962.

Laurie, Henry. *Scottish Philosophy in its National Development.* Glasgow: J. Maclehose & Sons, 1902.

Lovejoy, A. O. *Reflections on Human Nature*. Baltimore, Md.: Johns Hopkins Press, 1961.

McCosh, James. *The Scottish Philosophy: Biographical, Expository, Critical From Hutcheson to Hamilton*. New York: R. Carter, 1875.

MacLeod, John. *Scottish Theology in Relation to Church History Since the Reformation*. Edinburgh: Publications Committee of the Free Church of Scotland, 1943.

Miller, Perry. *Errand Into the Wilderness*. Cambridge, Mass.: Harvard University Press, Belknap Press, 1956.

———. *Jonathan Edwards*. New York: Meridian Books, 1949.

Mossner, Ernest Campbell. *Bishop Butler and the Age of Reason: A Study in the History of Thought*. New York: Macmillan Co., 1936.

Niebuhr, Reinhold, *The Children of Light and the Children of Darkness*. New York: C. Scribner's Sons. 1944.

Orr, John. *English Deism: Its Roots and Its Fruits*. Grand Rapids, Mich.: Eerdmans, 1934.

Parrington, Vernon Louis. *The Colonial Mind (1620-1800)*. Vol. 1 of *Main Currents in American Thought*. New York: Harcourt, Brace & Co., 1927.

Riley, I. Woodbridge. *American Philosophy, The Early Schools*. New York: Dodd, Mead & Co., 1907.

———. *American Thought From Puritanism to Pragmatism and Beyond*. New York: Henry Holt & Co., 1923.

Roche, John P., ed. *Origins of American Political Thought: Selected Readings*. New York: Harper & Row, 1967.

Schlesinger, Arthur M., Jr. and White, Morton M., eds. *Paths of American Thought*. Boston: Houghton Mifflin Co., 1963.

Schneider, Herbert Wallace. *A History of American Philosophy*. New York: Columbia University Press, 1946.

——— and Scheider, C., eds. *Samuel Johnson, President of King's College*. 4 vols. New York: Columbia University Press, 1929.

Sidgwick, Henry. *Outlines of the History of Ethics for English Reuders*. London: Macmillan & Co., 1949.

Sorley, William Ritchie. *A History of English Philosophy*. Cambridge: At the University Press, 1920.

Stephen, Leslie. *History of English Thought in the Eighteenth Century*. 3d ed. 2 vols. New York: Peter Smith, 1949.

Strauss, Leo. *The Political Philosophy of Hobbes, Its Basis and Genesis*. Translated by Elsa M. Sinclair. Chicago: University of Chicago Press, 1952.

Swabey, William Curtis. *Ethical Theory From Hobbes to Kant*. New York: Philosophical Library, 1961.

Thompson, Clifford Griffeth. *The Ethics of William Wollaston*. Boston: R. G. Badger, 1922.

Townsend, Harvey Gates. *Philosophical Ideas in the United States*. New York: American Book, 1934.

Willey, Basil. *The English Moralists.* London: Chatto and Windus, 1964.

Zeller, Eduard. *Outlines of the History of Greek Philosophy.* Translated by L. R. Palmer. Revised by Wilhelm Nestle. 13th ed. New York: Harcourt, Brace & Co., 1931.

3. Works on the American Revolution

Andrews, Charles M. *The Colonial Background of the American Revolution: Four Essays in American Colonial History.* Rev. ed. New Haven, Conn.: Yale University Press, 1931.

Bailyn, Bernard. *The Ideological Origins of the American Revolution.* Cambridge, Mass.: Harvard University, Belknap Press. 1967.

Baldwin, Alice M. *The New England Clergy and the American Revolution.* Durham, N.C.: Duke University, 1928.

Becker, Carl Lotus. *The Declaration of Independence.* New York: Harcourt, Brace & Co., 1922.

Billias, George Athan, ed. *The American Revolution: How Revolutionary Was It?* American Problem Series. New York: Holt, Rinehart & Winston, Inc., 1965.

Bridenbaugh, Carl. *Mitre and Sceptre: Transatlantic Faiths, Ideas, Personalities, and Politics, 1689-1775.* New York: Oxford University Press, 1962.

Brown, Robert E. *Middle-Class Democracy and the Revolution in Massachusetts, 1691-1780.* Ithaca, N.Y.: Cornell University Press, 1955.

Colbourn, H. Trevor. *The Lamp of Experience: Whig History and the Intellectual Origins of the American Revolution.* Chapel Hill, N.C.: University of North Carolina Press, 1965.

Cross, Arthur Lyon. *The Anglican Episcopate and the American Colonies.* New York: Longmans, Green & Co., 1902.

Davidson, Philip Grant. *Propaganda and the American Revolution, 1763-1783.* Chapel Hill, N.C.: University of North Carolina Press, 1941.

Gipson, Lawrence H. *The Coming of the Revolution, 1763-1775.* The New American Nation Series. Edited by Henry Steele Commager and Richard B. Morris. New York: Harper, 1954.

Greene, Evarts Boutell. *The Revolutionary Generation, 1763-1790.* Vol. 4 of *A History of American Life.* Edited by Arthur M. Schlesinger and Dixon Ryan Fox. New York: Macmillan Co., 1943.

Greene, Jack P., ed. *The Reinterpretation of the American Revolution, 1763-1789.* New York: Harper & Row, 1968.

Howe, John R., Jr. *The Role of Ideology in the American Revolution.* American Problem Studies. New York: Holt, Rinehart & Winston, Inc., 1970.

Jameson, J. Franklin. *The American Revolution Considered as a Social Movement.* Princeton, N.J.: Princeton University Press, 1926.

Jensen, Merrill. *The Articles of Confederation; An Interpretation of the Social-constitutional History of the American Revolution, 1774-1781.* Madison, Wis.: University of Wisconsin Press, 1948.

Kemmerer, Donald L. *Path to Freedom: The Struggle for Self-Government in Colonial New Jersey, 1703-1776.* Princeton, N.J.: Princeton University Press, 1940.

McCormick, Richard P. *Experiment in Independence in New Jersey in the Critical Period 1781-1789.* New Brunswick, N.J.: Rutgers University Press, 1950.

Miller, John C. *Origins of the American Revolution.* Boston: Little, Brown & Co., 1943.

Morgan, Edmund S. *The Birth of the Republic, 1763-1789.* The Chicago History of American History of American Civilization. Edited by Daniel J. Boorstin. Chicago: University of Chicago Press, 1956.

—— and Morgan, Helen M. *The Stamp Act Crisis: Prologue to Revolution.* Chapel Hill, N.C.: University of North Carolina Press, 1953.

Morris, Richard B. *The American Revolution Reconsidered.* New York: Harper & Row, 1967.

Oliver, Peter. *Origin and Progress of the American Rebellion: A Tory View.* Edited by Douglass Adair and John A. Schutz. San Marino, Calif.: Huntington Library, 1961.

Robbins, Caroline. *The Eighteenth-Century Commonwealth: Studies in the Transmission, Development and Circumstances of English Liberal Thought From the Restoration of Charles II Until the War with the Thirteen Colonies.* Cambridge, Mass.: Harvard University Press, 1959.

Rossiter, Clinton. *Seedtime of the Republic: The Origin of the American Tradition of Political Liberty.* New York: Harcourt, Brace & Co., 1953.

Schlesinger, Arthur M. *The Colonial Merchants and the American Revolution, 1763-1776.* New York: Columbia University Press, 1918.

——. *Prelude to Independence: The Newspaper War, 1764-1776.* New York: Knopf, 1957.

Thornton, John Wingate. *The Pulpit of the American Revolution.* Boston: Sheldon and Company, 1860.

Trevelyan, George Otto. *The American Revolution* 3 vols. New York: Longmans, Green and Co., 1899-1907.

Tyler, Moses Coit. *The Literary History of the American Revolution, 1763-1783.* New York: Barnes & Noble, 1941.

4. *Other Secondary Works*

Armstrong, M. W.; Loetscher, L. A.; and Anderson, C. A., eds. *The Presbyterian Enterprise*: Sources of American Presbyterian History. Philadelphia: Westminster Press, 1956.

Boykin, Edward, ed. *The Wisdom of Thomas Jefferson.* New York: Doubleday & Co., 1941.

Brant, Irving. *James Madison.* 6 vols. Indianapolis, Ind.: Bobbs-Merrill Co., 1941–present.

Breed, William Pratt. *Presbyterians and the Revolution*. Philadelphia: Presbyterian Board of Publication, 1876.

Cunningham, John. *The Church History of Scotland, From the Commencement of the Christian Era to the Present Century*. 2 vols. Edinburgh: J. Thin, 1859.

Dalzel, Andrew. *History of the University of Edinburgh*. Edinburgh: Edmonston and Douglas, 1862.

Fisher, Edgar Jacob. *New Jersey as a Royal Province From 1738 to 1776*. New York: Columbia University, Longmans, Green & Co. Agents, 1911.

Foote, William Henry. *Sketches of Virginia*. Philadelphia: William S. Martin, 1850.

Grant, Alexander, *The Story of the University of Edinburgh During Its First Three Hundred Years*. 2 vols. London: Longmans, Green & Co., 1884.

Haddow, Anna. *Political Science in American Colleges and Universities, 1639-1900*. Edited with an introduction and concluding chapter by William Anderson. New York: Appleton-Century, 1939.

Heppe, Heinrich. *Reformed Dogmatics Set Out and Illustrated From the Sources*. Foreword by Karl Barth. Revised and edited by Ernst Bizer. Translated by G. T. Thomson. London: Allen and Unwin, 1950.

Hofstadter, Richard and Smith, Wilson, eds. *American Higher Education: A Documentary History*. 2 vols. Chicago: University of Chicago Press, 1961.

Humphrey, Edward Frank. *Nationalism and Religion in America, 1774-1789*. New York: Russell & Russell, 1965.

Johnson, Samuel. *A Dictionary of the English Language*. 2 vols. London: Printed by W. Strahan, 1755.

Morison, Samuel Eliot. *The Founding of Harvard College*. Cambridge, Mass.: Harvard University Press, 1935.

Pomfret, John Edwin. *The New Jersey Proprietors and Their Lands, 1664-1776*. Princeton, N.J.: Van Nostrand, 1964.

Pryde, George S. *Scotland From 1603 to the Present Day*. Vol. 2 of *A New History of Scotland* edited by William Croft Dickinson and George S. Pryde. 2 vols. London: T. Nelson, 1962.

Richardson, Lyon N. *A History of Early American Magazines*. New York: Nelson, 1931.

Stephen, Leslie and Lee, Sidney, eds. *Dictionary of National Biography*. 63 vols. London: Smith, Elder, 1885-1901.

Sweet, William Warren. *Religion in the Development of American Culture, 1765-1840*. New York: Scribner, 1952.

Taylor, William M. *The Scottish Pulpit From the Reformation to the Present Day*. New York: Harper and Brothers, 1887.

Trinterud, Leonard J. *The Forming of an American Tradition: A Reexamination of Colonial Presbyterian*. Philadelphia: Westminster Press, 1949.

Walsh, James Joseph. *Education of the Founding Fathers of the Repub-

lic: Scholasticism in the Colonial Colleges. New York: Fordham University Press, 1935.

5. *Articles*

Ahlstrom, Sydney E. "The Scottish Philosophy and American Theology." *Church History* 24 (September 1955): 1–18.

Baldwin, Alice M. "Sowers of Sedition: The Political Theories of Some of the New Light Presbyterian Clergy of Virginia and North Carolina." *William and Mary Quarterly* 5 (January 1948): 52-76.

Ford, P. L. "The Authorship of Plain Truth." *Pennsylvania Magazine of History and Biography* 12 (1888-89): 421-24.

Greene, Jack P. "Political Mimesis: A Consideration of the Historical and Cultural Roots of Legislative Behavior in the British Colonies in the Eighteenth Century." *The American Historical Review* 75 (December 1969): 337-60.

Nichols, James Hasting. "John Witherspoon on Church and State." *Journal of Presbyterian History* 42 (September 1964): 166-74.

Robinson, Stewart MacMaster. "Notes on the Witherspoon Pamphlets." *Princeton University Library Chronicle* 27 (Autumn 1965): 53–59.

Smylie, James H. "Madison and Witherspoon: Theological Roots of American Political Thought." *The Princeton University Library Chronicle* 22 (Spring 1961): 118-32.

Index of Subjects

American Revolution, 13-24; Boston Massacre, 13-14; Boston Tea Party, 16; Continental Congress, 17-24; Declaration of Independence, 22-23; Lexington hostilities, 17; Revolutionary activities of Princeton students, 13-16; Stamp Act, 13
Aristocracy, 142-44, 146

Calvinism, 38-41, 46-50, 85-86, 88-89, 108, 129-30, 148
Civil Society, 140-47
Contracts, 43, 168-73

Declaration of Independence, 1, 22-23
Democracy, 142-44, 146
Depravity, 37, 39, 48-50, 60, 66, 148
Epicureanism, 187-88
Epistemology, 30-34, 70-76
Ethics, 30, 34-8, 95-121

God, duty to, 103-7, moral perfections of, 102-3; natural perfections of, 98-99; proof of, 95-98

Idealism, 30-32, 73-74, 76
Just War theory, 43, 151-56
Jurisprudence, 159-65

Law of nations, 43, 150-56
Lectures on Moral Philosophy, Analysis, 25-53; Circulation, 51-52; Influence, 51-52; Nature, 1-2; Text, 64-188

Marriage, 135-33
Monarchy, 142-44, 146
Moral duty to man, 109-12

Moral duty to ourselves, 114-16
Moral philosophy, 25-26, 64-66, 186-87
Moral sense theory, 35-38, 78-81

Oaths, 43, 176-78

Political theory, 40-50, 122-85
Prayer, 106-7
Property, 126-28, 178-79

Recapitulation, 186-88
Relation of master and servant, 136
Relation of parents and children, 135-36
Religious freedom, 159-61, 166
Resistance, right of, 15, 46-47, 145-46
Rights, 110-112, 179-82

Scottish Common Sense philosophy, 27, 31, 33-34, 50-51, 96-97
Slavery, 45, 59, 125-26, 137
Social contract, 28-29, 45-46, 75, 122-25, 128-130, 140-41, 145
Society of Dissenters, 11
Stoicism, 107-8, 116, 187-88
Synod of New York and Philadelphia, 10-12, 18-19, 24-25

Virtue, 83-94, 115-16, 186-87

Whiggism, 27, 41-42, 44-45, 50, 58-59
Witherspoon, John, American Presbyterianism, 10-12, 18-19, 24-25; American Revolution, 16-24; Continental Congress, 22-24; early life in Scotland, 3; Evangelical-Moderate dispute, 4-7; later life, 24-25; pres-

idency at Princeton, 7–16, 24–25; University of Edinburgh, 3, 4, 26

Witherspoon, writings of, "Address to the Natives of Scotland Residing in America" (1776), 48; "Dominion of Providence Over the Passions of Men" (1776), 21; "Ecclesiastical Char-acteristics" (1753), 5; "Ignorance of the British with Respect to America" (1771), 13; Pastoral Letter of 1775, 18; "Serious Inquiry into the Nature and Effects of the Stage" (1757), 6; "Thoughts on American Liberty" (1774), 17

Index of Biblical Passages

Index of Proper Names

Leibniz, Gottfried Wilhelm (1646–1716), 187, 189
Leland, John (1691–1766), 100, 107–8, 187, 190
Livius, Titus (59 B.C.–17 A.D.), 158
Locke, John (1632–1704), 27, 29–32, 41, 45–47, 74–76, 78, 100, 128–31, 138–39, 148–49, 158, 166, 187, 191
Lycurgus (ca. 396–324 B.C.), 159, 165
Machiavelli, Niccolo (1469–1527), 187, 191
Madison, James (1751–1836), 15, 40, 44, 49–50, 55, 60, 139
Mandeville, Bernard (ca. 1670–1733), 35, 89, 162
Mather, Cotton (1663–1728), 29, 39, 64, 68, 100
Montague, Edward Wortley (1713–1776), 187, 191
Montesquieu, Charles Louis de Secondat (1689–1755), 15, 27, 44, 139, 148–49, 165–67, 187, 191
More, Thomas (1478–1535), 127, 132
Nettleton, Thomas (1683–1742), 187, 189
Newton, Isaac (1642–1727), 98, 100–101, 186, 188
Ovid (ca. 43 B.C.–17 A.D.), 69
Paine, Thomas (1737–1809), 20, 49
Pictet, Benedict (1655–1724), 4
Plato (ca. 427–347 B.C.), 120, 165, 187–88
Pouilly, Louis-Jean Levesque de (1692–1750), 187, 190
Pringle, John (1707–1782), 26

Pufendorf, Samuel von (1632–1694), 15, 26–27, 42–43, 156–58, 173–75, 182–83, 187, 190
Reid, Thomas (1710–1796), 26, 31, 33, 75, 100, 187, 190
Riccaltoun, Robert (1691–1769), 65, 68
Robertson, William (1721–1793), 7
Rousseau, Jean Jacques (1689–1755), 44
Rutherford, Samuel (ca. 1600–1661), 46
Selden, John (1584–1654), 187, 190
Seneca (ca. 4 B.C.–65 A.D.), 107
Shaftesbury, Anthony Ashley Cooper, Lord (1671–1713), 6, 35–37, 67, 69, 71, 75, 79, 82, 84, 89, 92, 94, 112–13, 121–22, 138–39, 190
Smith, Adam (1723–1790), 5, 26, 75, 84, 88, 187, 190
Smith, Samuel Stanhope (1750–1819), 24, 32, 51–52, 76
Solon (ca. 638–559 B.C.), 159, 165
Sydney, Algernon (1622–1683), 187, 191
Tacitus (ca. 55–117), 29, 94
Taylor, Jeremy (1613–1667), 113
Vattel, Emmerich (1714–1767), 43
Washington, George (1732–1799), 18, 23
Wilson, Andrew (1718–1792), 65, 68, 97, 100
Wollaston, William (1659–1724), 39, 84, 88–89, 187, 189
Xenophon (ca. 430–354 B.C.), 159, 165